MARY QUEEN OF SCOTS'
SECRETARY

MARY QUEEN OF SCOTS'
SECRETARY

WILLIAM MAITLAND
POLITICIAN, REFORMER AND CONSPIRATOR

ROBERT STEDALL

PEN & SWORD
HISTORY

AN IMPRINT OF PEN & SWORD BOOKS LTD.
YORKSHIRE – PHILADELPHIA

First published in Great Britain in 2021 by
PEN AND SWORD HISTORY
An imprint of
Pen & Sword Books Ltd
Yorkshire – Philadelphia

ISBN 978 1 52678 779 8

Typeset in Times New Roman 11.5/14 by
SJmagic DESIGN SERVICES, India.
Printed and bound in the UK by TJ Books Ltd.

Pen & Sword Books Limited incorporates the imprints of Atlas, Archaeology,
Aviation, Discovery, Family History, Fiction, History, Maritime, Military,
Military Classics, Politics, Select, Transport, True Crime, Air World,
Frontline Publishing, Leo Cooper, Remember When, Seaforth Publishing,
The Praetorian Press, Wharncliffe Local History, Wharncliffe Transport,
Wharncliffe True Crime and White Owl.

For a complete list of Pen & Sword titles please contact
PEN & SWORD BOOKS LIMITED
47 Church Street, Barnsley, South Yorkshire, S70 2AS, England
E-mail: enquiries@pen-and-sword.co.uk
Website: www.pen-and-sword.co.uk

Or

PEN AND SWORD BOOKS
1950 Lawrence Rd, Havertown, PA 19083, USA
E-mail: Uspen-and-sword@casematepublishers.com
Website: www.penandswordbooks.com

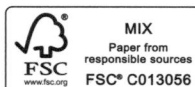

MIX
Paper from
responsible sources
FSC
www.fsc.org   FSC® C013056

Contents

List of Illustrations

Front cover

William Maitland of Lethington, Mary's Secretary of State, whose doubtful loyalty caused him to be dubbed the 'chameleon' by George Buchanan. (Oil on panel / Lennoxlove House Limited / scran.ac.uk / 000-000-027-976-R)

Picture section

Also by the same author

Hunting from Hampstead: The Story of Henry and Lucy Stedall and their Children (Book Guild Publishing, 2002)

A two-volume history of Mary Queen of Scots:

The Challenge to the Crown, Volume I: The Struggle for Influence in the Reign of Mary Queen of Scots 1542–1567 (Book Guild Publishing, 2012)

The Survival of the Crown, Volume II: The Return to Authority of the Scottish Crown Following Mary Queen of Scots' Deposition from the Throne (Book Guild Publishing, 2014)

Men of Substance: The London Livery Companies' Reluctant Part in the Plantation of Ulster (Austin Macauley Publishers, 2016)

Mary Queen of Scots' Downfall: The Life and Murder of Henry, Lord Darnley (Pen & Sword Books Limited, 2017)

The Roots of Ireland's Troubles (Pen & Sword Books Limited, 2019)

Elizabeth I's Secret Lover: Robert Dudley, Earl of Leicester (Pen & Sword Books Limited, 2020)

Website: www.maryqueenofscots.net

Introduction

My initial interest in the period of Mary Queen of Scots arose out of research that I was undertaking on my wife's grandmother's family, the Erskines of Mar. With the Earls of Mar having served Mary Queen of Scots and being responsible for the upbringing of James VI, I was magnetically drawn to her story with the murders of David Riccio and her husband, Henry, Lord Darnley. I thus embarked on her biography, initially viewing it from the point of view of the Scottish nobility. The more I researched, the more I realised that there was no consensus about who was involved in the murders and of the part that Mary played in them.

There is, of course, a huge literature on this well-trodden subject. More recent scholarly studies by Lady Antonia Fraser, John Guy and Alison Weir, for example, paint Mary as an innocent in the midst of intrigue, let down by those who might have helped her, and debased by politically motivated propaganda. They portray her as a Catholic martyr (as she wished her audience at Fotheringhay to believe), unfairly condemned both in her lifetime and by history. Their view is not shared by Dr Jenny Wormald, Roderick Graham or Susan Doran, who see Darnley's murder as a political necessity, in which Mary was involved. To each of these eminent historians I owe a debt of gratitude for their scholarship, but the more I have researched, the less convinced I have become of the conclusions that they reached. I then developed a hypothesis, based on all the plausible evidence, to conclude that the murders involved a conspiracy developed by Maitland, Moray and Cecil to depose Mary, as a Catholic, from the Scottish throne and to prevent her from succeeding Elizabeth in England. This resulted in my two-volume history of Mary Queen of Scots and of James VI until he inherited the English throne in 1603, published by the Book Guild in 2012 and 2014.

I was then approached by Pen & Sword History to write a biography of Darnley, which was published in 2017. This involved more research on him, particularly on the period prior to his arrival in Scotland, and it tested my hypothesis using a different central character. It was with this mindset that I approached Pen & Sword History to write this biography of William Maitland of Lethington, who has always stood out as being a profound influence over the murder plots, but seemingly changing his loyalties as his career unfolded. There has not been a full-length biography published on Maitland for more than one hundred years, although John Skelton wrote a three-volume history in 1887–9 and E. Russell wrote another in 1912, which largely supersedes Skelton's magnum opus. There is also a huge thesis, *The career of William Maitland of Lethington,* written by Mark Loughlin for his Ph.D. at the University of Edinburgh in 1991, which is available online. This has broken new ground in researching Maitland's life, with copious quotations in contemporary Scots. While this makes reading it quite challenging, it provides an invaluable source of original material, painstakingly put together.

Despite his later support for Mary Queen of Scots, I now see Maitland as being closer to the heart of the conspiracy causing her undoing than I had previously envisaged. This only reconfirms the hypothesis that I have developed.

Robert Stedall, January 2021

Preface

By far the most able but enigmatic of the personalities surrounding Mary Queen of Scots during her personal rule in Scotland was her Secretary of State, William Maitland of Lethington. He had also been the trusted Secretary of her mother, Mary of Guise, during her time as regent. He was a man of charm and academic stature, but his changes of loyalty caused him to face mistrust.

Maitland was a man of the Renaissance. Having travelled extensively in Europe as part of his impeccable education, he was far-sighted and politically brilliant. After studying the new religious doctrines being developed on the Continent, it was he who recognised that consolidating Scotland's Reformation would depend on breaking the Auld Alliance with Catholic France. He also worried that the Scottish government was being dominated by French officialdom rather than its traditional aristocracy. As soon as Elizabeth had established authority on the English throne and could admit to her Protestant affiliation, Maitland steered Scotland towards 'amity' with its erstwhile bitter enemy to provide mutual protection from Continental Catholic superpowers. His approach was welcomed by William Cecil, Elizabeth's Secretary of State. They had much in common and became close friends, so that Cecil did all he could to support him.

Maitland was never a leader of men, always working on behalf of others. He often explained his actions by claiming to subsume his personal beliefs to those of his mentors. The ends of his negotiations seemed to reach conclusions which contradicted his personal objectives and often lacked any sentiment of loyalty. Despite being the trusted Secretary of Mary of Guise, the queen regent, he provided undercover support for the Protestant Lords of the Congregation who were bent on undermining her government. To cement an English alliance, he tried to arrange for the Earl of Arran, second in line to the Scottish throne after his father, to marry Elizabeth I so that Mary's Catholic daughter, Mary Queen of Scots, who was still in France, could be deposed.

That Maitland was mistrusted is not in doubt. David Calderwood (1575–1650) in his *The Historie of the Kirk of Scotland* published in 1646 sums up his character: 'This man was of a rare witt [intelligence], but set upon wrong courses, which were contrived and followed out with falsehood. He could conforme himself to the times and was compared by [George Buchanan] to the chameleon [in a discourse] wherein all his syles [devious moves] and tricks were described.'[1]

Buchanan wrote *The Chameleon* as a biting satire on Maitland's ability to hide his true feelings. It caused embarrassment to Maitland, who went to great lengths to have it hushed up, and it was only published in the eighteenth century, although manuscript copies were circulated in his day. Knox's secretary, Richard Bannatyne, in his *Memorials of Transactions in Scotland*, his 'precious repository of information about Scottish political life', refers to Maitland as Machiavelli, describing him as the 'the father of traitors' and 'the head of wit called Mitchell Wylie'.[2] Machiavelli's name is used in several puns, such as 'Meikle Wylie' (Much Wily), all as allusions to Maitland's political craftiness. Machiavelli believed that a prince had a right to be devious to protect the State; Maitland was devious to promote his personal objectives.

A good example of Maitland's complex scheming involved his discussions with de Quadra, the Spanish ambassador in London in 1563, with whom, on Mary's instruction, he promoted her marriage to Don Carlos, the heir to the Spanish throne. This was a project diametrically opposed to the interests of the Scottish Reformation and the English alliance. Nevertheless, Maitland made sure that their discussion was leaked to record his apparent support for the marriage and a Scottish Counter-Reformation. There has been much debate on his objective. Was it to 'frighten' the English into accepting Mary as Elizabeth's heir so that the marriage negotiation was brought to an abrupt end? Was it to demonstrate that Mary, as a Catholic, was too dangerous to be queen of either Scotland or England? Or was he simply trying to gain his mistress's esteem by negotiating something against the odds, regardless of Scottish domestic interests? Despite their hitherto warm relationship, Cecil, as might be expected, appeared to be greatly disquieted on learning of Maitland's negotiation. Nevertheless, Cecil could be equally devious, and there is reason to believe that he put Maitland up to it to demonstrate that Mary was inappropriate, not only as Elizabeth's potential successor, but even to remain as Scottish queen.

PREFACE

Maitland's unorthodox diplomacy often included hidden objectives that did not immediately become apparent. Because of the difficulty of unravelling his real intentions, the great Victorian biography by John Skelton offers an apologia to explain away Maitland's underhand approach. Perhaps historians have been coloured by his undoubted charm. In my earlier books on this period, I have sympathised with his dilemma of being forced into actions with which he did not agree. It is with regret that, when the spotlight is on him, I can only see a snake in the grass; a greater nemesis for Mary even than Cecil. When they realised that she could not be moulded to their Protestant will, Cecil, Lord James Stewart, Earl of Moray, and Maitland set about to destroy her. Maitland later claimed that he was being blackmailed, but the evidence suggests that he was at the heart of the plotting.

Maitland was guided by an absolute belief in his political abilities and felt threatened by those with the temerity to challenge his preeminent role in Scottish government. Until late in his life, when by all accounts his young wife, Mary Fleming, had him twisted round her little finger, he felt no obligation to demonstrate unfailing support for her mistress. So long as the Scottish queen's objective to ascend the throne of both nations coincided with his personal ambition for Scotland's union with England, he would support her. Nevertheless, this required her to adhere to a Protestant religious policy. If she deviated from his masterplan or threatened his authority, he would do what he could to bring her down, despite their previously close working relationship. It was only later in life, when Mary was safely under house arrest in England, that he felt contrition for the plight that he had engineered for her. He knew that the evidence of her part in the murder of her husband had been falsified; much of it had had been created by himself. Although her determined Catholicism made her unacceptable as the means of uniting the Scottish and English crowns, he came to realise that this did not provide valid grounds for her deposition in Scotland, and so he became determined to make amends. When he masterminded a plan for her to marry the Duke of Norfolk, the senior English peer, he lost the respect of his former allies, particularly Moray and Cecil. His meddling was unwise. It resulted in Norfolk's execution and compounded Mary's woes. By this time, he was terminally ill, suffering from a wasting paralysis, but this did not stop him continuing a futile cause célèbre in defending Edinburgh Castle on her behalf.

PART I

A BRILLIANT BUT DEVIOUS SECRETARY

Chapter 1

Maitland establishes his standing under Mary of Guise

The story of Maitland's pivotal role in Scottish history really begins with the English Reformation. Although Henry VIII sought a divorce from Catherine of Aragon in the hope of begetting a male heir, it was turned down by the Pope. The deeply religious king now nominated himself as head of the English Church in the Pope's place. His purpose was entirely political, and he retained Catholic Church dogma in his 'Henrican' church services, although Archbishop Thomas Cranmer of Canterbury attempted to steer him towards Lutheranism. It was abuses within the Catholic Church which had allowed Lutheranism to sweep through Northern Europe, and Henry needed allies to defend his stance. He faced the wrath of the European Catholic superpowers, France and Spain, who threatened to launch a Counter-Reformation in England to restore the 'old religion' under the Pope's authority.

Henry's most immediate danger came from Catholic Scotland. Following the death of James V, his widow, Mary of Guise, the queen dowager, was determined to protect the Scottish throne from English belligerence for her infant daughter, Mary. She upheld the Auld Alliance with France, which 'valued Scotland chiefly as a weapon against England'.[1] Henry's most obvious tactic was to seek a marriage between Mary and his infant son, Prince Edward, thereby uniting the two crowns. (Much later, Maitland lamented Scotland's failure to support this marriage.)[2] The queen dowager deplored his bullying tactics and preferred a French marriage for her daughter to underpin the French alliance and to uphold Scotland's adherence to the Catholic faith.

To assert his authority and to promote the English marriage, Henry resorted to a series of lightening military strikes into Scotland better known as the 'Rough Wooings'. Despite his undoubted military superiority, he faced the logistical difficulties of provisioning a sizeable army on the meagre produce available from Scottish soil. Furthermore, accurate maps for planning purposes were in short supply. In need of French assistance, the queen dowager managed to negotiate Mary's marriage to the French dauphin, Francis. Not only was this an exceptional coup for her Guise relations, but the French agreed to provide garrisons of battle-hardened French troops to protect Scotland from English aggression.

Despite this setback, Henry did not immediately give up hope of arranging Mary's marriage to Prince Edward, but he needed another line of attack. He had always blamed the Scottish Catholic Church, headed by Cardinal David Bethune (or Beaton), for failing to support an English marriage for Mary. He now used evangelist preachers to infiltrate the Scottish Church and challenge Catholic dominance by reforming its religion. Many of these preachers were Scots who had been converted to Lutheranism while travelling on the Continent. They were only waiting for the opportunity to promulgate their new-found beliefs in their homeland. The Scottish Catholic Church was an easy target. It was extremely wealthy, the result of persuading aristocratic landowners and burghers to provide it with bequests on death in return for redemption in the afterlife. This left it well able to bankroll the Scottish Crown and maintain its Catholic allegiance. It was also corrupt. It spent little of its wealth on providing education or in supporting the poor and the sick. Instead, its monastic foundations were maintained in great opulence. Its bishops lived as lairds in their own castles, with little interest in theology, often maintaining a string of mistresses, generally from aristocratic families.

It took little to persuade Scottish lairds and burghers that the Reformed Church offered a less financially demanding and corrupt regime upon which to focus their Christian faith and munificence. The Catholic Church, however, did not take criticism lightly. When George Wishart began to whip up enthusiasm for Lutheran teaching around Edinburgh, he was arrested and brought before the cardinal at St Andrews, where he was condemned for spreading heretical doctrine. In March 1546, he was burnt at the stake, making him a martyr to the Reformers' cause. Two months later, with support for Protestant thinking already growing in southern Scotland, a group of Fife lairds managed to gain access to Bethune's castle. The cardinal was dragged from his rooms before being hung, drawn and quartered. Henry VIII was euphoric on hearing of his death, but the lairds were holed up there for fifteen months with about 150 supporters, besieged by Scottish government and French troops. Although they were provisioned by the English from the sea, their support came to an end when Henry died in January 1547. Eventually, the French sent a powerful naval force to bombard the castle, bludgeoning the besieged 'Castilians' into surrender.

One of the Reformers who had made his way into the castle at St Andrews in April 1547 was a former Catholic priest, John Knox. After being converted by Wishart, Knox had become his close associate. He did much to encourage the lairds with his evangelical rhetoric, but, like his fellow prisoners, found himself serving for nineteen months afterwards on French galleys. Following English negotiations for their release, Knox made his way to England, where he was licensed to preach at Anglican services in Berwick-upon-Tweed. Such was his impact that he was soon preaching in Newcastle, from where he was picked to become one of six royal chaplains to Edward VI. Not for the last time in his career, Knox's lack of political tact let him down. When John Dudley, Earl of Warwick, masterminded a coup to replace Edward Seymour, Duke of Somerset, as protector, Knox failed to recognise the political imperative for change and condemned Warwick's action in a sermon. Although Warwick – later Duke of Northumberland – had misgivings about Knox, he did not bear grudges and brought him to London to reinforce his own more Puritan leanings. When Knox challenged the dogma of the new 1552 prayer book drafted by Cranmer, Warwick tried to assuage his criticism by offering him the Bishopric of Rochester, but Knox's growing Calvinist faith meant that he already opposed a hierarchy of bishops and refused the appointment. He returned to Newcastle, but Cranmer received instructions to appoint him as Vicar of Allhallows in London. Knox came back to preach before Edward VI and the court but turned down the Allhallows post, moving less controversially to Buckinghamshire. When Mary Tudor became queen and restored England to Catholicism, Knox was forced, in January 1554, to flee to the Continent and, after making his way to Geneva, studied under Calvin. This led to his final break with Cranmer's Anglican theology.

In August 1555, Knox paid a visit to Scotland, during which he travelled extensively. After his departure from St Andrews in 1549, there had been no evangelical theologian of stature to provide leadership. He now gained almost universal support when he described the Scottish Catholic clergy as a 'greedy pack'.[3] Yet the priesthood was greedy only because its charges for baptisms, marriages and burials, together with the dispossession of excommunicates, provided the principal sources of its meagre income. Knox was now espousing Calvinism in all its militancy. He converted many to the reformed faith. One of the first of these was Alexander Cunningham, 5th Earl of Glencairn, who housed Knox at Findlayston. Others were Gilbert Kennedy, 3rd Earl of Cassillis, James Douglas, 4th Earl of Morton, Andrew Stewart, 2nd Lord Ochiltree, Patrick, 3rd Lord Ruthven, and Robert, 5th Lord Boyd. When, in 1556, Lord James Stewart, an illegitimate half-brother of Mary Queen of Scots, Archibald Campbell, 4th Earl of Argyll, and John, 6th Lord Erskine, heard Knox preach at Calder, they too joined the growing group of like-minded Reformers among the Scottish nobility. Another secret adherent was Maitland, despite being Mary of Guise's Secretary.

Maitland had been born in about 1528 into one of only a handful of Scottish professional families fulfilling governmental, legal and diplomatic roles on the Crown's behalf. This coterie lived by their wits and charm rather than as aristocrats, who wielded power as landowners and soldiers in their own fiefdoms. Maitland was nothing if not a snob. His father, Sir Richard Maitland, was a grandson of the 2nd Lord Seton. The family were Anglo-Norman, whose name originated as Maltalent (evil genius), making William's later association with the name of Machiavelli seem all the more appropriate.[4]

Sir Richard had held various court appointments, latterly as a distinguished Lord of Session, and was to become Keeper of the Privy Seal after Maitland's appointment as Secretary. He was also a poet of some note, but his chief recreations, despite suffering from failing eyesight, were his books and his garden at Lethington, a handsome tower house near Dunbar (now called Lennoxlove). William's mother was Mary Cranston of Crosbie. Together, they saw to it that William, the eldest of their seven children, gained an unrivalled education, initially at the grammar school at Haddington. In 1540, he attended St Leonard's College, St Andrews, and in 1542, like so many of his well-to-do contemporaries, travelled to Paris to attend the Scots College, where he became proficient in Latin, French and English. His letters show that he also enjoyed French, Italian and probably Greek literature.[5] If he were born in 1528, as it is thought, he was aged twelve when he arrived at St Leonard's and fourteen when he went to Paris. His movements from 1542 to 1550 are not known, but he is likely to have undertaken studies elsewhere on the Continent, and for a layman became 'exceptionally well equipped theologically', being familiar with the 'new learning'.[6] Elizabeth, no mean academic in her own right, later described him as 'the flower of the wits [brains] of Scotland'.[7] It was not just his academic ability that marked him out: 'He was an accomplished man of the world, with a genius for affairs, a skilful and persuasive diplomatist, much assisted by a good presence and a fascinating address, by imperturbable self-possession, and a charming gift of wit and repartee.'[8]

In 1553, Maitland married Janet Menteith of Kerse although she died before 1558 after providing him with a daughter, Marion. In 1554, at the age of twenty-six, he was appointed assistant to David Paniter, the Catholic Bishop of Ross and Secretary of State. This was at the time that Mary of Guise took over as regent from James Hamilton, Earl of Arran, whose policies were in tatters. In 1543, Arran had faced strong opposition for edging Scotland towards an alliance with England, to be cemented by the marriages of Mary to Prince Edward, and of his own son, James, to Princess Elizabeth. Cardinal Bethune only prevented this by questioning Arran's legitimacy, thereby forcing him to revert to Catholicism and the Auld Alliance (see Endnote 1). When they realised that the Scots had cold feet, the English resorted to a further round of military aggression. In 1547, Arran's hastily gathered Scottish troops were defeated at Pinkie Cleugh, forcing him to flee the field 'scant with honour'. The Scots needed French support. Mary of Guise gained the nobility's backing for her daughter's betrothal to the French dauphin, conditional on her being sent to France for her education. In the following year she travelled from Dumbarton on a galley sent by Henry II. Arran was appeased with the French dukedom of Châtelherault and an income of 10,000 livres. Although he retained nominal control as regent, he had lost credibility and Mary of Guise's status was boosted by the arrival of French troops and political advisers to protect the Scottish government.

By 1554, Mary Tudor had become the English queen and there were fears that her marriage to Philip of Spain would result in Spanish-led aggression to combat French interests in Scotland. At last, Mary of Guise persuaded the Scottish government that she should replace Châtelherault as regent. She still needed support against the Hamiltons and their allies who were now being spearheaded by his illegitimate half-brother, John Hamilton, Archbishop of St Andrews. This left her under an obligation to a growing group of Scottish Reformers led by

Lord James Stewart, who promised her their backing in return for her confirmation of religious tolerance. With Mary Tudor on the English throne, they had no hope of English support, so tolerance was their best option. This made it politically desirable for the queen regent to bring representatives of this reforming clique into her service.

Maitland had rapidly gained in respect as an Assistant Secretary. He added a Scottish dimension to the advice the queen regent was receiving, which Henry Cleutin, Sieur d'Oysel, her senior French adviser, could not offer. 'The Regent herself did not always understand the people she ruled, and therefore fell into serious mistakes, from which a little knowledge of Scottish history would have saved her.'[9] It was perhaps thanks to Maitland's position that when Knox visited Scotland in 1555 he was surprised at the religious tolerance of the queen regent's regime. Being established as the religious leader of the reforming movement, he found its cause making steady progress under her mild rule.[10] Nevertheless, he was shocked that Reformers would attend Catholic services in addition to their own assemblies.

Although Maitland was converted by Knox, he defended the need for compromise, recognising the precarious basis upon which the queen regent's show of tolerance rested. A conference of Reformed leaders was held at the home of John Erskine of Dun, an old and tried Lutheran, during which Maitland demonstrated his 'theological equipment' by challenging Knox and claiming that St Paul had attended Jewish services to allay accusations of prejudice.[11] He was on a hiding to nothing. Knox cited the accepted view among all reformed creeds that the Mass was 'formally idolatrous', making it dishonest for convinced Protestants to follow a double course. To avoid further confrontation, Maitland climbed down, but in all probability continued his compromising practice despite becoming the Reformers' political leader. With Knox witnessing growing support for Reformed doctrine, he wrote to the queen regent demanding that she too should become a Reformer or face her 'dejection to torment and pain everlasting'.[12] She contemptuously treated his letter as a joke, and he soon returned to Geneva.

With Mary Tudor still on the English throne, Maitland was 'acutely aware of the Congregation's inherent weakness and their poor prospects of success without English aid'.[13] In June 1557, with England being inveigled, entirely against the will of its people, into Philip II's war on the Continent against France, Henry II coerced the regent into raising a Scottish army to invade England from the north. Although she called a convention of Scottish nobles to join her at Newbattle Abbey, the failures of their earlier incursions at Flodden and Solway Moss had left them with no appetite to imperil their safety in the interests of France.[14] On d'Oysel's advice, her French troops built a fortress at Eyemouth to threaten the English garrison at Berwick. When this provoked the English into crossing the border, the Scottish nobles had no choice but to attend a call to protect Scottish soil. Nevertheless, when the English retired again, the Scots refused to cross into England to support d'Oysel's French troops, which had pushed ahead to besiege Wark. Furthermore, they demanded, on pain of treason, the return of Scottish cannon that d'Oysel had taken with him. Unluckily for Maitland, he had come to Kelso with the queen regent, and found himself in the invidious position of being sent by her to require the Scots to counter their demands. Having faced personal threats, he returned to the queen regent with their flat refusal. D'Oysel had no choice but to return across the Tweed with the Scottish guns. His incursion caused petty belligerence, which was to continue in the Border region until the signing of the Treaty of Cateau-Cambrésis in April 1559.

With Mary Tudor's Spanish connections making an Anglo-Scottish alliance impossible, the Reformers needed to support the queen regent's government to assure their freedom of worship and to retain religious peace in Scotland. This involved them in some apparently contradictory decisions. In November 1557, Châtelherault, George Gordon, 4th Earl of Huntly and Argyll, who had refused to support the queen regent in her proposed English invasion, threatened to overthrow her government. Maitland realised that Châtelherault's restoration to authority would only accelerate religious conflict at a time when the Protestant Lords in Scotland could have no expectation of English support. He thus encouraged Lord James, Glencairn, Sir William Kirkcaldy of Grange, and probably Morton to rally to the queen regent's support, even seeking additional French troops for her. Yet the Reformers also needed to deter her from embarking on another Scottish invasion of England.

To diminish Châtelherault's authority, the lords even proposed the restoration of Matthew Stuart, 4th Earl of Lennox, to his titles and estates. The significance of this needs to be understood. After marrying Henry VIII's niece, Margaret Douglas, Lennox had supported the English King. This had resulted in the attainder of his Scottish estates after leading an English army into Scotland as part of the Rough Wooings. His lands around Glasgow were now occupied by the Hamiltons, and his restoration would require their return. Yet the principal issue was the question mark over Châtelherault's legitimacy originally raised by Cardinal Bethune in 1543. If upheld, this would make Lennox the heir to the Scottish throne (Bethune's argument is explained in detail in Endnote 1). Although it is difficult to find the cardinal's view credible, it worried Châtelherault at the time and was politically convenient for those like James VI, Lennox's grandson, who later wanted to assert the prior claim of the Lennox Stuarts to the Scottish throne. With Châtelherault backing down, the plan for Lennox's restoration at this time was dropped.

It was not until 3 December 1557, after Knox's departure, that a 'band' known as the 'First Covenant' was signed in Edinburgh for the formation of the Lords of the Congregation. The original signatories were Argyll, his son, Archibald, Lord Lorne, who inherited as the 5th Earl in the following year, Glencairn, Morton and Erskine of Dun. (After 1560, Dun became one of the first superintendents of the Kirk.) Initially, this group was aimed entirely at reforming the Scottish Church and Maitland made no sign of supporting them. They issued two resolutions: to introduce the Book of Common Prayer of Edward VI and Protestant services into churches that individual Reformist magnates controlled in accordance with their feudal jurisdiction; and 'to hold private assemblies for the reading and exposition of the Scriptures', thereby 'laying the foundation for a national Protestant establishment'.[15] These resolutions were echoed by the burgh's councils, which claimed similar authority over churches in their precincts. These steps made the queen regent extremely anxious and met with opposition from the Catholic Church hierarchy.

In February 1558, Maitland's diplomatic skills were put to the test on a mission as the queen regent's ambassador to the court of Mary Tudor in London before travelling on to France. He was accompanied by Ives de Rubay, the queen regent's legal adviser. Their objective was to conclude a peace between England and Scotland in which France was to be included. With England, to its consternation, having recently suffered the loss of Calais, Mary Tudor would not countenance any peace terms involving France. With the mission doomed to failure, plans for Maitland and de Rubay to travel on to France were dropped. The queen regent now realised that she had no hope of gaining Mary Tudor's support to uphold the Catholic faith in Scotland. Maitland later admitted that his visit had enabled him to meet with Cecil to discuss opportunities for assisting the Reformers that might arise when Mary Tudor died, an objective that conflicted with his brief from his mistress.

Following Mary Tudor's death in the following November, it soon became clear that Elizabeth, as her successor, would restore Protestantism in England. About a month later, the queen regent appointed Maitland as her Secretary following Paniter's death. According to Buchanan, it was Lord James and Cassillis, her newly appointed Lord High Treasurer, who sponsored him. Sir Richard Maitland was no doubt also influential. Writing after his father's death, Maitland's son, James, claimed that she would have preferred to appoint a French diplomat. When she argued that there was no suitable Scottish candidate, the Protestant lords remonstrated that Maitland, who was now aged thirty, was equal to the role.[16] This gained him a seat on the Privy Council, which also included Lord James and Morton, the leader of the powerful Douglas clan, as members. His 'shining abilities, intellectual and practical' made him an instant success.[17] As the role of Secretary in both Scotland and England was to supervise foreign policy, Maitland's period in France and close interest in England made him ideal, and the queen regent found his advice invaluable. 'His great abilities were reinforced by his personal charm. His natural gaiety and his large accomplishments, his geniality and kindliness, his tact and his consideration ... must have greatly commended him to an able and highly-bred woman like Mary of Guise.'[18]

Maitland was now a familiar figure both in the Privy Council and at court, which still retained important executive powers. His 'impressive cultural [and Renaissance] background' enabled him to play 'a full part in the masques and celebrations of the court and [he] was also [an adept] card playing companion of the Queen Dowager'.[19] He was forever seeking friendships, and she much appreciated his qualities, which in some measure she shared.

Despite the importance of his position, Maitland found that the queen regent's French advisers were supervising his role. In addition to being French ambassador, d'Oysel held the title of Lieutenant of the King of France in Scotland.[20] He was supported by the Comptroller, Bartholomew de Villemore, and de Rubay. The positions of Chamberlain and Treasurer were deliberately left vacant. Scottish nobles of all faiths objected to their traditional posts in Scotland's government being occupied by French diplomats. Although Huntly, a staunch Catholic, had backed Mary of Guise's appointment as regent, he failed to quell an uprising in the north in October 1554. This resulted in him being imprisoned for five months in Edinburgh Castle. She demoted him as Lieutenant-General, handing the Great Seal of Scotland, which he held as Lord High Chancellor, to de Rubay. He was not going to forget these slights. The Reforming lords also found themselves required to accept French policies, of which they did not approve, if order were to be maintained. The queen regent may have been genuine in professing 'a supreme regard for the [Reforming] interests of Scotland', and maintained peace by playing lip-service to their religious concerns.[21] Nevertheless, Maitland began to fear French influence, not just in terms of protecting the throne for Mary Queen of Scots, but as an attempt to subsume Scotland under French and Catholic domination.

Elizabeth's accession to the English throne signalled a change of policy for the Lords of the Congregation. At last, the Scottish Reformers could hope for English backing. For the time being, Maitland chose to remain in the employment of the queen regent. Nevertheless, he had been duplicitously serving the interests of the Protestant lords long before this. He was, of course, of far more use to them as a member of government. As early as 1558, John Spottiswoode had named him as one of the principal advocates of religious reform.[22] Despite this, he used all his consummate tact to remain as Secretary. Although it has often been claimed that he resigned, E. Russell makes clear that he did not. He resumed his role under the provisional government set up by the Lords of the Congregation and was reconfirmed in it following Mary Queen of Scots' return to Scotland. His determination to remain was not motivated by financial consideration, but it provided a platform for him to steer Scotland towards union with England and to prevent a renewal of the Auld Alliance.

Maitland was 'acutely aware of the Congregation's inherent weakness and their poor prospects of success without English aid'.[23] Although the beliefs espoused by the Lords of the Congregation were based on genuine personal conviction, membership provided a convenient political platform from which to challenge the queen regent and her dominant French ministers. It was not just Reformers who felt threatened; Huntly felt the same. He was backed by fellow Catholics, including John Gordon, 11th Earl of Sutherland, and George Sinclair, 4th Earl of Caithness. If it came to a confrontation between the queen regent and the Reformers, Huntly and his allies were likely to support them to re-establish Scottish sovereignty.

Chapter 2

The Lords of the Congregation challenge French authority

It is important to draw distinctions between the key architects of the Reformation in Scotland, as each of them had slightly different objectives.

Knox was entirely motivated by his growing belief in the new religious dogma. He was determined to install Calvinism as the 'established' church of Scotland to the exclusion of all other forms of Christian worship. He was horrified by the lack of Christian knowledge of most Catholic priests, and at their failure to provide universal schooling, health care, and support for the elderly. He disapproved of the profligate and sometimes debauched lifestyles found in the monasteries and among the bishoprics. He was determined to lead the people towards a church that served its communities to better spiritual and practical effect. This required the overthrow of Scotland's Catholic government.

Lord James Stewart, who emerged as the natural leader of the Lords of the Congregation, was devoutly religious but had ambitions for power. If the queen regent's Catholic government could be defeated, and, if he could establish his legitimacy as the eldest child of James V, he wanted to become regent for his half-sister in France or to become king. He used his position with the Lords of the Congregation to promote his ambitions under the guise of seeking a Scottish Reformation. Nevertheless, his illegitimacy was irrefutable, and he lacked military clout. He was reliant on the great magnates at the heads of their clans for support. He garnered help from Argyll, Glencairn and many others, but to challenge the queen regent's hardened French troops he needed universal backing. He was uncertain of Châtelherault, who, as heir to the throne, saw Lord James's ambitions as threatening, and of Huntly, who remained adamantly Catholic, despite falling out with the queen regent. He was also uncertain of Morton, who for a time remained politically neutral, and of James Hepburn, 4th Earl of Bothwell, who never veered from his unfailingly loyalty to the regency.

Maitland had a slightly different agenda. From the outset, he realised that a Scottish Reformation could only be achieved with English support. This conveniently fitted with his concern that Scotland was being subjugated to French rule, threatening the traditional position of Scots in government. His objective was to break the longstanding Auld Alliance with Catholic France and to replace it by amity with England. With Elizabeth's accession likely to restore England to Protestantism, a union of Britain's Protestant interests offered the lords an opportunity to end Scotland's religious schism of the previous fifteen years. Furthermore, permanent union would end centuries of conflict.

Following the marriage of Mary Queen of Scots to the French Dauphin Francis on 24 April 1558, the queen regent in Scotland received additional military support from France. The rising tide of Reformist unrest had prevented her from leaving Scotland to attend the ceremony herself, but she continued to rely on Maitland for advice. She kept him beside her to draft correspondence, despite having a conflicting desire to have his diplomatic skills available at her daughter's wedding in France. The marriage gave her a greater sense of security and made her more aggressive. On 28 April, hoping to halt a burgeoning of Reformist services, she approved the burning at the stake of a former priest turned Reformer, Walter Myln, at St Andrews. The inevitable backlash provided the lords with a cause célèbre to incite what Knox dubbed the 'rascally multitude' to oppose her rule. She now had a fight on her hands, and the lords demanded the revocation of the heresy laws, under which Myln had been charged. When Mary Tudor died seven months later the queen regent compounded her difficulty by proposing another invasion of England, this time to support her daughter's claim to the English throne, but the Scots again refused to support it. With the English being aware of the queen regent's hostility, the lords at last had hopes of English backing to challenge her and to implement the Scottish Reformation.

Most importantly, James, Earl of Arran, Châtelherault's son, returned from France as a committed Protestant and persuaded his wavering father to join the Protestant lords. Many traditional Hamilton allies followed suit. Arran had already gained repute as a soldier in France and soon joined Lord James as one of their military leaders. Knox also returned and set about spreading Reformist evangelism. In 1557, while waiting at

Dieppe for a ship to cross the Channel, he had written his *First Blast of the Trumpet against the Monstrous Regimen* [Rule] *of Women,* a diatribe against the rule of both Mary Tudor and the queen regent, which was published in early 1558. He saw it as 'a subversion of good order, of all equity and justice' for women to rule men.[1] His timing was unfortunate as Elizabeth succeeded Mary later in the year. To make amends he wrote to her conveying his unfeigned love and reverence, but then told her that she ruled by the will of the people and not by dynastic right. Elizabeth now saw him as an anathema and would not have his name mentioned. He remained oblivious to criticism but was destined to return to Scotland rather than gain a more glittering Protestant post in England.

There was another important factor. The superpowers, France and Spain, were exhausted by continuous war. Their representatives were meeting at Cateau-Cambrésis to negotiate a peace, which also involved England. The terms included the reinstatement of large areas of Europe won and lost in earlier years. However, England came off badly and failed in its efforts to gain the restoration of Calais, its last remaining outpost on the Continent. Negotiations were inevitably tortuous and were knocked sideways by the death of Mary Tudor on 17 November 1558. This caused a break in the discussions while opposing sides reassessed the political and religious implications of ending England's close alliance with Spain and its probable reversion to Protestantism.

Although Scotland's part in the negotiations was being undertaken on its behalf by France, Maitland was already demonstrating his abilities to a wider audience at the heart of Scottish politics and diplomacy. While he remained in the queen regent's service, he watched with trepidation as the French continued to dictate Scottish government policy. He persuaded his Scottish colleagues that the French were seeking to extinguish Scotland's independence. In France, the young queen-dauphine had quartered her arms with the royal arms of England, implying provocatively that Elizabeth was illegitimate. This aligned the English with Scotland's Reformist interests.

Maitland was soon in close contact with Cecil. It is an interesting coincidence that they both came from middle-class professional backgrounds, and their families were to achieve a *noblesse de robe* during the succeeding century, although 'Cecil's origins were a good deal more obscure than Maitland's'.[2] Maitland later told him: 'Sence the first beginning of our acquwentence I have ever set you before my eyes as a patterne wyshing I might conforme myself and all my actions to the imitacion of yours.'[3] Cecil carefully cultivated his association with both Lord James and Maitland, seeing them as well-educated, astute, discreet, and arguably the most able men in Scotland. Theirs was not just a political relationship. Cecil became their genuine friend, and Maitland stayed at his house on visits to London, where they shared a mutual love of French and classical literature.

Lord James Stewart's religious faith meant that he was widely trusted. Like Maitland, he was impeccably educated, having attended: 'St Leonard's College at St Andrews, of which, as Commendator of the Priory, he was the nominal head. At the age of seventeen or eighteen, he went to Paris where he studied under the celebrated Ramus in the College of Prèsle. Under various influences, including that of Knox, he became a convinced and earnest Protestant.'[4] He readily supported Maitland, 'giving him full scope in the management of public affairs and reserving to himself only a moderating influence'.[5]

When the Scottish Parliament met on 29 November, news of Mary Tudor's death gave no hint of any anti-French feeling other than a request by a growing band of Reformers for legal confirmation of religious toleration, which the queen regent managed to evade. She had been criticised from France for her lax religious policy, which had allowed Reformist numbers to reach a level that conflicted with French interests. Furthermore, she now faced the prospect of Protestantism being restored in England.

In January 1559, Maitland's underhand diplomacy came to the fore. He secretly brought Châtelherault for a meeting on the Scottish border with Sir Henry Percy, Deputy Warden of the Middle March, and Sir James Croft, governor of Berwick, ostensibly to end belligerence on the border, which had continued since d'Oysel's incursion to Wark in 1557. On arrival, he steered his English counterparts towards alliance with the Lords of the Congregation, seeing English support as a necessary precursor to embarking on a Scottish Reformation. 'From this point Maitland acted as an undercover agent for the Congregation whilst in the pay and service of the Regent.'[6] Cecil shared the desire for an alliance, believing that English security could only be assured if Scotland returned to the status of an English suzerainty. He concluded that, if the queen-dauphine remained an absentee ruler, a council of Scottish nobles should be appointed 'to govern the whole realm'. If she disagreed, she should be deposed.

Unsurprisingly, there is no complete record of Maitland's discussion, as he took few into his confidence. In all probability even Knox was kept in the dark, even though he had been nominated as the Lords of the Congregation's secretary. Percy was impressed by 'the young Laird of Lethington' with his frank explanation of their objectives. Maitland's proposals were endorsed by Châtelherault on the Hamiltons' behalf, but probably sweetened by the prospect of Arran's marriage to Elizabeth. Maitland dismissed the queen-dauphine's claim to the English throne, 'which never entered into any wise man's head'.[7] He also met privately with Croft to establish whether England remained inextricably bound to Spain. If the superpowers failed to come to terms at Cateau-Cambrésis, he wanted assurance that this would not prevent England from reaching a separate agreement with the Scottish lords. Croft thought that it would not.

Following the meeting at Berwick, Maitland duped the queen regent into allowing him to travel on to London, where he arrived on 19 March. She even sent him 750 crowns for the purpose. To add credibility to his mission, he was accompanied by Sir Robert Melville, who was to remain Maitland's close ally, and David Forrest, the Master of the Scottish Mint. He was immediately interviewed by Cecil and met Elizabeth for the first time. He argued 'that the French sought to use Scotland as but a "futstole" from which to attack England: "Ye are the marke they shote at, they seke our realme but for an entry to yours."'[8]

Maitland also suggested that France's domestic difficulties made them incapable of waging a successful war against a combined English and Scottish force. It would be better and less costly for the English to join with the Scots to defeat the French on Scottish soil than to wait until Scotland became a bridgehead for an invasion of England. By pointing out the folly in delaying, he was well received and, after overcoming initial English scepticism, gained support in principle for a 'godly' union and for England's military intervention in Scotland. He then travelled to France, where he saw Francis and Mary. With the Treaty of Cateau-Cambrésis having at last been signed on 3 April, he returned from Fontainebleau on 21 April with a copy ratified by them. He broke his return journey in London, holding further discussions with Elizabeth and Cecil, and only left for Scotland at the end of May. With France being hostile to Elizabeth's accession, the creation of an alliance with the Scottish Reformers was now of even greater importance to her.

Knox reached Scotland before Maitland's return. It was already clear that a religious revolution was gestating. There was 'a seething mass of popular discontent with the monastic system that it would be difficult to restrain'.[9] The wealth, idleness, luxury and immorality of the Catholic monasteries was a problem not unique to Scotland. Reformers produced a placard, known as the 'Beggars' Summons', which was attached to the doors of most friaries and hospitals.[10] It provocatively demanded the monks' evacuation to make way for afflicted poor, widows and orphans.

After his arrival, Knox came to Perth where he preached at St John's on 11 May 1559. Even he was staggered at the power of his oratory. His sermon caused such a riot that the rascally multitude sacked and looted nearby monasteries. Although the French garrison attempted to suppress the insurgency, Ruthven, as provost, failed to provide them with assistance and joined 2,500 Reformist troops raised by Glencairn and Ochiltree. The queen regent sent reinforcements, backed initially, in accordance with their pact, by Lord James and Argyll (the 5th Earl), although both later claimed to be trying to moderate her stance. Their arrival forced Glencairn and Ochiltree to withdraw. When Ruthven was removed as provost, he signed a bond with them to bring about the 'liberty of the congregation' by ousting the French from Scotland. When it was learned that England might provide them with support, Lord James and Argyll quickly joined them.

The Lords of the Congregation were determined to show the English that they had the military strength to challenge the queen regent, despite her receiving reinforcements from France. On 4 June 1559, a force of 300 Reformers left Edinburgh to link up with others from St Andrews. Although she went after them, they remained a step ahead of her. Ruthven arrived at Cupar in Fife with 100 horse and 800 men from Perth. Within a week, they had 13,000 troops from further afield encamped on Cupar Muir. When Patrick, Master of Lindsay (later 6th Lord Lindsay of the Byres), joined them, he came with his father. The elder Lindsay was a vehement Reformer and an experienced soldier who added greatly to the lords' prestige. There were now pockets of Reformist support in Edinburgh, Dundee, Perth, Ayr and St Andrews.

On learning of their strength, the queen regent called an eight-day truce to avoid confrontation. Although she attempted to meet privately with Lord James and Argyll in the mistaken belief that they would be more amenable, on 13 June the lords sent the elder Lindsay to negotiate.

She agreed to their demand that French troops should leave Fife, but when she failed to call a promised meeting at St Andrews, they insisted on the French garrison leaving Perth. Although she had hoped for Huntly's assistance, he shared the general concern at French motives and remained aggrieved at her earlier treatment of him. By withdrawing his men from Perth before the Protestant lords' arrival, the French garrison was forced to surrender. Nevertheless, Huntly was shocked when its townsfolk ransacked Scone Abbey. During July, he collected the Catholic treasures of Aberdeen Cathedral for safekeeping at Strathbogie and even persuaded the provost of Edinburgh, George 5th Lord Seton, to reintroduce the mass at St Giles'.

Despite remaining in the queen regent's employment, Maitland's principal preoccupation was in securing Châtelherault, Huntly and other ditherers to the Lords of the Congregation's cause. With Châtelherault being of uncertain loyalty, and Huntly having a reputation for double dealing, Maitland needed at least to assure their neutrality to avoid them threatening the impending stand against the regency. Neither of them had any great religious interest, but each hoped for benefit. Just as in England, it was clear that the resources of the monasteries would be redistributed. Much of their property had already been granted to senior nobles, although their tenure was uncertain. Huntly controlled the bishoprics of Galloway and Aberdeen, while Châtelherault laid claim to St Andrews and Argyll, with the abbeys of Arbroath, Paisley and Kilwinning. Maitland had some sympathy with their claim to church lands, which had been carved out of their estates in times past. He had 'nothing of Knox's democratic fervour. As an intellectual aristocrat, his sympathies were with the traditional feudal regime.'[11] While Knox wanted the Reformed Church to assume control of the Catholic Church's patrimony, Maitland told him that his ideas were 'devout imaginations'.[12] While Knox envisioned a church-controlled state, Maitland wanted a state-controlled church.

With the Lords of the Congregation at last having some military clout, the burghers of Edinburgh, Dalmellington and St Andrews appointed Reformist ministers. Knox went to St Giles' in Edinburgh to galvanise support for the impending challenge against Catholicism. Thomas Randolph, the English ambassador, claimed: '[He] is able in one hour to put more life into us than five hundred trumpets continually blustering in our ears.'[13] Knox strongly advocated military action and deprecated Lord James's and Argyll's apparent support for the queen regent at Perth.

While Knox spearheaded religious conversion, Maitland, acting in the background, managed the political issues to achieve backing from England and in the Scottish Parliament. Meanwhile, the lords gathered troops. Lord James, who was now recognised as their military leader, marched with Argyll to Stirling and then to Linlithgow. Their strategic objective was to prevent supplies and reinforcements being delivered to French garrisons north of the Forth. He adopted a religious façade to cloak his personal ambition to oust the queen regent, who retreated to Dunbar. On 29 June, the lords entered Edinburgh unopposed. She counter-attacked and denounced Lord James for seeking the Crown, which he hotly denied. Without English support, the lords had no choice but to withdraw from Edinburgh, and, with a French garrison already stationed at Leith, D'Oysel fortified its port to provide access from France by sea. On 19 July, Kirkcaldy was sent south with an urgent letter from Maitland to Cecil seeking English help.

On 10 July, Henry II of France died following a jousting accident. By the shattering of a lance, Mary had become the queen consort of France, and the Guises were able to use her new position to take control of French government. They immediately sent additional military support to their sister in Scotland, instructing her to eradicate the Scottish Reformers and ameliorate the nobility with a liberal distribution of French 'pensions'. When she reluctantly adopted their confrontational approach, Maitland pushed the Lords of the Congregation into an English alliance. Cecil exhorted Lord James and Argyll to protect England's northern border by assuming control of Scottish government. Not unnaturally, Lord James believed that the English would provide military support, but Elizabeth was nervous of challenging the regency. She argued that the legitimate Scottish succession should not be overridden by religious preconditions.

Three months earlier, Mary and Francis had overlooked Elizabeth's doubtful legitimacy by confirming her as the rightful English queen. Their letter was sent via the queen regent in Scotland, and Maitland brought it to London. Elizabeth dared not contravene the terms of the Treaty of Cateau-Cambrésis so soon after its signing and concluded that she could not provide the Lords of the Congregation with overt support. Cecil still hoped that she would come to recognise England's security as more important than protecting Mary's Scottish throne. When providing money alone proved insufficient, he wrote at length to his fellow English Council members to justify military action, even if it meant backing rebels against an anointed queen.

Cecil explored every avenue. He advised his agents in Scotland to 'anywise kindle the fire, for if quenched the opportunity will not come again in our lives'.[14] Yet he remained pessimistic of the lords achieving success. In August, he spirited Arran, who had visited Geneva, to London to consider once more his suitability to become Elizabeth's spouse and to replace Mary on the Scottish throne. It is known that Maitland advocated this as a means of uniting Scotland with England, and it had probably been mooted at the meeting with Percy earlier in the year. Cecil also wanted to assess Arran's potential as an alternative to Lord James as Scottish regent. Nothing came of these discussions and it is possible that Arran was already showing signs of his inherited insanity. Eight months later, in April 1560, he was forced to leave camp outside Leith due to mental illness.

In September, Lord James called a conference of Reformist nobles at Stirling, which was joined by Châtelherault and Arran. On 21 October, at a convention in the Tolbooth in Edinburgh, Châtelherault signed documentation to suspend the queen regent. As heir to the throne, his signature gave this step a semblance of legality, but she ignored it. Lord James again appealed to England, and although Cecil saw it as 'a heaven-sent opportunity to remove the threat of France' from Scotland, Elizabeth refused to invade in support of a rebel cause.[15] She was worrying that Spain would combine with France to place Mary on the English throne. Even Cecil recognised that she faced 'steadfast enmity abroad but no steadfast friendship'.[16] She provided Lord James with more financial backing, while hotly denying any involvement to the foreign ambassadors in London, 'at which she was expert to the point of genius'.

On 21 October, Lord James returned to Edinburgh with 15,000 men, but found the queen regent bedridden at the castle suffering from dropsy. Erskine, the governor, refused to desert her, but she was moved to Leith, where its garrison of 3,000 French troops was being used to good effect. It sallied out to waylay a convoy of Lord James's provisions stuck in heavy ground at Restalrig, causing the loss of more than 1,000 of his men. To make matters worse, on 31 October Randolph was sent secretly to deliver £3,000 from Elizabeth, but the queen regent had warning and called on Bothwell to intercept it, which he achieved successfully. With Bothwell being one of the few Scottish lords still supporting her, he faced lasting antagonism from Lord James and his allies, including Maitland.

The lords realised that they still lacked the skills and artillery to challenge the French without military support. With concerns over Erskine's 'ambiguous attitude' as a 'hesitating reformer' at the castle, they again withdrew from Edinburgh.[17] Maitland, who did his utmost to dissuade them from leaving, now took the momentous decision to desert the queen regent openly by travelling with them to Stirling on that 'dolorous night' of 6 November.[18] It has been suggested that his undercover diplomacy had come to light, forcing him to flee in danger of his life.[19] Despite its delay, his defection was of huge significance and added 'respectability and credibility to the Congregation's cause'.[20] Until then the lords were justifiably labelled by the queen regent as rebels, but, as a government official, Maitland's support gave them kudos. It is interesting that, despite Maitland's changing allegiance, his father, Sir Richard, remained in the queen regent's service and, as a Catholic, disapproved of his son's action.

On arrival at Stirling, Knox breathed new heart into the disappointed Reformers, but 'without the help of England by land and sea, they were impotent against the power of France'.[21] With Maitland now seen as their 'accredited envoy', he was sent by sea from Stirling to Berwick to garner support. On 10 January 1560, when Mary of Guise ignored her undertaking to call Parliament, she was seen as 'the enemy of the rights and liberties of the kingdom and was justly deemed unworthy to be trusted with its government'.[22] Forty-nine signatures, including those of seven earls, were placed on a bond to expel the French and appoint Châtelherault as leader of a provisional government.

Maitland, who was accompanied by Randolph, reached Berwick on 24 November for a lengthy secret meeting with Elizabeth's envoy, Sir Ralph Sadler, deputed by Cecil to handle the negotiation. Maitland then continued to London for a meeting with the Council, arriving in early December. Sir Nicholas Throckmorton, the English ambassador in Paris, who was advocating open intervention in Scotland, also arrived, and Cecil made reference to their unique opportunity to make it an English dependency. With many Council members still in receipt of Spanish pensions, the majority opposed him. With Elizabeth not yet securely positioned on her throne, she feared that incursion into Scotland could only lead to war with France. With Cecil seeking to support Scottish heretics against their legitimate sovereign, he had no prospect of Spanish support. He argued that Elizabeth would be acting in self-defence by pre-empting a French-led invasion from the north to support Mary's claim to the English throne.

Cecil eventually threw down the gauntlet, threatening to resign unless Elizabeth grasped her opportunity. She realised that she had to back him but had no great love for the Scots and hated Knox. She still prevaricated. Although she quartered 4,000 foot and 2,000 horse at Berwick, she refused to send them across the border. Instead, she instructed Admiral William Winter to prepare an English fleet at Berwick to harry French reinforcements and supplies arriving in the Forth. Although his orders were dated 16 December, he was only instructed to leave Berwick eleven days later and, if caught, was to claim that he was seeking out pirates without her authority. He was nearly too late, but a storm badly damaged a fleet of French reinforcements in the North Sea, drowning many troops on board.

Maitland played an important part in persuading Elizabeth to intervene. On 20 January 1560, he produced an 'anonymous' tract setting out the whole case for an armed alliance between the two nations for mutual defence. Their common religion was drawing the two realms together, severing Scotland forever from friendship with France. Elizabeth at last sent a further 2,000 men under Lord Grey of Wilton, and placed the young Thomas Howard, 4th Duke of Norfolk, Lieutenant of the North, in overall command. They gathered at Newcastle, before joining those already at Berwick. On about 16 February, Maitland left London for Berwick to complete a new treaty of alliance with the English representatives. On arrival seven days later, he was joined by Lord James, Ruthven, Sir John Maxwell and the Master of Lindsay for negotiations with Norfolk. Under the Treaty of Berwick, signed on 27 February, the English agreed to protect the Scots 'in their old freedoms and liberties' for so long as Mary remained in France (and for one year longer).[23] In return, the Scottish lords undertook to support the English in Ulster by using Argyll's military power to police Highland Scots, who were fomenting unrest there. Elizabeth unwisely failed to take up this offer.[24] The English 'advanced no claim to superiority, sought no unfair advantage and scrupulously respected Scottish susceptibilities'.[25] The lords even confirmed loyalty to Francis and Mary as their rightful king and queen.

With the treaty signed, Maitland returned to London, as the lords wanted it confirmed under the Great Seal of England. This was to 'impress the neutral nobles – those who had not yet joined them – perhaps also to impress Elizabeth, and to guard against any further vacillation'.[26] This proved a wise precaution. The French ambassador in London, the Chevalier Michel de Sèvre, made strenuous efforts to prevent its ratification. After some prevarication, Elizabeth confirmed the terms, arguing that they were not hostile to France, but an attack on Guise interests being promoted in Scotland. It was convenient that the Guises were losing their authority in France. With English help now assured, Maitland returned to Berwick, but dared not cross the border ahead of the English invasion force. Even so, he managed to work on those lords who were wavering to gain more support. These included Morton, whose estates round Tantallon were threatened by the queen regent's forces. Elizabeth's prevarication and parsimony, however, gave the Scots little encouragement.

While the lords waited for the English, the queen regent's troops, under Bothwell's command, captured Linlithgow. They then regained Edinburgh, which had been left undefended. Bothwell went on with 800 men to capture Stirling, from where he advanced into Fife, linking up with other French forces to challenge Lord James and Arran at Cupar Muir. Buoyed up by a sermon from Knox, the lords kept the French at bay for twenty-one days, despite being outnumbered. This enabled Winter to capture two French men-of-war and vessels carrying supplies. Being left short of provisions, the French were forced back through Stirling to Leith. Despite their need for reinforcements, the Guises were no longer positioned to provide them. Furthermore, the queen regent was dangerously ill. Mary begged her mother to take care of her health and promised undying love but could do no more.

On 29 March, Norfolk's troops crossed the border, meeting up four days later with Scots led by Lord James and Glencairn at Prestonpans to prepare for an advance on Leith. A week later they were joined by Châtelherault and Huntly and received promises of support from other Scottish Catholics. For her own safety, the queen regent was restored to Erskine's care at Edinburgh Castle, but was in no mood to capitulate.

It was not plain sailing. Elizabeth would have preferred to stem her prohibitive costs by coming to a settlement. Her earlier prevarication had left Norfolk with inexperienced and under-provisioned men. 'Poor leadership, exacerbated by clashes of personality between Lord Grey and the Duke of Norfolk, resulted in the debacle of the siege of Leith.'[27] On 7 May, a combined Scottish and English force was soundly rebuffed by its French garrison. A group of Scottish whores, determined not to lose their French clientele, caused considerable injury to the attackers by throwing burning coals on them from the battlements. Furthermore, an English commander was captured. On 10 May, the disappointed Scots held a Parliament outside the walls, but could do little more than ratify the Treaty of Berwick, hoping that Elizabeth would send more men. Although Leith remained under siege, Maitland was fearful that the English would break the treaty and retire. He was determined not to lose this opportunity for perpetual 'amity' but needed the French garrison's removal. He worried that a compromise would lose him the support of the waverers he had wooed so hard to join them. Although Cecil sympathised with Maitland's predicament, even he implied that the Scots would have to come to terms.

By holding Leith, the French were positioned to receive further reinforcements by sea, making the siege ineffective. Despite her grave illness, the queen regent sent Bothwell to France for more support. Although negotiations continued, Maitland saw her for the last time on 10 May. She died at Edinburgh Castle on 11 June, swollen and in great pain. Such was the respect for her that Lord James, Argyll and Glencairn visited her on her deathbed. As heir to the throne, Châtelherault was reappointed regent, with Lord James as his deputy. They now assumed control to force out the French.

The French government was exhausted by war and instructed their ambassador, Charles, Sieur de Randan, to achieve peace before their expenditure in Scotland led to 'the ruin and desolation of France'. With Mary's Scottish throne now at risk, Philip II was asked to mediate to defend Scotland's Catholicism. As he needed England as an ally, it suited him to be pragmatic. He did not want Mary on the English throne, linking it to France and threatening his means of communication through the Channel. Without consulting her, Spanish and French representatives negotiated in Edinburgh with Châtelherault, Lord James, Maitland and Cecil, who arrived from London.

The Guises considered the Treaty of Edinburgh, signed on 6 July, as a sell-out. Elizabeth was recognised as the rightful English queen, and Mary's claim was dropped. All French and English troops were required to leave Scotland (with their recent fortifications being demolished), except for a token force of sixty French at Inchleith and Dunbar 'to provide a colour of sovereignty'.[28] Châtelherault and Lord James were reaffirmed as governor (regent) and deputy respectively to head a council of twenty-four Scottish nobles for so long as Mary remained abroad. Catholic services were banned. Mary still had her throne, but at a price. If Francis and Mary failed to ratify its terms, England could intervene to uphold the Scottish Reformation. For Maitland, it was a personal triumph despite the disaster of the military campaign, but it is hard to imagine how the negotiators expected France to endorse it, and their commissioners may well have assumed that they would refuse.

Cecil had generally found the Scottish lords self-seeking and difficult to deal with, but warmly acknowledged the services of Lord James and Maitland, which only cemented their friendship. He mentioned Maitland with special distinction, reporting to Elizabeth that he 'was very helpful' and 'worth six others', being 'of most credit and wit [wisdom],' bearing 'all the burden of foresight' by anticipating problems before they arose.[29] Russell describes him as 'probably the most accomplished statesman of his day … a man of great moral courage'.[30]

The lords sent a 'collective letter of thanks' to Elizabeth and, on 19 July, a thanksgiving service was held at St Giles' with 'the whole nation rejoicing at its deliverance from French soldiery'.[31] On returning to London, Cecil fully expected a reward both for the Scottish negotiators and for himself, but Lord Robert Dudley, his political opponent, had Elizabeth's ear. Cecil received nothing, despite facing considerable personal expense, and his request for pensions for the key Scottish lords was turned down. Cecil argued that Elizabeth 'had procured the conquest that none of her progenitors with all their battles had ever obtained – the conquest of the whole hearts and goodwills of the nobility and people of Scotland – which surely is better for England than the revenues of the Scottish Crown'.[32] She responded that she had spent £247,000, more than a year's revenue, providing men and equipment to free the Scots from France and they had benefited enough. They had also failed to negotiate the restitution of Calais.

From the safety of France, Mary refused to ratify the Treaty of Edinburgh, which she had played no part in negotiating, and failed to endorse the subsequent 'Reformation' Parliament. To do so would have compromised her position on the Scottish throne. As a Catholic, she could not accept the banning of papacy, and she had no intention of forgoing her claim to the English throne. This became a battle of wills with Elizabeth which would last for the rest of her life. There was no certainty that the French would stay away. 'There was still a nucleus of a French party in the bishops and churchmen, leagued with the disappointed Cock of the North [Huntly]' and his supporters.[33] Huntly wanted his share of the cake. He expected to be recognised as Lieutenant of the North with semi-regal status. This was nothing new. Scotland had been a loose affiliation of earldoms, each of which held judicial sway in their own areas and did not see themselves as bound by central authority. The Reforming Lords saw Huntly as the chief obstacle to Scottish unity. Both Lord James and Maitland worked hard to detach the other northern lords from his disruptive influence, causing many of them to attend the parliament designed to shape Scotland's future structure.

Knox did not wait for royal approval before meeting to dismantle the Scottish Catholic Church. Presbyterianism was now to become the 'established' faith of Scotland. He had, in the meantime, been commissioned to prepare a 'polity' for the new Scottish Reformed Church. Even Huntly recognised that the Reformation had become unstoppable. By May, Knox had already produced the first draft of a Book of Discipline setting out its dogma. Although he was its driving force, his lack of tact or interest in statecraft was an impediment. It was Maitland who 'framed' it, taking responsibility for:

> organising all the forces whose co-operation he believed to be necessary for carrying out, with safety and some prospect of permanence, the revolution which was inevitable, and which alone would end the schism that for a generation had distracted Scotland and made it a prey to its neighbours … He brought into it the political forces, without which he believed success to be impossible … Hence the increased emphasis he placed on national and patriotic considerations.[34]

The opening of Parliament was delayed by Mary's failure to send commissioners in accordance with the requirements of the Treaty of Edinburgh, but objections to their absence were overruled after heated debate, and it was formally opened on 9 August. Although he was Lord Chancellor, Huntly also conveniently absented himself, apparently suffering a 'sore leg', but more than 100 lairds attended. Huntly's absence allowed Maitland to take control as 'harangue maker', and he became its driving force to make it 'a massive, conclusive display of support for the Congregation' and a mandate for the new legislation.[35] He spoke with tact and efficiency, pointing out the debt that was owed to England and the need for the lords to work as a unified group. It was soon agreed that six representatives from among Knox's supporters should be elected to sit and vote with the Lords of Parliament at each new session and to join the Lords of Articles, who acted as the legislature when Parliament was not in session. Parliament now amounted to thirty-six members, including ten prelates, ten earls and lords, ten burgesses (mainly the provosts of the large towns) [collectively the 'three estates'] and the six representatives of Knox's followers.

Parliament's chief task was to change Scotland's religion, and Maitland spoke to confirm the abolition of papacy. This involved three acts: the first abolished the Pope's jurisdiction; the second annulled the old heresy laws; and the third prohibited the celebration of Mass. Given Maitland's close relationship with Cecil, these were modelled on corresponding English laws passed only in the previous year. It had always been the intention that this legislation should stand as a backstop to be used by the executive with discretion.[36] It was general practice within Europe for each state to adopt only one form of faith, but 'to be vastly more humane in enforcing it'.[37] There is no real evidence of religious persecution by Reformers in Scotland. The Catholic Church offered little resistance. Archbishop James Bethune of Glasgow (a nephew of the Cardinal) departed for Paris along with the French garrisons. The primate, Archbishop Hamilton of St Andrews (Chatelherault's illegitimate half-brother), kept a low profile while awaiting Mary's return. 'Their do-nothing pleas for patience and prayer only excited derision.'[38]

The next task was to approve the formation of the Scottish Reformed Church, now being dubbed 'the Kirk'. With the Reformers probably in a majority in Scotland and dominating the burghs, Parliament called on Knox to present 'the sum of the doctrine' that he wanted established.

Four days later, he presented his Confession of Faith, and it was agreed that it should be reviewed by Maitland and John Wynram of St Serf with their more moderating views. Maitland sent a copy to Cecil, whose advice was being sought throughout.[39] Knox was able to demonstrate that it was 'in substantial agreement with all the other reformed confessions'.[40] Despite attempts to tone down some of his strong wording and to omit a chapter on the civil magistrate, it was approved without amendment by a large majority.[41]

On Parliament's instruction, Knox organised a committee of Reformers to refine his draft of the Book of Discipline so that the Catholic hierarchy of bishops could be replaced by a General Assembly to provide the Kirk's administration. A Scottish Confession was also developed as a clear statement of Calvinist faith. Neither of these was debated in Parliament as Maitland feared that this would be divisive, when Parliament's aim was to present a united front. Knox's vision of a centralised Kirk to supervise religion, education for all classes and care for the poor and afflicted was supported by Maitland with some 'vehemence' and was quickly adopted in the burghs.[42]

Inevitably, Knox tested his hitherto harmonious relationship with Maitland by trying to go a step further. He hoped that the General Assembly would be authorised to supervise both Crown and government. Maitland knew that providing it with overarching powers would never find favour with the Scottish nobility, who benefitted from income drawn from church and monastic lands and would find their authority being subsumed. He realised that only the most extreme of those who had plundered church land for their own benefit would readily part with it and was unconvinced that they should.

With the terms of the Treaty of Edinburgh being approved in Scotland, Parliament selected twenty-four councillors to govern during Mary's absence in France (and for one year longer). These included Maitland and, after the meeting of Parliament, he became its Speaker. He wrote to Cecil of the 'great victory', and that the bishops had 'uttered their ignorance to their own confusion'.[43]

It was soon clear that the treaty would not be ratified by the French, who may never have had the intention of doing so. The Scots still needed the assurance of English aid in the event of a French invasion. On 11 October, a deputation seeking an English alliance set out for London headed by Maitland, with Morton and Glencairn. They were also supported by Robert Melville. To underline their hopes, Maitland reopened the prospect of Elizabeth marrying Arran, despite his mental instability, to replace Mary Queen of Scots on the Scottish throne. This was no 'light-hearted escapade'.[44] It was widely supported in Scotland, and Maitland came under huge Hamilton pressure to gain approval. Even Lord James appears to have backed it, although probably to assist the union rather than the Hamilton interest.[45] While Maitland admitted that 'Scotland is here in a corner of the world separated from the society of men', he was fully aware of its tactical and strategic import.[46] He argued 'that Scotland by divine geographical appointment offered England more advantages than [any suit from the Continent]'.[47] The marriage would create 'an Imperial Britain embracing England, Ireland and Scotland united under a common creed, language and crown', providing 'the best possible defence against Continental aggression'.[48] It would also provide a remedy for the cost of continual warring between them.[49]

The Scots reinforced their enthusiasm by tactlessly seeking Francis's and Mary's blessing, which was not, of course, forthcoming. Elizabeth had little enthusiasm for it.[50] She was at the height of her romance with Dudley and made clear that she was 'not presently disposed to marry'.[51] Furthermore, she was not prepared to countenance an anointed queen's deposition.[52] Randolph also voiced disapproval, but this is likely to have been based on his concern about Arran's 'imperfection'.[53] He considered the embassy to be 'as mad a journey as any that ever was made'.[54] He also 'felt that Maitland's unifying presence could ill be spared from the centre of government'.[55] Arran and Châtelherault were left extremely disappointed.

The Reformers' prospects looked uncertain. There was still a major constitutional problem. So long as Mary refused to ratify the Treaty of Edinburgh and failed to call Parliament, there was no approved mechanism for governing the country. Plundering the treasury without formal authority would be treasonable. Then, as if by some miracle, news came that, on 5 December, Francis II had died. Suddenly the Guises had lost power and 'the nightmare of a succession of a French prince was dissipated'.[56] Knox saw it as 'a wonderful and most joyful deliverance'.[57] When it became clear that Mary was likely to return to Scotland, Arran turned his marriage ambitions onto her. The English approved. It was also supported by Knox, who hoped that an ardent reformer might soften her Catholic stance. Nevertheless, the other Scottish lords feared the Hamiltons' resultant growth in power. To their relief, Mary showed no interest; the Guises had more important suitors to be wooed. There was some wry amusement in Scotland at Arran being thwarted for a second time. Mary's return, however, did not bode well for the Scottish Reformation. Maitland warned Cecil that many Scots were making efforts 'to put themselves in her good graces'.[58] It would also bring the alliance brokered with the English at the Treaty of Berwick to an end. 'If the amity was to be maintained', another bond for union would be needed.[59]

Chapter 3

The return of the widowed Mary Queen of Scots

It is important to assess the slightly differing attitudes of Maitland, Lord James, Knox, Cecil and Elizabeth to the prospect of Mary's return.

To preserve the amity, Maitland had to hope that Mary's ratification of the Treaty of Edinburgh would gain her Elizabeth's recognition as her heir. Having supported the marriage of Arran to Elizabeth, he needed to rebuild his bridges. He fully expected that, once separated from her Guise relations, she would be more amenable to the Reformist faith and would make a marriage acceptable to the English interest in return for the glittering prospect of inheriting the English throne. All his early correspondence with Cecil infers this assumption. He later hoped Elizabeth and Cecil would accept that if Mary became politically Protestant and made a marriage acceptable to them, she might remain personally Catholic. This proved not to be the case.

Lord James had a somewhat different agenda. As the eldest child of James V, albeit illegitimate, it always rankled with him that he could not be king, a role for which, in Cecil's eyes, he was eminently suited. He still hoped that this could be arranged but realised that he had to wait to be called and could not press his claim. If he could not be king, he wanted authority. This might be as regent or as the *eminence grise* behind the Scottish throne, but he wanted to be head of government and was not averse to heading a Scottish republic. As a staunch Reformer, he strongly favoured amity with England to dispense with the Auld Alliance and saw that this could be cemented by Elizabeth recognising Mary as her heir. This would oblige England to protect Scotland from Catholic aggression, particularly from France or from the Scottish Catholic nobility led by Huntly. He was determined that Mary should return to Scotland as an uncommitted widow to prevent her from bowing to ultra-Catholic Guise influence if she remained abroad. Her marriage to a Catholic potentate would threaten the Scottish Reformation and his own position. Like Maitland, he believed that Mary, once back in Scotland, would see the pragmatic imperative of becoming a Reformer to underpin a Protestant government and to promote her acceptability as Elizabeth's heir. He wanted her to choose a husband, who he would be able to work with while he remained as head of state. He was attracted by a foreigner who might spend time with Mary abroad, leaving his management of day-to-day affairs unfettered.

Knox, whose outspokenness was already making him less influential in political matters, was only interested in maintaining Scotland's Reformation, which he had initiated. He did not oppose Mary's return as queen but took for granted that she would be required to become a Reformer. He believed that a Catholic monarch could only cause schism and conflict, thus paralysing government action. He was critical of Lord James for permitting her to hold Catholic services in private. After living in Geneva, he would have preferred Scotland to become a Calvinist republic. Buchanan later developed a more sophisticated model of republicanism than Knox's *Monstrous Regimen of Women* to oppose the divine right of monarchy. This upheld the ideals of a free state, as espoused by Greece and Rome. He believed that rulers were accountable to the people. If they failed in their duties, they should be replaced, even if this called for tyrannicide.

Cecil also hoped for union between Scotland and England and strongly favoured Lord James and Maitland as anglophiles supervising Scottish government. He wanted to avoid Elizabeth acknowledging a Catholic heir, but was happy to string Mary along, as she would hardly adopt a Catholic policy in Scotland with the prize of the English throne, as she assumed, within her grasp. When Elizabeth later proposed that Mary should marry her paramour, Dudley, creating him Earl of Leicester for the purpose, Cecil made clear that her nomination as Elizabeth's heir would still need parliamentary approval. His lack of enthusiasm may have been coloured by Leicester being his political opponent, though Leicester was also lukewarm to the idea of the marriage and did all he could to extricate himself without offending Elizabeth.

Elizabeth's view was rather different from that of Cecil. She did not want religious preconditions to stand in the way of Mary as an anointed Tudor queen returning to her Scottish throne. At the same time, she was determined to avoid nominating any heir to the English throne, fearing that it would make them the focus of plots against her rule, just as she had been during the reign of her sister, Mary I. While admitting that there was no one she preferred to Mary, she told Maitland that she would not acknowledge her claim. She never veered from this stance, even in the last days of her reign, much to the later frustration of James VI. She would have liked to have had the power to nominate a successor in her will, as her father had done.

Mary returned to Scotland as a widow fully expecting that her position as Elizabeth's heir could be negotiated. She had been led to believe this by both Lord James and Maitland, although they expected her to become Protestant. As a former queen consort of France, it was the prospect of the English throne rather than the certainty of ruling out-of-the-way Scotland that was the attraction both for Mary and her Guise relations, but never would she consider subsuming her Catholic beliefs to political necessity. In this she demonstrated a political naivety that afflicted the important decisions of her reign.

To establish Mary's future, the first consideration was her remarriage. Sir Nicholas Thockmorton, the English envoy in Paris, reported that she was 'wise and prudent beyond her years and might prove dangerous'.[1] Her Guise uncles needed a suitor who would restore their flagging influence, but Catherine de Medici was determined to prevent this in the hope of taking greater control as regent for her younger sons. She quickly vetoed the suit of the ten-year-old Charles IX, now king of France, leaving the Guises to look further afield. Within a fortnight they were considering Philip II's son, Don Carlos, despite Catherine's opposition. Philip was not enthusiastic. He had no desire to encourage the Guises' hawkish ambitions so soon after the signing of the Treaty of Cateau-Cambrésis. His principal objective was to stay on cordial relations with Elizabeth in England. With Mary being her dynastic heir (if not rightfully queen), the English would consider marriage to his son as hostile. This did not prevent him continuing in negotiation to see what came of it.

Philip's other problem was that he did not want to admit that Don Carlos, whose mother, the Infanta Mary of Portugal, had died in childbirth, was displaying mental and physical shortcomings, which might have seemed even more off-putting than those of Francis II had they been more generally known. He was a hunchback with twisted shoulders, who never weighed more than six stone. He was also a sadist, who roasted live rabbits and tortured horses to hear them scream. He became brain damaged after fracturing his scull falling downstairs while chasing a servant girl whom he enjoyed flagellating. Although his life had been saved by a trepanning operation, he was left epileptic and homicidal, making any marriage completely inappropriate. Yet all of this appears to have remained hidden from the diplomatic community.

Cecil, Lord James and Maitland watched from afar in fear and trepidation. They needed to distance Mary from the Continental marriage market at the earliest opportunity by returning her as an unattached widow to her Scottish throne. 'The Guises, with the secret help of Spain [and with the militant Catholicism of Europe at their backs], might soon recover their lost ground.'[2] Mary's devout Catholic faith, though, would not sit comfortably with Knox and the newly established Kirk. There were rumours that she was encouraging a coterie of Scots, led by Huntly and Bothwell, to challenge the Lords of the Congregation. When her envoy, Gilles de Noailles, Abbé du l'Isle, appeared in Scotland, Knox records that he demanded the restoration of the Catholic clergy and bishops. The Scots said this would need parliamentary approval, which it was unlikely to provide. Nevertheless, Noailles stayed on in Edinburgh to discuss with Huntly and Bothwell the means of addressing the Protestant lords' power.

Other French envoys arrived to build bridges and to authorise a meeting of Parliament in the following May. They brought a liberal distribution of 'pensions' with a request for a renewal of the Auld Alliance. Maitland warned Cecil that this would be difficult to resist. He wanted Cecil's assurance of England's continued commitment to union, despite Elizabeth having rejected marriage to Arran. He also wanted her to make a gesture to attract Mary to the amity. He hoped to reconcile their interests by bringing 'over the Scottish Queen to the Protestant side'.[3] Ratifying the Treaty of Edinburgh was not enough. Cecil would not agree that Mary as a Catholic should be recognised as Elizabeth's heir, but Maitland applied pressure by warning that the Scottish Reformers were split into two camps, with the Hamiltons bent on arranging her marriage to Arran, and the remainder wanting her to return unattached.

The Protestant lords chose Lord James to visit Mary in France 'to grope her mind [as Maitland phrased it] from his great position and high character and his relationship to the Queen'.[4] He left on 18 March 1561 with a considerable retinue, carrying instructions to invite Mary to return, provided that she did not interfere with the Scottish Reformation and came with 'no armed force and no foreign council'. The plan, which was largely Maitland's, was agreed with Cecil when Lord James reached London on his way to France. Mary could return to her Scottish throne and hold Catholic services in private, if she undertook to maintain the religious status quo and not to reverse the Scottish Reformation so recently established. They shared Maitland's view that once separated from her Guise relations she would become more amenable in religion. By choosing a spouse approved by the English, she would become more acceptable as Elizabeth's heir.

Huntly and his northern allies did their best to derail the plan. They sent the persuasive Catholic priest, John Leslie, to visit Mary in France. After travelling by sea, he reached Mary ahead of Lord James. He invited her to return via Aberdeen, from where Huntly and other northern Catholics would escort her with 20,000 men to overthrow the Protestant government in Edinburgh. She realised, astutely enough, that the power of the Reformers made this a romantic fantasy and turned down the offer, but she respected Leslie, who later became Bishop of Ross and her closest adviser in captivity.

Leslie was closely followed by Lord James, who caught up with Mary on 15 April at St Dizier in Champagne, where she was accompanied by her uncle, the Cardinal of Lorraine. On the advice of d'Oysel, and even of her uncles, Mary had already decided to support the Protestant party in Scotland, 'as the most powerful in the Kingdom, and to make Lord James and Lethington her principal ministers'.[5] Brother and sister were candid over their religious differences, each trying to convert the other. (Lord James was even offered a cardinal's hat.) Nevertheless, he used his considerable powers over a period of four or five days to persuade her to accept the deal and to defer her remarriage. She would be required to ratify the Treaty of Edinburgh, which included her acknowledgment of Elizabeth's title to the English throne but could expect to be recognised as her successor if the English queen died childless.[6] This encouraged Mary, and it achieved the immediate objective, which was 'to sever [her] from the subversive designs of her uncles and the Catholic powers'.[7] There can be no doubt that Lord James and Maitland underestimated the difficulty of persuading Mary to adopt Protestantism, but Lord James seems to have overstated Elizabeth's and Cecil's willingness to nominate her as heir to the English throne. Elizabeth wanted Mary kept dependent on her goodwill for the fulfilment of her hopes: '[If Mary] were to remain a Catholic, and to hold herself openly or secretly at the disposal of the Catholic powers, there was reason to fear that her recognition by the English Parliament as the next heir would, sooner or later, be followed by Elizabeth's assassination.'[8]

Throckmorton, who had been fearful of the outcome of Lord James's discussion in the presence of the manipulative Cardinal of Lorraine, met up with him on his return to Paris and was impressed with his negotiating skills. As Lord James had travelled at his own expense, Throckmorton sought a reward for him from Elizabeth. She did not honour this, despite respecting his achievement, but, according to Leslie, Lord James asked Mary for the Earldom of Moray. This title was held by the Crown, but its estates were mainly in the hands of Huntly, who occupied the adjacent area. The objective was to clip Huntly's wings.

After returning to Edinburgh on 29 May, Lord James reported his negotiations to a convention of Scottish lords. Mary had made three requests: firstly, the calling of Parliament should be delayed until her arrival in Scotland, which was agreed (but Maitland had no intention of adhering to it); secondly, she wanted Bartholomew de Villemore, the former French Controller, to be retained in his old capacity, but this was refused; and thirdly, she pressed for Catholic bishops and churchmen to be restored to their benefices, as previously requested by Noailles, but this was emphatically resisted. Noailles left Scotland on 7 June, having tried unsuccessfully to persuade Huntly and Bothwell to prevent the convention from meeting by taking 'military possession of the capital'.[9] Lord James wrote to Mary to explain the convention's views. To thwart a Counter-Reformation, the convention asserted the Reformers' authority by appointing commissioners to destroy Catholic church artefacts all over Scotland. This 'was a political, quite as much as a religious measure, adopted in view of the Queen's return'.[10] Lord James and Maitland were detailed to handle the north 'to beard the reputation of the lion in his den'.[11] Huntly thought better of opposing them. 'According to Spottiswoode, these visitations were carried out amidst an orgy of violence, pillage and fire.'[12] 'The volumes of the fathers, councells, and other books of humane learning with the Registers of the Church [were] cast into the streets and consumed with fire.'[13] By spending forty days on this mission, Lord James and Maitland remained largely out of contact at a crucial time. As Maitland admitted, the victory of Protestantism was far from secure with its supporters being 'diverse in their commitment to the faith' and to the amity.[14] It was not so much a conflict between Catholic and Reformer, as between those supporting the Auld Alliance and those backing amity with England.

Despite her Catholicism, Mary seemed to provide a means of achieving union with England to replace the Auld Alliance. She knew that effective government in Scotland depended on her being recognised as heir to the English throne. It would then be treasonable for her subjects to appeal to England against her religious persuasion. She offered an advantage over Elizabeth's marriage to Arran by avoiding controversy with France, and he was a very poor prospect. However, she failed to appreciate that this required her to become a Reformer. Maitland hoped to find 'ways enough to induce her to favour the religion'.[15] He banked on the attraction of the English throne to bring her round, just as the opportunity of the French one was to persuade the Huguenot Henry of Navarre that 'Paris is worth a Mass'.

Maitland hoped that, with a successful negotiation, he would regain Mary's goodwill after having promoted Arran's marriage to Elizabeth. He was extremely nervous of how she would perceive him and was panic-stricken on hearing rumours that he was to be sent as the Scottish envoy to France.[16] He wrote to offer her 'faithful service' and she replied on 29 June, making clear that she knew exactly what he had been doing. She would forget the past and judge him only by his future loyalty but, 'as the principal instrument' of the 'practices' attempted against her, she told him to curtail his 'intelligence' with Cecil.[17] She wrote: 'Nothing passes among my nobility without your knowledge and advice. I will not conceal from you that if anything goes wrong after I trust you, you are the one that I shall blame first. I wish to live henceforth in the amity of the Queen of England and am on the point of leaving for my realm. On arriving, I shall need some money for my household and other expenses. There must be a good year's profit from my mint.'[18] This was imperious stuff from an eighteen-year-old, and Maitland was quickly reinvented as a faithful servant, despite sending Cecil a copy of her letter. With the exception of Huntly, Maitland had swayed most of the Scottish lords to support him, and gratefully accepted Elizabeth's assurance of her continued backing.[19]

Before leaving France, Mary held a meeting with Throckmorton, who, on Elizabeth's instruction, again sought her ratification of the Treaty of Edinburgh. She again refused, on the pretext that she needed to discuss it with her government, which might take a different view when she was back in Scotland. She also confirmed her determination to uphold Catholicism despite being tolerant of other beliefs. Elizabeth worried that, after a receipt of French pensions, the Scottish government might not pressurise her to ratify the treaty, and wrote to express her concern after all she had done for them, even suggesting that it should be made a precondition of Mary's return.

To Throckmorton's embarrassment, Elizabeth refused Mary's request for a passport to travel to Scotland through England. This upset Maitland, who was bent on fostering the amity. Nothing daunted, Mary was ready to set out regardless, making Maitland nervous at her temerity, and he advised Elizabeth 'to keep some good force at Berwick' until reaction to her arrival became clear. She may have planned to land 'somewhere north of the Humber ... pursuing her journey overland through the Catholic counties of the north', no doubt wooing the local communities as she went.[20] Instead, she travelled in two of France's royal galleys, which could outstrip any English vessel with designs on impeding her course. In reality, Elizabeth would never have risked affronting the French by interfering with her journey.

On 19 August 1561, after only five days at sea from Calais, Mary, dressed in her mourning clothes, landed at Leith with her entourage, including three of her Guise uncles. 'The mist was so thick and dark that scarce might any man espy the length of two pairs of boots.'[21] She was ahead of schedule and only her half-brother, Lord Robert Stewart, the Commendator of Holyrood Abbey, was available to greet her. He hastily arranged for Holyrood to be made ready. The lords soon appeared and received her arrival with great celebration. Even Huntly came from the north in great state. Knox admitted that the crowd outside Holyrood rejoiced with bonfires, and 'honest musicians gave their salutations at her bedroom window'.[22] Pierre de Bourdeille, Abbé de Brântome, who had accompanied Mary, was less fulsome, complaining that five or six hundred 'knaves of the town' played fiddles, rebecs (stringed instruments) and sang psalms 'so badly and out of tune that nothing could be worse!'[23] Mary showed consummate tact by thanking them in colloquial Scots. On 31 August, with her uncles and other members of her entourage, she attended a formal welcome with a banquet in the city. Lord James was immediately recognised as head of government and Maitland was hugely relieved when Mary affirmed her trust by reconfirming him as Secretary.

Having been away from Scotland for thirteen years, Mary delivered Charles IX's request to send an ambassador to renew the Auld Alliance. Nevertheless, Knox kept anti-Catholic propaganda close to the surface, preaching from the pulpit of St Giles' for two hours every Sunday as a prophet of doom. He declaimed that 'one Mass was more fearful to him than ten thousand armed enemies being landed in any part of the realm'. This upset Lord James, who needed all his powers of persuasion, with help from Argyll, Morton, Lord Robert Stewart and Maitland, to honour his pledge for Mary to hold Catholic services in private. The more zealous Reformers, including Knox, Arran, Glencairn and Patrick, Master of Lindsay, took issue with this. On her first Sunday in Scotland, the Master of Lindsay heckled her while she attended Mass in the Chapel Royal with her French guests and servants. With a group of fellow extremists, he shouted out that the 'idolater priest should die the death'. Lord James stood sentry at the door to provide protection, but the chaplain carrying the altar furniture and candles 'was trodden in the mire' and had to be rescued by Lord Robert Stewart.[24] The priest was so frightened that he had difficulty lifting the host for the elevation. This resulted in a proclamation, probably devised by Maitland and the queen, to prevent further disruption to her services. Eventually the Council formally confirmed her right to hold Mass with her household in private but drew the line at it being sung. She avoided conflict by approving an Act of the Privy Council to allow her Reformist government to operate without religious intervention.

Mary had alienated Catholics by confirming her agreement with Lord James to seek to celebrate Mass only for herself in private, but, by leaving the Catholic Church banned, the Crown's control of its income provided a strong practical incentive not to interfere on its behalf. Unlike in England, Scotland never needed a formal break from Rome to gain control of Church wealth. Its revenues had been collected by James V as early as 1535, when the Pope granted him the formal right to nominate Catholic bishops (although, given the distance of Scotland from Rome, this had been in practical effect since 1487). Mary used Church assets, as her father had done, to benefit loyal supporters among the nobility.

On Maitland's advice, the Act of Reformation of 1560 had not granted control of Catholic Church income to the Kirk, as so much of it was already received by the nobility. It thus remained under the Crown's jurisdiction, supplementing royal coffers. Nevertheless, he strongly supported the compromise, ultimately agreed in 1562, whereby one-third of each benefice was to be used to finance the Court of Session and the Kirk, leaving two-thirds in liferent (lease) to the present possessors. This was a timely financial arrangement that raised money for Mary's government and the impoverished Reformed church without having the appearance of taxation. It also curried favour with the English.

The Catholics were, however, determined to defend their religion. Being without freedom of worship, they embarked on a crusade to restore papacy. From the safety of the north, Huntly infuriated Lord James by claiming he could 'set up Mass in three shires'. Despite lacking authority there, Lord James hoped to wean him away from leading a Counter-Reformation. Neither Archbishop Hamilton of St Andrews – who had granted significant benefices to the Hamilton family – nor Archbishop Bethune of Glasgow – now based in Paris – were in any position to challenge the deal agreed with Mary, and she steadfastly refused to disturb the religious status quo in place on her return. Although Catholic services, other than those for herself in private, had been officially banned, she hoped to achieve religious tolerance, seeing herself as 'the chosen vessel of the Counter-Reformation', and 'was well aware of her value on the political chessboard of Europe'.[25] She was determined that her guests among the nobility and her servants should take Mass with her, unmolested, in private. She handled this tactfully, while gaining respect and popularity. Sir James Melville reported that she behaved 'so princely, so honourably and so discreetly, that her reputation spread in all countries'.[26] Michel de Castelnau, Sieur de Mauvissière, the French envoy, confirmed that she delighted the Scots. Nevertheless, Arran objected that she was taking advantage of a concession granted only to her. He accused attendees of 'idolatry' and scared off several of those invited. Although the Pope encouraged her to confront the heretics, this conflicted with her hopes for recognition as Elizabeth's heir.

It would have been difficult for Mary to follow precisely 'the path marked out for her by Maitland and Lord James'.[27] She would have needed to 'forfeit her French dowry, the favour of her Guisian kindred, the friendship of France, the sympathies of Catholic Europe, and the chances of [becoming consort to] the throne of Spain, not to speak of the immortal fame to be earned as the restorer of the lost dominions of the Catholic Church – and all for the sake of the doubtful friendship of Elizabeth, and the remote chances of the English succession'.[28] She was no zealous missionary for the Catholic faith. She disregarded papal and other Catholic advice when it did not suit her immediate purpose. In 1562, she refused to welcome the papal nuncio, who arrived uninvited to advise on restoring the Catholic faith. She transferred church lands under her supervision without seeking papal sanction. She married Henry, Lord Darnley, before receiving papal approval. She even adopted Protestant rites to wed Bothwell.

Realising that Knox was fomenting anti-Catholic propaganda, Mary summoned him to Holyrood. Even while in France, she had told Throckmorton that Knox was the most dangerous man in her kingdom. He was now aged forty-seven, the successful architect of the Scottish Reformation, and a profound irritant. He had already composed a prayer to be said after Grace with his family: 'Deliver us, O lord, from the bondage of idolatry. Preserve and keep us from the tyranny of strangers.' Suddenly he was face to face with the eighteen-year-old in a test of her religious faith, believing that she threatened to undo all that he had achieved. He was not about to pull any punches on grounds of her youth and sought to present her in the most unfavourable light.

Mary challenged Knox's comments in *The First Blast of the Trumpet against the Monstrous Regimen* [Rule] *of Women,* which referred to women as 'weak, frail, impatient, feeble and foolish creatures'.[29] She objected to him inciting armed revolt against an 'idolatrous ruler', especially a female ruler. This conflicted with the Tudor vision of the monarchy's divine authority. He admitted that his complaint was with Mary Tudor for breaking the 'covenant' between the English nation and God by repealing its Protestant legislation, but Mary pointed out that his book referred to all women rulers. She asked whether subjects should have the power to resist princes, and Knox was clear that if princes exceed their just authority, they should be opposed. It was an act of 'obedience' to resist rulers who opposed the true faith 'until that they be brought to a more sober mind'. As a Tudor monarch, Mary was stunned by the inference that she was subject to her people. Knox magnanimously agreed to tolerate her for the time being, claiming backhandedly 'to be as well content to live under your grace as Paul was to live under Nero'.

Despite leaving Mary in tears of frustration, Knox respected her religious conviction. He wrote to Cecil: 'Her whole proceedings do declare that the Cardinal's lessons are so deeply printed in her heart that the substance and the quality are likely to perish together … If there be not in her a proud mind, a crafty wit and an indurate heart against God and his truth, my judgement faileth me.'[30] He was not hopeful of persuading her to conform to the Protestant faith. This was not what Cecil, Lord James and Maitland hoped to hear.

Knox sought another interview with Mary to persuade her to the true path of the Reformers. As soon as they met, she again attacked him for undermining her position by opposing women rulers. Although he conceded that he would not disallow her rule on grounds of her femininity alone, they reached an impasse over religion and her absolute right to govern. She confirmed to him: 'Ye are not the Kirk that I will nurse. I will defend the Kirk of Rome, for, I think, it is the true Kirk of God.' Knox retorted: 'Conscience requireth knowledge, and I fear right knowledge ye have none.' She responded: 'But I have both heard and read.'[31]

Maitland did not approve of Knox's confrontational approach, realising that these showdowns could provoke her into a less conciliatory religious stance. He wanted her to become a Reformer but believed a more persuasive line would be more effective. He wrote to Cecil that she doth 'declare a wisdom far exceeding her age'. He went on: 'The Queen my mistress behaves herself so gently in every behalf as reasonably we can require. If anything be amiss, the fault is rather with ourselves. You know the vehemency of Mr. Knox's spirit, which cannot be bridled, and yet doth sometimes utter such sentences as cannot easily be digested by a weak stomach. I would wish he would deal with her more gently, being a young princess unpersuaded.'[32]

It was clear that Knox and Maitland were drifting apart, and Lord James was cast in the role of conciliator. To limit Knox's more controversial demands, Maitland managed to withdraw the requirement for the Book of Discipline to be signed by the nobility. When, on 2 October, the Edinburgh Town Council issued a proclamation placing Catholic priests in the same category as prostitutes and whoremongers, Mary was able to have it suppressed, with its members being deprived of their privileges.

In contrast to Knox, Mary's working relationship with Lord James began well, particularly as he was left to manage the government on her behalf. Maitland and Morton became his two closest advisers. With Lord James holding sway throughout this early period, Mary deferred to them. Despite his rough exterior, Morton was an outstanding administrator, but with a propensity for feathering his own nest. The Council contained six Reformers – Erskine as Lord Treasurer, Morton, Argyll, Châtelherault, Glencairn, Bothwell, and William Keith, 4th Earl Marischal, – and four Catholics – Huntly as Lord Chancellor, George Hay, 7th Earl of Erroll, John Stewart, 4th Earl of Atholl, and William Graham, 2nd Earl of Montrose. The remainder were the Officers of State, who had previously served under the queen regent; Maitland as Secretary, Robert Richardson as Treasurer, James MacGill of Rankeillor as Clerk-Register and John Bellenden of Auchnoul as Justice Clerk. Huntly and his allies, 'who had hoped for Catholic predominance under a Catholic queen, were deeply disappointed, and remained restive and discontented'.[33]

Lord James installed able military leaders to settle petty feuding between local lairds and to create an environment for peace with England in the Border region. On 4 September 1561, Sir John Maxwell was appointed warden of the western Marches to end its long-standing history of local bloodletting. Sir Andrew Ker of Cessford, one of the more powerful local magnates, became warden of the middle Marches.

Being close friends of Cecil, Lord James and Maitland seemed to offer the best hope of Mary being recognised as Elizabeth's heir. With their control of the Council, the practice of having six nobles present soon lapsed. It was generally only the Reformers who attended. All the Officers of State backed Lord James and would continue to support him through most of the upheavals of the next six years. He treated Mary in a bluff, dominating manner, while Maitland was more obsequious. Council statutes had the force of Acts of Parliament. Parliament's business was delegated to a committee, the Lords of Articles. When Parliament sat, its role was to sanction its committee's actions. As the Lords of Articles were chosen by those in power, they rubber-stamped Lord James's and Maitland's actions and Maitland did not need to attend. The issue was not in gaining approval for new legislation, but in implementing it. Traditionally, this had been undertaken by the great magnates in their hereditary roles, but this involved despotism and corruption. The queen regent had weakened their position by appointing civil servants as officials, both as her executive for government and to administer the courts. This policy was vigorously upheld by James VI on taking the reins of power.

Mary only rarely attended meetings, spending her time exuding charisma in her private apartments, cocooned within a close circle of courtiers such as the Setons, Livingstons and Flemings, who seemed suspiciously pro-French and Catholic. Buchanan reported: 'She was graced with surpassing loveliness of form, the vigour of maturing youth, and fine qualities of mind.'[34] Even Knox grudgingly admitted that she held 'some enchantment whereby men are bewitched'.[35] Despite captivating those at court, her failure to involve herself in government was markedly in contrast to her mother, and her son, James, when he came of age. She was not a 'reluctant ruler, displaying marked indifference to the problems of her native land', but willingly undertook extensive progresses to be seen by the Scottish people.[36]

With the revenues of the Duchies of Touraine and Poitou as Queen Dowager of France, and the inheritance from her mother's estates as Duchess of Longueville, Mary was financially secure. She cultivated an agreeably cosy atmosphere involving music and dancing. At Christmas 1561, overcoming his Calvinist scruples, Randolph reported: 'The ladies be merry, leaping and dancing, lusty and fair ... My pen staggereth, my hand faileth farther to write ... I never found myself so happy, nor never so well treated.'[37] Knox saw dancing as an invention of the devil, but his was a lone voice while Mary was becoming much loved. Progressively, people turned a deaf ear to his ranting. He complained that they were seduced from extremism by the court's gentle and civilising influence. Scandals, such as they were, fell on him. In 1563, at the age of forty-nine, he seriously damaged his credibility by marrying Ochiltree's daughter, the seventeen-year-old Margaret Stewart.

Chapter 4

Diplomatic efforts to establish Mary as Elizabeth's heir

Even while still in France, Lord James and Maitland realised that Mary's primary interest would be to gain recognition as Elizabeth's heir. At this stage, they both hoped that, when separated from her Guise relations, she could be brought round to the political necessity of becoming Protestant.

Her claim to the English throne was convoluted. Depending on one's religious persuasion, she was either the rightful claimant ahead of Elizabeth or had no claim whatsoever. Elizabeth's right to the throne was open to doubt. In Catholic eyes, Henry VIII had not validly divorced Catherine of Aragon at the time of her birth. This made Elizabeth illegitimate. In Protestant eyes, Henry had received a legal divorce, thus validating his marriage to Anne Boleyn. Although Elizabeth had been declared illegitimate by Act of Parliament in 1536 to protect the claims of Henry's children by Jane Seymour, and this had not been revoked in the meantime, she had been named in the succession under Henry VIII's will. Mary Tudor had been declared illegitimate in 1533, but this had not prevented her from succeeding her brother, Edward VI. Thus, in English eyes, Elizabeth was the legitimate queen. While Mary Queen of Scots was her dynastic heir, being the senior descendant of Henry's elder sister, Margaret Tudor, the former Queen Consort of Scotland, she was barred under the Act of Succession of 1536, having been born outside England, and had been overlooked in Henry VIII's will, under which he had parliamentary authority to nominate his successors. Thus, Mary's claim would need Elizabeth's approval, which in turn required Parliament's ratification.

With Mary having quartered her arms in France with the royal arms of England, it seemed clear that she had no intention of forgoing her claim to be Elizabeth's successor, even if she might defer her immediate claim.

This was confirmed by her refusal to ratify the Treaty of Edinburgh. Lord James and Maitland knew that the English throne held far more appeal for her than returning as queen to a relatively minor country.

Before Lord James visited Mary in France, Maitland had been extremely nervous of her return. He wrote to Cecil arguing that, as soon as she set foot in Scotland, she would win hearts with her charisma. Her Catholicism was unlikely to detract Scottish support as the Reformation had not sufficiently taken root and many lords remained Catholic. Even Reformist nobles, being 'inconstant' and 'covetous', could be bought off. If she pursued a Catholic policy, the Scottish Reformation would be in tatters, ending any prospect of union with England. Even though Lord James returned from France knowing that Mary would accept the religious status quo in Scotland, he knew that she would need inducement to convert to Protestantism. He wrote to Elizabeth with what he called a 'middle way' to test whether she would 'allure' Mary with the prospect of becoming her heir if she converted and subsumed her immediate claim to the English throne behind Elizabeth. He would then attempt to bring her 'to some conformity' in religion.[1] (See Endnote 2.) He regretted her adoption of the English coat of arms while in France, blaming it on poor Guise family advice. While his approach would never be acceptable to Elizabeth or Cecil, it provided the opening for Maitland's later negotiations.

As soon as Mary returned to Scotland, she wanted to resolve her English claim before considering marriage. As early as 1559, Elizabeth had told the English Parliament that she did not intend to marry, although this may have been a political manoeuvre to hold Philip II's suit at bay during the negotiations of the Treaty of Cateau-Cambrésis. Her decision to remain unmarried resulted in her being dubbed even then as the 'Virgin Queen'. Yet in 1560, she seriously contemplated marrying Dudley, with whom she was infatuated (see Endnote 3). They enjoyed a fling, lasting about five years, which was made all the more scandalous because he was married to Amy Robsart. The Spanish ambassador reported: 'Lord Robert has come so much into favour that he does whatever he likes with affairs and it is even said that her Majesty visits him in his chamber day and night.'[2]

Maitland was the obvious person to promote Mary's cause with Elizabeth and Cecil. He was the most able and experienced Scottish diplomat. He always gave the impression of being on the side of whoever he was talking to, a practice that resulted in Buchanan later describing him as a 'chameleon'. Maitland's objective was to cement the amity, which remained undocumented as it was considered merely a 'familiarity'.[3] At the time of Arran's suit to marry Elizabeth, the great attraction for England had been to protect its northern border. With the Reformers now in power in Scotland, this concern was not so critical.

While the Scottish government saw that the acceptance of Mary as Elizabeth's heir would provide England with protection from Continental Catholic aggression, the English concern was whether they could trust Mary to adhere to an anglophile political policy and maintain the Reformation in both countries. Maitland saw three stumbling blocks: firstly, Mary was not proving as compliant as hoped in converting to Protestantism; secondly, Elizabeth had to be persuaded to nominate a successor, despite seeing any heir as the focus for challenge to her rule; thirdly, Mary had to be persuaded to ratify the Treaty of Edinburgh, but this required Elizabeth to modify the condition that Mary should forgo any future claim to the English throne.

On 2 September 1561, only thirteen days after Mary's return from France, Maitland, now aged thirty-three, set off for London for a series of meetings with Elizabeth, who was attended by Cecil and Dudley. Elizabeth was quietly amused that this man who had argued so eloquently in favour of her marriage to Arran was now promoting Mary's claim to the English throne. She pulled his leg by claiming that she was expecting him to confirm Mary's long-delayed ratification of the Treaty of Edinburgh. Maitland took this seriously, explaining that in the period prior to his departure from Scotland, there had been insufficient time to call a Scottish Parliament and that Mary had not expected to have to answer so quickly. He claimed not to have discussed it with her, but, in his opinion, the treaty as drawn was prejudicial to her interests and she was unlikely to confirm it. He argued that it would be preferable to reach an accord that might endure, rather than something that would be ineffectual. His willingness to criticise the treaty's terms shows the familiarity of his relationship with Elizabeth.

Maitland now repeated Lord James's earlier request that Mary should withdraw her immediate claim to the English throne in return for recognition as Elizabeth's heir. He pointed out that when Margaret Tudor married James IV, Henry VII had not debarred her descendants from the succession. He then offered Mary's ratification of the treaty insofar as it confirmed Elizabeth's title, if Elizabeth would recognise Mary's claim to the succession, but admitted that this would require modification to its wording. Elizabeth expressed sympathy, but openly explained her concern for her security. While confirming that there was no claim she preferred to Mary's, she could not acknowledge her as her heir. Once confirmed, there was no going back; it was a right. She argued that, instead of friendship, it was likely to produce 'a contrary effect'.[4] 'Think you,' she asked, 'that I could love my winding-sheet, when as examples show, princes cannot even love their children who are to succeed them?' She was frank when she said: 'I know the inconstancy of the English people, how they ever mislike the present government and have their eyes fixed upon the person that is next to succeed ... They are more prone to worship the rising than the setting sun.' She admitted having been the focus for plots against Mary Tudor, sometimes without knowledge of them, and this left the second person in the realm at their mercy: 'There were occasions in that time I stood in danger of my life ... so never shall my successor be.'[5]

As a concession, Elizabeth agreed to appoint commissioners to modify the treaty terms. Mary would forego her claim only during Elizabeth's lifetime, thus upholding the dynastic succession that both queens held so dear. She told Maitland to correspond with Cecil to agree this. He believed this had been a good opening. Elizabeth was offering benevolent neutrality in return for Mary's friendship. By admitting there was no claim that she preferred to Mary's, she was not threatening to debar her under the terms of Henry VIII's will. Mary's religion was not discussed, but it can be assumed that she was expected to become Protestant, as the objective of union would otherwise be meaningless. Elizabeth greatly respected Maitland's part in trying to bring Mary to conformity and provided an English pension to cement his loyalty.

Although Maitland was back in Scotland by 24 September, an absence of only twenty-two days, his mission had laid out the ground rules for future diplomacy. Despite all his future efforts, an impasse had been reached. 'Elizabeth [had] concocted ... a cocktail of diplomatic finesse: a torpid combination of delay, prevarication and faint promises designed to give Mary the impression that a favourable response to her claim was negotiable.'[6] There were obvious benefits of keeping 'the Scottish Queen's affairs hanging in uncertainty'.[7]

In Elizabeth's eyes, Mary's rival claimants all had shortcomings, which weakened their position. If Mary were debarred for being born outside England, the next in line was Lady Margaret Lennox – Margaret Tudor's daughter by her marriage to the 6th Earl of Angus – followed by her two sons, Darnley and his brother, Charles Stuart. Henry VIII had vetoed her under his will, and their Catholicism was no more acceptable to the English Parliament than Mary's. After them, the next in line dynastically was twenty-three-year-old Catherine Grey, sister of the ill-fated Jane, and grand-daughter of Henry VIII's younger sister, Mary. She had the merits of being both Protestant and born in England, and was first in line under Henry VIII's will, but Elizabeth considered her totally unsuitable and had placed her in the Tower after her clandestine marriage to the Earl of Hertford (see Endnote 4). Her sister, Mary Grey, was never a serious contender. She was almost a dwarf, with a curvature of the spine, and may have been mentally deficient. In 1565, she secretly married the Sergeant-Porter, Thomas Keyes, a giant of a man, and their disparity in size caused wry amusement. When this came to light, she too was placed in the Tower, remaining there until her husband's death in 1572. They had no children, but she lived on in some poverty until 1578.

For those seeking a male heir, there was the twenty-five-year-old ultra-Protestant Henry Hastings, 3rd Earl of Huntingdon. He was descended from the Countess of Salisbury, niece of Edward IV, and was the leading Plantagenet representative. He was Dudley's brother-in-law, but had no children and no ambition for the throne. With the Tudors being well established, his claim was remote. When Elizabeth was ill with smallpox in the spring of 1562, Parliament identified four serious candidates: Mary Queen of Scots, Lady Margaret Lennox, Lady Catherine Grey and Huntingdon. The Spanish ambassador, Alvares de Quadra, Bishop of Aquila, reported that there was no certainty about the outcome, but no one supported Mary, who would need Elizabeth's backing to uphold her dynastic claim.

Finally and fairly implausibly, another claimant was the Infanta Isabella of Spain, the daughter of Philip II and Elisabeth de Valois, born in 1566. She claimed entitlement as a descendant of John of Gaunt. The Spanish Armada was later launched in her support, and she was again promoted in 1594 by the Jesuit Robert Parsons in his book, *A conference about the next succession to the Crowne of Ingland*. It cannot be believed that the English took her claim seriously, but Parsons's book was designed to gain papal support for her.

It seems clear that Elizabeth expected Mary to succeed her, if she: a) confirmed Elizabeth as the rightful queen; b) gave up any league with France and remained friendly towards England; and c) made an acceptable marriage with ultimate conversion to Protestantism. Nevertheless, she wanted Mary to take her claim on trust while she demonstrated her Protestant affiliation. This gave Mary none of the assurance she was looking for. Regardless of dynastic entitlement, the English government was determined on a Protestant monarch, and Elizabeth would be acting against its wishes if she favoured Mary, who remained mistrusted as a member of the Guise family. Maitland believed that Mary was not irretrievably committed as a Catholic. He told Cecil: 'Surely I see in her a good towardness, and think that the Queen, your sovereign, shall be able to do much with her in religion if they once enter in a good familiarity.'[8] Despite the Scottish praise for his negotiation, it was clear that, if Mary remained Catholic, neither Cecil nor the English Parliament would countenance her claim.

Although Elizabeth had agreed to renegotiate the treaty's unacceptable terms, this was never done. Six weeks after Maitland's return to Scotland, she demanded ratification in its original form. Mary had nothing to gain and everything to lose by agreeing. In January 1562, Sadler opposed Mary's claim to become Elizabeth's heir in the House of Commons, arguing that 'our common peoples and the very stones in the streets should rebel against it'.[9] With intrigue among English Catholics always close to the surface, a recognised Catholic heir would fuel doubts over Elizabeth's legitimacy and Cecil had persuaded her to change her mind. If Mary's stock rose, Philip's support for Elizabeth, upon which she depended, was unlikely to continue.

While everyone recognised the English desire for a Protestant succession, Mary's stand-off with Knox forced Maitland to try another tack. He hoped that Cecil would accept Mary as Elizabeth's heir if she made an acceptable Protestant marriage, even though she might remain personally Catholic. But Cecil would not agree. Her accession depended on her renouncing her Catholic faith.

Mary needed another approach. It was logical for the two monarchs to meet, as was recognised even by Mary's Guise uncles, who were still sidelined in France. To engineer this, Maitland had initially planned

Mary's return to Scotland via London, where the two queens could establish an acceptable basis for Mary to succeed Elizabeth. As has been seen, Mary's refusal to ratify the treaty ended this plan. Once back in Scotland, she approached Randolph, believing that a meeting would so inspire Elizabeth that any differences would melt away. She had told Francis Russell, 2nd Earl of Bedford while still in France: 'We are both in one isle, both of one language, both the nearest kinswoman that each other hath, and both Queens.'[10] By reaffirming their kinship, she hoped that Elizabeth would be persuaded to recognise her rightful dynastic claim. On 5 January 1562, Mary wrote: 'We will deal frankly with you, and wish that you deal friendly with us; we will have at this present no judge of the equity of our demand but yourself ... If God will grant a good occasion that we may meet together, which we wish may be soon, we trust that you shall more clearly perceive the sincerity of our good meaning than we can express by writing.'[11]

While Elizabeth enjoyed a natural affinity with male company, Mary always preferred women and told her: 'It is fitter for none to live in peace than for women, and for my part I pray you think that I desire it with all my heart.'[12] Although Elizabeth was receptive, the English Privy Council was divided. Despite Mary's religious tolerance being well received, Cecil preferred to follow Henry VIII's will by promoting the Protestant Catherine Grey, even though Elizabeth found her unacceptable. Despite this, Elizabeth considered making Mary her *de facto* heir, but without naming her as such. She was a respectable widow and had not put a foot wrong. This terrified Cecil and, much to Maitland's frustration, he did all he could to prevent the meeting. Both Maitland and Lord James now found Dudley more amenable than Cecil in promoting it.

Despite Scottish Catholic opposition, Mary persuaded her Council to approve her visit to England. On 25 May, Maitland returned to London, remaining there until July to finalise details for a meeting at York in August or September. He was nervous of the outcome and, before leaving Scotland, had written to Cecil: 'I pray you let me tak no voyage on hand oneless the success may fall out according to my desire for I list not always to travel in oncertayntees, he that will hasard must sometimes lose.'[13] The planning reached an advanced stage with masques being written to cover three evenings. Nevertheless, Cecil continued to put a damper on it, complaining at the expense, estimated at £40,000.

Then bad news came from France. On 1 March 1562, while travelling with his men from Joinville to Paris, the Duke of Guise had attacked a group of Huguenots holding an unauthorised service in a barn at Vassy in Champagne. His men left twenty-three dead and over 100 wounded. Cecil saw this as the start of a Guise-inspired religious crusade, which might spread to England. In France, Catholics and Huguenots took up arms, with Spain likely to offer the Catholics support. To curb Guise power, Catherine de Medici expressed sympathy for the Huguenots, who were now led by the Prince of Condé. Throckmorton told Elizabeth that, by backing the Huguenots, she could gain Calais, Dieppe or Le Havre, and perhaps all three. With England poised to challenge her Guise relations, Mary called in Randolph to dissociate herself from her uncles' 'unadvised enterprise'. Although Elizabeth still wanted to meet Mary, Cecil sought a postponement, citing wet weather and a shortage of 'wine and fowls' at York.[14] Without seeking her approval, he sent Sir Henry Sidney to Scotland to cancel it.

By 25 June, the fighting in France had fizzled out. Maitland, who had 'shuffled the cards anew', continued to lobby Elizabeth, who was at Greenwich, and, to his relief, on 6 July, she overruled Cecil, confirming the meeting, despite the Council's universal opposition. 'It is both groaned at and lamented of the most and the wisest', wrote Sidney to Throckmorton. Mary received a safe conduct to meet sometime between 20 August and 20 September with 1,000 attendants and provision for Catholic worship in private. Although she had to pay her share of the cost, Scottish coin could be exchanged on arrival. Cecil was beginning to feel that the amity's benefits were no longer mutual, but, through gritted teeth, he arranged for an elephant to participate in the pageant.

Maitland returned home in triumph, but news of the meeting received only a muted reception in Scotland. Châtelherault excused himself with a poisoned arm and Huntly was incapacitated by a sore leg. Despite Mary's excitement, the Scots were highly suspicious of Elizabeth's motives. On 12 July, the day of Maitland's return, Elizabeth prevaricated. Fighting had again broken out in France, and England might have to intervene. The meeting would greatly strengthen Guise standing and could lead to the formation of a Catholic league against Protestantism. Elizabeth would not forgo the opportunity to incite France's internal troubles and was committed to supporting the Huguenots.[15] Sidney returned to Scotland to postpone the meeting for a year. When Mary received him, 'it was with great grief ... divers manifest demonstrations ... and watery eyes. She fell into such a passion as she did keep her bed all that day.'[16]

Mary was caught in the middle of a conflict between her uncles and England. If she supported her family, she would be opposing Elizabeth. If she supported Elizabeth, she would be backing heretics against her family and their lawful sovereign. She was well aware that her pension as Dowager Queen of France, upon which she was dependent, funded her Scottish government. She kept her head down, but assured Randolph of her neutrality, confirming that her uncles would have acted out of duty. The best she could do was offer herself as mediator between 'oure dearest friendis, England and France', but she had little expectation of this being accepted.[17]

With time on her hands, Mary was persuaded by Lord James to challenge the overly powerful Gordons in northern Scotland. On reaching Aberdeen, she received Elizabeth's letter justifying her support for the French Huguenots. 'Necessity has no law,' it said. 'We have no choice but to protect our own houses from destruction when those of our neighbours are on fire.'[18] Charles IX would see her as a good neighbour for preserving the Huguenots and destroying tyranny. She provided graphic details of the Catholic butchery, confident that Mary would not ignore her uncles' terrible crimes. 'I would write more,' she said, 'but for the burning fever that now holds me in its grip.'[19] She was suffering from smallpox, which could be fatal. This gained Mary's attention, and she prepared herself to claim the English throne. Nevertheless, when the English Privy Council discussed the succession at the height of Elizabeth's illness, only a single voice favoured her claim.

From the outset, English involvement in the war in France proved a disaster. In October 1562, Guise captured Rouen from the Huguenots after a long siege. He then coerced them into combining with Catholics to evict the English, who were pushed back to Le Havre. Mary showed a lack of tact by holding a series of balls in praise of Catholic victories. This was hardly likely to soothe the Reformers. Knox voiced disapproval when 'the dancing began to grow hot' and was disgusted at her celebration of Protestant deaths. With the English fearing an attempt by the Guises to place Mary on the English throne, Elizabeth's correspondence with her dried up.

Chapter 5

Lord James (soon to be Earl of Moray) and Maitland establish authority

Throughout Scottish history, bitter sores between warring clans have caused feuds lasting several generations. With Lord James being the illegitimate son of James V, and Maitland being a member of the diplomatic class, they were isolated from such rivalries. Nevertheless, they were open to challenge from three groups jealous of their power: the Hamiltons, led nominally by Châtelherault; the Gordons, led by Huntly; and the Hepburns, led by Bothwell. Each commanded enough wealth and military support to cause a nuisance.

Despite being a Protestant, Bothwell had supported the queen regent. He had ambushed funds being sent from England to support the Lords of the Congregation against her French garrisons, causing him to fall out with them. As Lord High Admiral, he had come to Calais to escort Mary home, taking charge of the merchant ships chartered for her baggage. After a cumbersome journey through the North Sea, these arrived at Leith several weeks after the queen. On arrival, he was singled out for his loyalty to Mary's mother with gifts of land. Although he was appointed to the Privy Council, he did not attend regularly. With Arran showing signs of eccentricity, Bothwell was banished from court after treating him as a laughing stock. When his sister, Jean Hepburn, married Mary's and Lord James's half-brother, Lord John Stewart, Bothwell hosted their reception at Crichton. He also arranged a stag party for the bridegroom. Late at night, Lord John was escorted on a drunken sortie through Edinburgh, where they called at the house of Arran's mistress, Alison Craik, 'a good handsome wench'.[1] As Arran was not there, they returned on the next evening, forcing him to escape by a back door. The General Assembly lodged a complaint, and, on the following night, the Hamiltons and the Hepburns arrived with armed supporters ready for an affray. It was only the last-minute intervention by Lord James, Argyll and Huntly that calmed matters. Mary saw the escapade as a joke that had gone badly wrong and banished Bothwell to Crichton for a fortnight, hoping that it would soon be forgotten, and Knox was asked to reconcile Bothwell and Arran.

With Arran showing signs of delusion, he claimed that Bothwell was encouraging him to rekindle his suit to marry Mary, making her extremely wary of him. He told Knox that Bothwell had advised him to murder Lord James and Maitland and to abduct the queen to Dumbarton as a prelude to marrying her. In all probability, Bothwell had spoken in jest, but Arran wrote to Mary and Lord James that Bothwell was trying to involve him in a power-sharing plan. This was treasonable, and Lord James was looking for an excuse to bring Bothwell to book. It is hard to judge whether Arran's story was told in spite after the attack on his mistress, or whether Bothwell was taunting him. Arran was clearly insane and Châtelherault had to restrain him at Kinneil, his house near Bo'ness.

Arran and Bothwell were both arrested and brought to Edinburgh Castle on 4 May. With nothing to hide, Bothwell willingly came forward for trial. Arran was interviewed by Erskine and Morton, both of whom found him apparently mentally fit, but he relapsed and was returned to his father's care, from where he escaped to see Knox. Knox reported that 'he began to rave and speak of devils, witches and such like, fearing that all men about came to kill him'.[2] Lord James now held him at St Andrews to await a confrontation with Bothwell before Mary and the Privy Council. On arrival, he again accused Bothwell of treason. Despite his obvious lunacy, Lord James imprisoned him in Edinburgh Castle, although he was 'ill-bruited for [such] rigorous entertainment'.[3] (See Endnote 5.)

Although Bothwell was exonerated without trial, Lord James wanted to avoid any mischief while he and Mary were in the north dealing with the Gordons. Mary thus gave approval for Bothwell to be held in Edinburgh Castle. Three months later, on 28 August 1562, he escaped and asked Knox to intercede, hoping that Mary would recognise the injustice of his imprisonment. Mary (who was sympathetic) allowed him to take a ship to the Continent. Unluckily, this was wrecked in a violent storm off the Northumberland coast. Although the English offered to return him,

Lord James requested a trial to be arranged in London, where he knew the English hated him. On 24 January 1563, Bothwell was moved to Tynemouth, from where he was sent by Elizabeth to the Tower, remaining there until Mary's marriage to Darnley three years later.

It was Lord James, not Mary, who was married, choosing Agnes Keith, Marischal's eldest daughter. On 10 February 1562, Mary hosted a wedding celebration for them at Holyrood. Much to Knox's disgust, this involved feastings and masques over three days. Recognising Lord James's role as architect of her return to Scotland, Mary granted him the earldom of Moray, a title he had always coveted. Its estates had previously been occupied by Huntly and the objective was to clip his wings. Although the title was granted on 30 January, it was not immediately made public. On 7 February, it was announced that he had been created Earl of Mar in recognition of his marriage.

It was not only Lord James who wanted to weaken Huntly's power; Mary had good reasons of her own. This had very little to do with religion, but was designed to bring the recalcitrant earl, who was spearheading efforts to prevent her conciliation with Elizabeth, to heel. Furthermore, the twenty-six-year-old Sir John Gordon, Huntly's third son, described by Buchanan as a man 'in the very flower of youth', was acting as if he were above the law.[4] He cut a dash at court and had been cynically encouraged by Lord James and Maitland to become Mary's suitor. Nevertheless, he was a rogue, who had caused an affray in Edinburgh. Although he had been placed under house arrest, under the supervision of the Hamiltons, he had escaped.

Together, Mary, Lord James and Maitland engineered a plan to bring the Gordons to heal, and to enable Lord James to gain control of the Moray estates. On 11 August 1562, with Maitland still in London, Mary and Lord James left Stirling with a well-equipped force led by Kirkcaldy and the Master of Lindsay. Their initial objective was to gauge Huntly's reaction from his Aberdeenshire base at Strathbogie, which was rich in treasures and furnishings, including the church ornaments from Aberdeen Cathedral, held for safekeeping until Catholicism could be restored.

Mary wanted Randolph to witness her challenge to the most powerful of the Scottish Catholic magnates. Despite travelling through appalling weather, they reached Aberdeen on 27 August, where the Countess of Huntly pleaded the cause of her son, Sir John. Mary insisted on his return to ward at Stirling, and, though he went, he again escaped, raising 1,000 horse to harry the royal party, with the intention, as he later admitted, of abducting Mary. She warily refused Huntly's invitation to Strathbogie, despite his reputation for 'marvellous great' hospitality.[5] There were rumours that he planned a coup to assassinate Lord James, Maitland and Morton, forcing her to marry Sir John. Mary was protected by the royal army, but Sir John continued harrying her party as it moved to Darnaway Castle, the Moray stronghold, which Randolph reported as 'very ruinous'.[6]

From the relative safety of Darnaway, Mary and Lord James provocatively announced his creation as Earl of Moray. After moving on to Inverness, Mary used all her guile by wearing highland dress to gain local support. She felt strangely at home with the Gaelic people, who spoke a language that she did not understand. Randolph was completely caught up in it all, reporting to Cecil: 'It may please you to know that in good faith where so many were occupied, I was ashamed to sit still, and did as the rest.'[7]

Sir John's plan was to separate Mary from Moray as they crossed the Spey. Although he hid 1,000 troops in the woods, Mary's escort of 3,000 men forced him to retire. Randolph had 'never seen her merrier, never dismayed, nor never thought that stomache to be in her that I find'. On 22 September, she received a great welcome on returning to Aberdeen. With a dearth of lodgings, Randolph found himself sharing a bed with Maitland, who had joined them from London. He was horrified when he learned that Huntly had intended burning their hostel to do away with his bed companion.

After being summoned to Aberdeen, Huntly was ordered to surrender the Crown's cannon he was holding at Strathbogie. When it did not appear, he was denounced as a rebel. His eldest son, George, Lord Gordon, was Châtelherault's son-in-law, so Huntly called on him to raise Hamilton support. He even contacted Bothwell, who had by then escaped from Edinburgh Castle. With no support being forthcoming, he lost his nerve and offered troops to help to capture Sir John, but Mary would not have the untrustworthy Gordons in her midst. Huntly was now forced into a willow-the-wisp existence to avoid capture, visiting Strathbogie only by day. Kirkcaldy hoped to surprise him at his midday meal. He approached the castle with twelve men, planning to hold the entrance until reinforcements arrived. Timing was of the essence, but his back-up force gave the game away by appearing too early. The portly Huntly managed to escape, without sword or boots, over a back wall onto a fresh horse, which outdistanced his pursuers.

With father and son now outlawed, Lady Huntly remained at Strathbogie to negotiate, but when Mary refused a meeting, she rejoined her husband. Witches then told her that his unmarked body would lie in the tolbooth at Aberdeen the next evening, so she persuaded him to attack Mary's forces. He positioned 800 men at Corrichie, fifteen miles from Aberdeen, with every expectation that Mary's troops raised locally would defect. When Moray appeared with 2,000 men led by Argyll and Morton, Huntly was hopelessly outnumbered. He was suffering from high blood-pressure and was too unwell to withdraw. When he eventually appeared at 10 o'clock the next morning, 1 November, his men were already committed. After an exhortation from Maitland, Moray's force raked Huntly's elevated position with fire, forcing him into attack, but Huntly, Sir John and his younger brother, Kenneth, were captured after being mired in swampy ground. At this critical moment Huntly 'burst and swelled' and fell dead from his horse.[8] His unmarked body was taken to Aberdeen, thus fulfilling the witches' prophecy.

Although Kenneth was reprieved, Mary attended Sir John's execution on the following day. He made her distraught by announcing from the scaffold his hopes of marrying her, and, when the executioner made a clumsy job, she fainted. After remaining in her chamber for a day, she had recovered sufficiently to take possession of the furnishings from Strathbogie, including elaborate tapestries and the ornaments from Aberdeen Cathedral, some of which were provided to Moray. Huntly's role as Lord Chancellor was given to Morton.

On 26 November, Gordon was handed over by Châtelherault and was also convicted of treason. He was transferred to Dunbar, but Moray persuaded Mary to defer his execution. He was forced to attend the attainder of his father's embalmed but disembowelled body in Edinburgh. 'The coffin was set upright, as if the Earl stood on his feet.'[9] Maitland expressed Mary's feelings by saying: 'I am sorry that the soil of my native country did ever produce so unnatural a subject as the Earl of Huntly hath proved in the end against his Sovereign.'[10] Gordon was not released until 1565 when Mary needed his support for her marriage to Darnley.

Moray was now the most powerful figure in Scotland. In addition to the spoils from Strathbogie, Mary increased his annual income by 1,000 marks, but, as always intended, withdrew the earldom of Mar. She had given the Reformers unassailable power but had no pangs of conscience. She wrote to both her uncle the cardinal and the Pope confirming her continued personal allegiance to the Catholic faith. Châtelherault reconfirmed his Reformist faith and sought Knox's help to gain a reprieve.

With the Gordons defeated, Maitland continued his efforts to arrange Mary's meeting with Elizabeth, telling Cecil that, after bringing down the senior Scottish Catholic earl, she needed better assurance in the English succession than relying on Elizabeth's trust. Mary assured Randolph that she 'never more heartily desired the Queen's Majesty's kindness and goodwill than she now doth'.[11] He took her side, telling Cecil that, despite her love for her uncles, 'yet she loveth better her own subjects. The amity meant more to her than a priest babbling at an altar.'[12]

Cecil remained unconvinced. When Parliament met on 11 January 1563, he tabled a Bill of Exclusion to debar Mary from the English throne. With the Huguenots weakening, 'France and Spain were drawing together', and it was not the time to '[take] the risks that Mary's recognition would entail'.[13] When Mary was told, she retired to bed for six days, but, on 13 February 1563, sent Maitland to London for one more push. He brought a letter from Moray, seeking to reignite a 'love once kindled'.[14] With Elizabeth recovered from smallpox, he hoped to prevent the bill from becoming law. Mary had told him that, if it were passed, he was to demand an audience with her. There was nothing he could do. Mary was a woman, a Guise, a Catholic and a foreigner. Although he offered Mary's services to arbitrate with France, he had no confidence in them being accepted.

Mary was understandably depressed at the failure of Moray's 'middle way'. She needed a new approach. She decided to secure her claim by finding a husband, even one who might lack Guise approval. She did not criticise Maitland. Despite his failure to arrange a meeting with Elizabeth, Mary recognised his worth by formally confirming him as Secretary of State. He now travelled on from London to open negotiations in France.

Chapter 6

The negotiations for Mary's remarriage

With Moray managing her government, Mary settled down to her introspective court life, every inch the model queen in her mourning clothes. Unlike Elizabeth, she made clear that she wanted to remarry, but Moray preferred others to take the lead in finding her a husband who might weaken his position. This made negotiations slower than she hoped. She was beginning to find his moralising demeanour irksome. By comparison, Maitland was amenable, and she began seeking his advice, relying on his diplomacy to identify a suitable consort. She saw marriage only in terms of providing the 'fortification of her estate' and reinforcing her dynastic claim to the English throne.[1] She would not necessarily subordinate herself to her husband but believed that the Scottish nobility would be more compliant if dealing with a man.

In January 1563, when Maitland took charge of her marriage negotiations, he, in effect, replaced Moray as her leading minister. Yet he lacked Moray's authoritative persona. In February 1563, he broadened the Council's representation by appointing Ruthven, who was an adamant Protestant and had led the Reformers in Perth. There is evidence that Maitland received lands in East Lothian as a pay off, and they remained close allies until his death in 1566.[2] Nevertheless, Ruthven was mistrusted, with a reputation for taking sides for personal benefit and for dabbling in sorcery. Randolph records Moray's disapproval of him, and Mary saw him as someone 'I cannot love', which Ruthven blamed on his use of enchantment. Her concerns were to prove justified when he played a leading role in Riccio's murder.

While Mary was in the north, a mob threatened a priest celebrating Mass at Holyrood. She blamed Knox for inciting the riot and, against Maitland's advice, sent him for trial before Parliament. He arrived with a substantial following, supported by both Moray, infuriated at his loss of authority, and Ruthven. Maitland warned her that she would lose the argument, and Knox was acquitted when even a Catholic bishop supported him. She needed Moray and, swallowing her pride, reinstated him beside Maitland as her joint chief minister.

The choice of Mary's husband, whether Protestant or Catholic, would disturb the careful balance between her private Catholic and public Protestant affiliation. The principal objective was to enhance her claim to the English throne. This precluded an overtly Catholic spouse. The English would feel threatened by a powerful prince with his own dominions, but, if he lacked influence, she gained nothing. If she left Scotland to reside permanently with someone with less authority, her throne would be at risk. A Scottish or English subject would be demeaning, unless he improved her claim to the English throne, and would cause jealousy with his peer group. Overcoming these issues would be difficult.

Widows were not generally the first choice for royal husbands, but at twenty Mary had youth, beauty and a crown in her favour. She knew that her dynastic claim to the English throne was of greater appeal than her assured possession of the Scottish one. Cecil feared that, if she chose a Catholic spouse, the Pope would declare Elizabeth illegitimate, causing English Catholics, still in a majority in the shires, to rise in Mary's favour. He saw that a Scottish royal family with children would win English hearts, winning allegiance for her from the childless Elizabeth. He advised that, without Elizabeth's prior approval, her marriage would be considered hostile. He wanted a delay, hoping that Elizabeth would marry before her.

Mary's initial objective had been to find a powerful dynastic prince to underline her 'greatness' and to restore the Guise family's flagging influence.[3] Yet there was only a handful of suitable candidates and, as she explained to Randolph, they were not falling over themselves to seek her hand. To Moray's and Maitland's dismay, her first choice remained Don Carlos, potentially the most powerful prince in Europe. Since her departure from France, negotiations with the Spanish had been handled though the secret intercession of her Guise cousin, Anne, Duchess of Arschot, daughter of Antoine, Duke of Lorraine. She was a close friend of Philip II's chief minister in the Low Countries, Antoine de Perrenot, Cardinal Granvelle. In February 1563, Maitland was sent to London to hold secret talks with the Spanish ambassador, de Quadra, on a mission that was to last four months.

Maitland's negotiating plan has been discussed in the Preface. By remaining Catholic, Mary was not following the script that had been devised for her. On arrival in London, he obeyed her instructions by meeting de Quadra to reopen the prospect of marriage to Don Carlos, whose physical and mental shortcomings remained hidden from the diplomatic community. Far from identifying impediments to the match, Maitland wholeheartedly encouraged it. De Quadra claimed that their marriage was 'the thing in the world that he most desired'.[4] He confirmed it as 'such a marriage as would enable her to assert her rights', reporting back that the eighteen-year-old prince was 'very far in love with her'.[5] Knowing the Spanish ambassador's loquacious tongue, Maitland might have been more circumspect, but he fanned rumours in directions that would have seen encouragement of the marriage as unwelcome. They even reached Knox and Catherine de Medici. If genuinely supportive, he would surely have remained more discreet. De Quadra reported that Maitland accepted that a Catholic husband 'would be bound to seek Catholic measures, and [the Scots] would have to put up with them'.[6] With the English facing the spectre of another Spanish king of England, it is not possible to reconcile Maitland's single-minded focus on the union with genuine backing for the marriage. Nevertheless, he convinced de Quadra, who wrote to Philip enthusiastically: 'Not only would you give your son a wife of such excellent qualities ... but you also give him a power which approached very nearly to [Pan-European] monarchy.'[7]

Maitland's approach has to be seen as a deception encouraged by Cecil to test Mary's willingness to consider such a match in the hope of deterring Elizabeth from nominating her as her heir. To maintain his cover, Cecil fired off a moralistic tirade to bring Maitland back into line and refocus him securely onto a tack upholding Protestantism and the union. It is difficult to believe that Cecil was genuinely critical of Maitland and their old familiarity was soon back in place. The ruse bears all the hallmarks of separate discussions with de Quadra conducted by Dudley's brother-in-law, Sir Henry Sidney, on his behalf in February 1561. This is explained in Endnote 6.

Russell also accepts that Maitland was not 'an earnest favourer of the match', which 'sits uncomfortably with his image of Maitland as an Anglophile proponent of the union'.[8] Nevertheless, he comes to a different conclusion on Maitland's motive. He argues that Maitland was exerting 'pressure on the English to frighten them into concessions regarding the succession and the amity'.[9] He concludes: 'There was in Maitland a growing arrogance, which tended to make him less careful of consequences in prosecuting his policy, especially in the face of opposition, which he thought unreasonable, and not a little contemptuous, not only to himself, but to his country.'[10] This view seems quite far-fetched for a diplomat of Maitland's stature. Russell also argues that Maitland attempted to protect Mary's claim to the English throne by confirming both her and Philip II's religious tolerance. He cites Philip's reluctance to support Mary Tudor's burning of English heretics and his pragmatic acceptance of the development of Protestantism in the Low Countries. Yet Maitland knew better than anyone that the English government was determined on a Protestant succession.

Another view is that Maitland's negotiating skills ran away with his more realistic objectives, reaching conclusions that he did not personally support. This also seems implausible. It is also suggested that Moray supported the Don Carlos marriage in expectation that Mary would be obliged to live in Spain, so that he could supervise the Scottish government without interference. It again seems unrealistic for the Spanish to permit a committed Reformer to administer a key part of their dominions without any ambition for a Counter-Reformation. Elsewhere it is suggested that, when Cecil learned of Maitland's negotiations, their former cordial relationship was fraught with suspicion. According to Randolph, Moray also expressed his disapproval. Despite this, their friendship quickly resumed, and it is more likely that Moray was in on the act. On one count, the rumours proved helpful to the Scottish Lords. When they surfaced, Archbishop Hamilton unwisely celebrated Mass over Easter, forcing Mary temporarily to imprison him.

On 17 April 1563, Maitland arrived in France to explain the de Quadra negotiation to Catherine de Medici but seems to have hinted that these did not reflect his own views. She felt understandably threatened at the prospect of an axis of Spanish power surrounding France. Despite wanting Philip's support against the Huguenots, she was not going to hand him the English throne. She did not realise that Philip was only playing along with the Don Carlos marriage to divert Mary from choosing the twelve-year-old Charles IX, unaware that this was opposed by Catherine. The Guises felt obliged to support Catherine. They were in no position to do otherwise. Two months earlier, while inspecting his army at Orléans, the Duke of Guise had been killed after being shot three times in the back of his shoulder by a Huguenot. On hearing this, Mary 'was marvellous sad, her ladies shedding tears like showers of rain'.[11] Randolph reported: 'Here we have not a little ado … I never saw merrier hearts with heavier looks since I was born.' Mary was now destitute of confidantes except for her four Maries, Mary Fleming, Mary Seton, Mary Livingston and Mary Bethune, who knew Scotland no better than she did. She confided in Randolph that she needed a husband, both personally and politically. On Randolph's persuasion, Elizabeth wrote her a much-cherished letter of condolence.

With Catherine de Medici having gained control of French government, she cajoled the Huguenots into an alliance to force out the English, their erstwhile allies, from their base at Le Havre. While in Paris, Maitland embarked on Mary's offer to mediate between France and England. He quickly negotiated the release of Sir Henry Killigrew, who had been captured at the fall of Rouen after leading an English contingent in support of the Huguenots. This gained Maitland the grudging respect of Sir Thomas Smith, the English ambassador. To Cecil's annoyance, Maitland also tried to steer the English towards withdrawal from France, but parried Catherine de Medici's attempts to renew the Auld Alliance. His job done, he left France on 22 May, travelling with Killigrew.

To resuscitate Guise standing, the cardinal wrote to Mary in August to promote the Archduke Charles's suit. His intervention annoyed Mary, who concluded that he 'careth not what becometh of me'.[12] As she later told the Duchess of Arschot: 'Not that I don't consider it great and honourable, but less useful to the advancement of my interest, as well in this country, as in that to which I claim some right.'[13] This did not stop the cardinal. By 15 June, he had sent Philibert du Croc to Edinburgh to gain her approval. Mary remained closeted with him for days, but, to Randolph's relief, nothing came of his persuasive efforts.

Elizabeth did not welcome the Archduke Charles's suit any more than that of Don Carlos, fearing that either could incite Habsburg demands for her excommunication, leading to English Catholics rising up to support Mary. She told Maitland that a husband chosen from the Austro-Spanish Empire would make Mary her 'mortal enemy'. She countered the threat by favouring the Archduke Charles for herself. Mary promptly demanded to know what husbands were 'sortable', and Elizabeth realised that she had to clarify 'whom we can allow and whom not; secondly what way we intend to proceed to the declaration of her title'. Mary realised that she had to listen.[14] Her control of Scotland depended on her being recognised as Elizabeth's heir to provide the means of ending Knox's insubordination. Maitland now classified English views on Mary's marriage into three categories: Elizabeth herself wanted Mary's husband to give her 'least cause to stand in fear';[15] the Papists sought a Catholic husband to put Elizabeth under maximum pressure; and the Protestants wanted one to defend their cause.

Maitland returned to Scotland on 24 June. With Knox and the hardline Reformers likely to oppose Mary choosing a Catholic husband, he wisely denied any marriage plans. When de Quadra provided him with lists of English partisans who would support Mary, he seems to have fed them to Cecil. There is no hint that Mary recognised his mission's underhand intent. On the contrary, it 'had done nothing but enhance his credit' with her.[16] He was now at the height of his prestige in both government and court. It was thanks to him that his father, Sir Richard, despite being blind, over sixty-five and remaining Catholic, was appointed Keeper of the Privy Seal. At the end of the year Maitland was granted the Abbacy of Haddington with an income of 2,000 marks (£1,333). This was three times the value of the earldom of Moray granted to Lord James, making him financially secure. He was now a widower and positioned to woo Mary Fleming. Meanwhile the Scottish queen naively continued the Don Carlos marriage negotiation, with the result that an embassy from Eric XIV of Sweden promoting his son, Gustavus Vasa, was peremptorily rejected.

It was only the death of de Quadra of the plague in London in September that ended any prospect of a Habsburg marriage, but with the English being forced out of Le Havre by an outbreak of plague, Elizabeth was on the defensive. Catherine de Medici was equally nervous. She proposed that Charles IX, now aged thirteen, should marry Elizabeth, who was thirty, and that his brother, Henry, who was twelve, should marry Mary, now twenty-one. Elizabeth politely turned down Charles IX as he was both too big (in terms of power) and too small. Mary believed, incorrectly as it turned out, that marrying Henry as the second surviving son would be demeaning after being queen consort to his brother, Francis, and she feared the consequences of having to leave Scotland.

Elizabeth resorted to rehabilitating one of Mary's rival claimants to the English throne, receiving Lennox and his wife, Lady Margaret, back into favour. Although only recently released from the Tower, Lady Margaret remained a focus for Catholic intrigue. She was maintained under virtual house arrest at court, where her son, the seventeen-year-old Darnley, sang and performed on the lute in the evenings 'as indeed he plays very well'.[17] In the previous February, Elizabeth had asked Mary to restore Lennox to his Scottish estates and end his exile in England. Mary ignored this, but sixteen months later, in June 1564, with Maitland still in London, Elizabeth again pressed for his rehabilitation. This was not initiated as a means of promoting Darnley as Mary's husband, but to fire a warning shot that the Lennoxes were plausible rivals for the English throne. Mary could see the advantage of marrying her male contender. His mother had furnished him with courtly graces and, although apparently Catholic, he did not seem vehemently so, regularly throwing his critics off guard by attending Protestant services. This made him less threatening in Scotland than Don Carlos.

Elizabeth, however, was soon regretting what she had started. She asked Maitland and Moray to block the passport she had so recently requested. Well aware of rumours of Darnley's shortcomings, they wryly advised Mary to grant it. They wanted to make the point that Mary did not forever change her mind. It has also been suggested that they hoped to reduce the power of the Hamiltons, who had most to lose from Lennox's rehabilitation. Not only would Lennox be positioned to threaten their claim to be heirs to the Scottish throne, but the Lennox estates occupied by the Hamiltons during his attainder would need to be restored. Even Kirkcaldy could see the inevitable outcome, when he suggested that Mary's 'meaning is not known, but some suspect she shall at length be persuaded to favour his son'.[18]

On 17 November, Randolph at last delivered Cecil's definition of an acceptable husband for Mary. Ideally, he should be 'some fit nobleman within the island', committed to the amity. If no one met these conditions she could seek English permission to marry a foreigner, provided that he lived in Scotland after their marriage. He must be 'naturally born to love this isle' and 'not unmeet'. No one from France, Spain or Austria would be acceptable. Elizabeth had intended that if Mary followed this advice, her dynastic claim would be reinstated. Yet Cecil changed the drafting to say: 'We do promise her, that if she will give us just cause to think that she will in the choice of marriage show herself conformable ... we will thereupon forthwith proceed to the inquisition of her right by all good means in her furtherance.'[19] Although Mary was a foreign head of state, he wanted her dynastic claim to succeed Elizabeth to be tried in an English court. In practice, she would need to become Protestant. Both Cecil and Maitland knew that she was unlikely to agree.

Knowing that Mary would see Cecil's letter as a bitter pill, Elizabeth sent a diamond ring as a 'token of affection'. Randolph delivered this first, reporting that it was 'marvellously esteemed, oftentimes looked upon, and many times kissed'.[20] On receiving the letter, the mixed messages confused her. She needed to reply but would not allow the English to nominate her husband and privately continued searching. She decided to give Randolph the appearance of being compliant. With help from members of her court, she taunted him. When she told him that she was expected to marry an Englishman, others asked if Elizabeth had become a man. When asked to name someone, he was under instruction not to answer, but replied rather lamely, 'whom you could like best'.[21] When pressured to be more specific, he recommended her sending a delegation to ask Elizabeth. The strain was telling and, as so often, Mary broke into weeping without apparent reason. Having danced late into the night on her twenty-first birthday, she remained in bed all the next day. Her symptoms persisted and she complained of an abdominal pain in her left side. This is the first record of her duodenal ulcer. Although her medicines did not initially offer relief, it did not deter her partying lifestyle.

Maitland again suggested a private meeting between Elizabeth and Mary to discuss acceptable husbands. Although Elizabeth continued to pay lip service to this, it was vetoed by the English Parliament and no suitable candidate was named. Mary made clear that although 'princes at all times have not their wills', she wanted 'nothing more' than Elizabeth's love and was 'without evil meaning' towards her. Randolph took her side and affirmed to Elizabeth that 'the word of a prince' was to be trusted, but although her love was genuine, it was not to be presumed upon.[22] Realising that she had to specify someone, Elizabeth concluded that she should offer Dudley, after the council's opposition to her marrying him herself (see Endnote 6). She had suggested this to Maitland in an off-the-cuff aside in the previous year, but he had taken it as a joke, replying tongue in cheek that she 'had better snap him up herself'. He then used all his diplomacy by saying that it was proof of the love she bore Mary, 'as she was willing to give her a thing so dearly prized by herself'.[23] He knew that Mary was describing him as 'Elizabeth's groom' (he was Master of the Horse) and would be gravely affronted at being offered Elizabeth's cast-off. In all probability Cecil, who gave every appearance of backing Dudley's suit, saw it only as a tactic to delay Mary opting for a more threatening alternative. Dudley had remained under a cloud following the unexplained death of his wife and was only the fifth son of the attainted Northumberland. He was not of royal blood and lacked titles.

In September 1563, Randolph outlined English preferences for Mary's choice of husband by advising her that Elizabeth wanted an Englishman, but he was not authorised to mention a name. Mary immediately realised that he had Dudley in mind and asked whether this would make her acceptable as Elizabeth's heir. Randolph thought that it might. 'How would it look,' she asked, 'if Elizabeth married and had children and she had created a commoner as King of Scotland. Would it not be better for England to match me where some alliance and friendship might ensue?' Randolph replied that Elizabeth's chief objective was 'to live in amity with Scotland', but Mary reiterated that she had demonstrated her continuing loyalty and should be permitted to marry whom she liked.[24] Despite explaining that she would choose for herself, she did not rule out completely a member of the English nobility, but 'would not abase her state by marrying a subject of Elizabeth without something in hand to maintain her reputation, "dearer than life itself", and to satisfy her friends; and they could not and would not advise her to it'.[25] Although Dudley's name was not made public, Moray privately favoured him. He saw him as a friend and wanted to act as his sponsor for the Scottish Crown. Maitland was also supportive, seeing it as a final chance of achieving the amity, but it all depended on Elizabeth accepting Mary as her heir. Unfortunately, Dudley had not been consulted and lacked any enthusiasm to be put out to grass in Scotland, even in marriage to Mary, and worked hard to scupper the suit without causing Elizabeth offence.

Although Randolph had reiterated Elizabeth's opposition 'to the children of France, Spain or Austria', in March 1564, the Emperor Ferdinand reopened the suit of the Archduke Charles, undertaking that he would live in Scotland and would be provided with two million francs on marriage and a further five million after the emperor's death.[26] Although he wanted an answer by the end of May, nothing came of it. When the Scots warned Randolph, he concluded that they were trying to force Elizabeth's hand and he made Leicester's suit public. Facing the reality of losing him, Elizabeth suggested nonsensically that they should live as a *ménage à trois* in an extended royal family in London. This was not a good example of ruling 'from the head' as Knox expected, and Mary saw it as unworkable.[27] Her husband would need to be with her in Scotland to maintain control.

With the Leicester suit having little prospect of success, Maitland told Cecil that, if Mary were to be kept 'tied to the Protestant settlement in both realms', they needed to use their great 'private friendship and familiarity' to establish 'the like between the two queens they served'.[28] But Cecil was also in contact with Knox, who was sceptical of Scottish support for the union. Maitland's efforts were in vain. With Mary remaining Catholic and still hankering after a Catholic marriage, 'Cecil was not to be allured'.[29] 'When the danger became too great, he could not be expected to sacrifice the interests of England and Protestantism, in order to save Scotland from troubles which were properly its own.'[30]

The ending of the Leicester suit caused Maitland to realise that Mary's Catholic faith made her inappropriate as the focal point for the union that he held so dear. He began to consider means of removing her from the Scottish throne. This has caused him to face reproach. Despite his infatuation for Mary's confidante, Mary Fleming, he adopted a sequence of actions designed to depose the queen: his encouragement of her marriage to the unpalatable Darnley; the plan to implicate her in the murders of Riccio and Darnley; his promotion of Bothwell, a man whom he hated, to marry her, notwithstanding his involvement in Darnley's murder; the propaganda he devised to entice the 'Confederate' lords to take up arms against her; and his falsification of the Casket Letters, all point to his determination to end her rule.

There can be no doubt that Maitland had the support of Moray and Cecil, but with Moray being forced into exile after his ill-fated rebellion, and Cecil being in London, it was Maitland who had to mastermind the plot to bring Mary down. He sat on the fence during Moray's rebellion, as it would have been fatal if both of them should be removed from office at the same time, but each worked for the other's restoration to authority when their respective chips were down. Who would replace Mary? The only appropriate candidate was Moray, whether as king, as he would have preferred, or as regent for James when he inherited the throne, or as the head of a republic, as both Knox and Buchanan would have chosen. It was only after Maitland married Mary Fleming, and when her mistress was imprisoned, that he felt some remorse and took steps to ameliorate their queen's lot, falling out with Moray in the process. By then, Mary had been deposed and Scotland was set on a course of Protestant government with a regency for James, which might be able to achieve Maitland's cherished union with England. It was not, initially at least, Maitland's intention to support Mary in overturning Moray's regency, but to provide her with a face-saving status, even though she would be without authority.

PART II

MARY TAKES PERSONAL CONTROL

Chapter 7

Mary's efforts to take up the reins of power

In the early years of Mary's return to Scotland, Moray and Maitland had held such a stranglehold over her government that it was perhaps inevitable that she would seek to spread her own wings. She gibed at Moray's constraining influence, but, after grasping the reins of government, she took decisions that showed a political naivety and misjudgement hard to reconcile with someone apparently so carefully groomed to govern.

With Moray acting as the power behind the throne, Maitland had mentored Mary to follow their advice. She saw Maitland, with his charm and persuasiveness, as the person most likely to gain for her the succession to the English throne. So long as their objectives concurred, Moray and Maitland remained in alliance. They had enjoyed a taste for power and wanted to retain it. Starting in 1564, several factors began to weaken their dominant position in guiding Mary, not least because the choice of her husband would soon be resolved. Although their views seemed to diverge, they remained at this period more closely associated than is sometimes thought.

Moray strongly opposed Lennox's restoration to his estates after his treasonable action in supporting Henry VIII during the Rough Wooings. He realised that this would lead to the promotion of his son, Darnley, as Mary's spouse. It would also threaten Moray's position as her principal adviser, upsetting his considerable achievement in ending old feudal factions to unite the nobility behind the Crown. The Hamiltons shared Moray's opposition to Lennox, seeing him as a threat to their position as heirs to the Scottish throne. Mary also remained wary of him but recognised the dynastic advantage of marrying his son. She tried to foster Moray's support by reinstating him ahead of Maitland as her senior minister with the title of Lieutenant-General of the realm.

Maitland seemed to encourage Lennox's repatriation. Acting as Speaker of the Scottish Parliament, he had no great difficulty in gaining approval for it after Mary explained that it was the dearest wish of her sister queen. Maitland's apparent support needs analysis. On the face of it, he had no more reason to want it than Moray. It has been suggested that he was encouraged to support it by Mary Fleming, whose brother-in-law, Atholl, was his kinsman and close ally. After his rehabilitation, Lennox went to stay with Atholl, to whom he confided his ambitions for Darnley to marry the queen. During this time, he became 'well friended of Lethington', who will surely have known of the marriage objective. Maitland was by then extremely doubtful that Leicester's suit would materialise and will have recognised that Darnley's royal blood enhanced Mary's claim to the English throne. Nevertheless, his Catholicism destroyed further hopes for English acceptance of the union. While in London, Maitland will have had time to assess Darnley's character. Even Randolph realised that his arrival in Scotland would cause 'mischief'. Did Maitland believe that Darnley, with his regular displays of Protestantism, could be brought round to the Reformed faith? Lady Margaret's Catholic scheming makes this seem implausible. It is more likely that he saw the marriage as the means of demeaning Mary's name, making her unacceptable to become Elizabeth's heir and even to remain Queen of Scots.

With marriage negotiations becoming temporarily deadlocked, Mary spent the first part of 1564 taking greater personal interest in government. Sensing Moray's and Maitland's opposition to her marriage negotiations, the content of diplomatic packages was not always shown to them. To broaden her activity away from 'courtly frippery', she reorganised the Court of Session to assure a proper hearing for the poor. Many judges, even those associated with Knox, were making judgements favouring rich and powerful friends. She increased stipends, requiring them to sit on at least three days per week in both morning and afternoon, even attending hearings herself. She arranged another progress to the Gaelic-speaking Highlands, listening to the harp, bagpipes and bardic poetry, with the court in highland dress. She became suspicious of members of her staff. Her French secretary, Augustine Raullet, an agent of the Cardinal of Lorraine, was replaced by the Piedmontese David Riccio (sometimes incorrectly spelt Rizzio), one of her valets de chambre, and an able musician, notwithstanding her need to correct his poor French.

Although Mary continued trying to revive her secret negotiations to marry Don Carlos, she wanted to meet Darnley. It was Sir James Melville, another able Scottish diplomat and a 'suave and dextrous courtier', who was sent to renew her claim to become Elizabeth's successor and to open further negotiations to find her a husband.[1] Maitland remained in Scotland to fulfil his government duties and to field any queries as they arrived. This enabled him to court Mary Fleming, whom he was to marry fifteen months later. Melville came to London with secret instructions for Lady Margaret to seek a passport for her son to visit his father. Although Leicester was favoured by Moray, Maitland and Knox, he was still resistant to marrying Mary, and she knew that it would not result in her confirmation as Elizabeth's heir. At Leicester's request, Cecil arranged for Elizabeth to grant a passport for Darnley, with its inevitable consequences. The English failed to appreciate that Mary's marriage to Darnley would destroy Moray's and Maitland's authority, upon which the amity depended. Randolph strongly disapproved of Darnley and was very confused by Cecil's apparent support for him.

In November 1564, Maitland and Moray met Randolph and Bedford at Berwick, where they complained at the lack of progress of Leicester's suit. They were furious when it was explained that Elizabeth would never willingly consent to Mary marrying anyone other than Leicester, but it would not result in her nomination as Elizabeth's heir. She was offered only a vague assurance that by marrying him, 'great good would ensew to both the realms'.[2] Maitland and Moray considered that they had been duped and criticised Cecil for his intransigence.

To address the build-up of opposition to Darnley, Mary needed allies. She decided to rehabilitate Bothwell, still being held in the Tower of London, and George Gordon, who was at Dunbar. As early as February 1563, she had instructed Randolph to demand Bothwell's release, after learning that her right to the English throne would be subject to trial. She did not want Bothwell, or any other Scottish lords, held in England against her will. Elizabeth was bombarded with letters, two from Mary and one from Mary Fleming, who also persuaded Maitland to write. Even Randolph wrote, probably being pushed into it by Mary Bethune (another of the four Maries), with whom he was enamoured.

Mary had still not entirely forgiven Bothwell for escaping from Edinburgh Castle. Randolph reported that she had wanted him to be 'reserved, though it were in prison, in store to be employed in any kind of mischief that any occasion may move'.[3] Knowing that Bothwell could threaten both Moray and the amity, he reported to Cecil: 'One thing I thought not to omit [is] that I know him as mortal an enemy to our whole nation as any man alive, despiteful out of measure, false and untrue as a devil.'[4] It was from Randolph's agent that Bothwell had intercepted the English money transfer four years earlier. At last, in June 1563, he was freed on parole from the Tower, but was not permitted to leave England. In December, being short of money, he wrote to Randolph from Northumberland to seek Mary's consent to go to France. In February 1564, he met up secretly with her at Dunbar while visiting his sister, Jean, following the death of Lord John Stewart after only two years of marriage. He then travelled to France, where Mary arranged his appointment as captain of the Scottish *Gens d'Armes*.

In February 1565, after a year on the Continent, Bothwell again petitioned to be allowed home. Without waiting for Mary's reply, he reached Scotland a month later. According to Randolph, his return was 'altogether misliked and she had sworn upon her honour that he shall never receive favour at her hands'. She was genuinely shocked at rumours that he had threatened to kill Moray, Maitland and Cecil. Randolph reported that Moray 'followeth the matter so earnestly that Scotland shall not hold them both'.[5] Nevertheless, when Moray demanded his arrest and attainder in relation to his old offences, she declared that 'she could not hate him'.[6] Bothwell was imprisoned to await trial, but she insisted on granting bail. When Moray surrounded the court with troops, she warned Bothwell not to appear. Despite being convicted of treason in his absence, Mary let him return to France before the verdict, refusing to forfeit his estates.

Chapter 8

Marriage to Darnley

After receiving a passport, Darnley left London on 3 February 1565, reaching Edinburgh ten days later while Mary was hunting in Fife. With Maitland wanting to show support for him, he stayed for a night at Lethington. Once in Edinburgh, he met Randolph, who lent him horses until his own arrived from England. Three days later he set out for Fife, where, on 17 February, he met Mary at the home of Sir John Wemyss of Wemyss. Lady Margaret had sent him with generous presents for Mary, Maitland and Moray. After two nights there, he met up with his father, who was staying with Atholl at Dunkeld, before rejoining Mary to take the ferry with her across the Forth on her return to Holyrood.

Mary gave no initial sign that meeting Darnley was more than a courtesy to her cousin, but she described him to Melville as 'the lustiest [most vigorous or athletic-looking] and best proportioned long man that I have ever seen'.[1] On first impressions, he went down well, but Moray saw him 'rather as an enemy than a preferer of Christ's true religion'.[2] He tried to win Moray over by accompanying him to St Giles' to hear Knox preach, but also privately attended Mass with Mary. After hearing Knox, he dined at Holyrood with Randolph and Moray, who suggested that he should partner Mary in a galliard. Even Randolph saw them as outwardly well suited and described him as 'a fair jolly young man', despite 'hoping against hope that the suit would fail'.[3] Due to violent snowstorms in Edinburgh they were confined indoors, where Darnley enjoyed cards and dice with Mary. He attended banquets and masques, but she did not show him undue attention, despite admiring his courtly skills as a poet, dancer and lute player. This brought him into contact with Riccio, with whom he developed a friendship.

Riccio was already one of Mary's closest confidants, being loyal, discreet and an amusing raconteur. He had a good bass voice and played the lute. Melville described him as a 'merry fellow', but 'hideously ugly' (he was deformed and probably a hunchback). He now controlled access to Mary, freely accepting bribes which no doubt financed his extravagant wardrobe. After his murder, £2,000 was found among his possessions and this could not have been amassed from his annual salary of £80. As he grew arrogant and greedy, Scottish courtiers considered him a 'sly crafty foreigner', and referred to him derogatorily as 'Seigneur Davie', but Mary would not be restrained from showing him favour.

In the face of hostility, Riccio's friendship with Darnley blossomed out of mutual self-interest. He believed that Lennox and Darnley would protect his position while he promoted Darnley's suit with Mary. He was admitted to Darnley's 'table, his chamber and his most secret thoughts'. They would even 'lie in one bed together', which must be construed as evidence of a homosexual relationship between them.[4] With Riccio gaining influence, he encouraged Mary to wrest government control from Moray and Maitland, seeing her marriage to Darnley as his opportunity to usurp Maitland's position as Secretary. Those opposing the marriage became shocked at the triangular relationship between Mary, Darnley and Riccio, seeing it as a Catholic conspiracy to undermine the Kirk.[5] With Moray and Maitland becoming increasingly concerned at the 'foreign practices' developing around them, they needed English help. They appealed to Cecil for a concession that might rekindle Leicester's suit for Mary, but neither Cecil nor Leicester would play ball. Cecil responded with a diatribe of complaints that he and Elizabeth were being pressurised. Mary's title to the succession 'could only come in due time and order'.[6]

No one expected Darnley's suit to prosper. With Randolph still promoting Leicester, he played down signs of a romance with Darnley, reporting that Mary's interest 'arose rather from her own courteous nature than that anything is meant, which some here fear may ensue'. Nevertheless, they shared a love of hawking and hunting, and Randolph was soon admitting that Darnley's behaviour was 'well liked, and hitherto he so governs himself that there is great praise for him'.[7] Buoyed up by his success, Darnley proposed marriage, which Mary just as quickly turned down. Yet Melville reminded her that it would 'put out of doubt their title to the succession'.[8]

At this stage, Mary would still have chosen either Don Carlos, remaining unaware of his incapacity, or Leicester, if she were proclaimed as Elizabeth's heir. As late as 24 March 1565, she tried unsuccessfully to revive the Don Carlos negotiations. On 16 March, Randolph was forced to advise that if she married Leicester, 'Elizabeth would advance her title to the succession in every way that she could but could not gratify her desire to have her title determined and published until she be married herself, or determined not to marry.'[9] This, of course, might never happen, and it ended Maitland's hopes of achieving the union through Mary's marriage to Leicester. Randolph blamed Leicester, who had never even met Mary. He could not believe that he would forgo such a woman of 'perfect beauty'. He wrote to Sidney: 'How many countries, realms, cities and towns, have been destroyed to satisfy the lusts of men for such women.' Leicester had spurned a kingdom and the chance to lie with her 'in his naked arms'.[10]

Randolph was soon being asked by Mary to obtain a passport for Maitland to travel through England to France. Maitland was showing every sign of supporting Darnley's suit and lent 500 crowns to Lennox, who was short of money, to keep the suit alive. As her most persuasive diplomat, he could be relied upon to promote it in the best possible light. Whatever she might say in public, Elizabeth knew that the Darnley marriage was now inevitable. Cecil did not want Leicester, his political opponent, as heir to the English throne, and Leicester showed no interest, with Elizabeth as the greater prize still apparently available. Moray was 'almost stark mad' with rage, seeing the danger to his position, and remained in close agreement with Knox.[11] He had 'seen through the vain self-sufficient youth,' and was quicker than Atholl to realise that his arrogant priggishness would eventually alienate all of them.[12]

Despite Maitland's apparent backing, he would not genuinely have supported a Catholic marriage for Mary. It would also position Darnley to promote Riccio as Secretary of State. Some historians have claimed that Mary Fleming's influence over Maitland was such that he was 'blinded to further and prosecute this marriage' out of love for her.[13] These views do not fit with his political ambitions for union and his desire to remain in office. Others have said that, while in London, he was unable to see Darnley's shortcomings for himself, but he would have assessed Darnley on earlier trips. His motive was to destroy Mary's credibility.

On Mary's instruction, Maitland left Scotland in late March and was in London from about 15 April to 13 May. He immediately demanded Elizabeth's approval for the Darnley marriage, arguing that he was both a member of the English royal family and an English subject. He had assumed that her granting of a passport signalled her approval. Instead, she voiced alarm and told the Privy Council that she was offended at Darnley's failure to seek permission before leaving England. She refused her consent, realising that the Scottish Protestant government, with whom she maintained such a good working relationship, was in great jeopardy. Maitland suggested that she should put forward a more acceptable English suitor, such as the recently widowed Norfolk, but Norfolk declined.

Maitland followed his brief by meeting Diego de Silva y Guzmán, the Spanish ambassador, to gain Philip II's support. Philip saw the marriage as assuring the 'success of [Mary's] claims and the quiet of her country'.[14] The papacy also expressed relief at a Catholic union. Catherine de Medici signalled approval, but then hedged her bets by telling Elizabeth that she opposed it, backhandedly hoping to establish closer English links if the amity with Scotland broke down.

At the beginning of April, Moray left court in disgust at the Catholic ceremony planned for Easter at Stirling. Mary let it be known that it confirmed his ambition to seek the Crown. With neither Moray nor Maitland in attendance, Mary took the opportunity to act independently. Although Maitland remained nominally as Secretary of State, Riccio practically superseded him. This shows Mary's extraordinary lack of judgement in allowing a court musician of doubtful integrity to usurp the position of her most trusted and experienced adviser. Maitland may have thought that he could return to influence on his return, but, if so, he reckoned without her growing infatuation for Darnley, whose veneer of charm was beginning to crack. Moray openly opposed the marriage, knowing that it would cause him to lose authority. With Knox and the Reformed Church 'in a state of latent mutiny', Moray began to test Elizabeth's support for him to take a more hostile stance.[15]

On 5 April, the court reached Stirling, with Mary and Darnley in the early stages of courtship. By some quirk of fate, he became ill, suffering a cold, followed by measles-like skin eruptions. These were accompanied by 'sharp pangs, his pains holding him in his stomach and in his head'. These are the symptoms of secondary syphilis, presumably contracted in England before his arrival. He occupied the royal apartments for a month, where Mary nursed him herself, compromising her reputation by visiting him at all hours. As he slowly recovered, royal decorum disappeared, and she was overwhelmed with sensations that she cannot have known she possessed. In the words of a poem of the period, it was: 'O lusty May, with Flora Queen.'[16] She did not realise that his temper tantrums were not just those of a fractious invalid, but symptoms of his disease. She was enthralled with a 'fantasy of a man, without regard to his tastes, manners or estate'.[17] Seeking Elizabeth's approval for their marriage had suddenly become irrelevant. She refused to travel even to Perth while he remained ill, but showered gifts on him. Randolph considered her 'in contempt of her people'.[18]

Darnley was delighted with his success, but was too narcissistic to become infatuated, seeing Mary only as a trophy, and their marriage merely as a necessary step on his way to the Crown of both Scotland and England. Everyone was taken aback by the model queen's unbridled passion. She later claimed that Moray had encouraged the suit to annoy the Hamiltons, thinking that he could change her mind when he needed to. This would explain why he let the relationship develop and implies that he accepted Cecil's assumption that she would soon recognise Darnley's shortcomings. It also suggests that he was more in tandem with Maitland's expectation that the suit would cause mischief than is sometimes thought.

The Privy Council was split, with Maitland, Atholl, Ruthven and Riccio showing apparent support, and Châtelherault, Argyll and Glencairn defending Moray's growing antagonism. With Moray developing his plans for rebellion to wrest power, Atholl became the focus for opposition to him and progressively took control. Maitland's more underhand approach called for him to remain in alliance with the couple.

On 20 April, Elizabeth confiscated Lady Margaret's Templenewsam estates and placed her under house arrest at Whitehall. Two months later, she was moved to the Tower, where her confinement was made 'hourly more severe'. She was released to Sheen only in March 1567 after Darnley's murder.[19] On 24 April, Throckmorton was sent to Scotland to convey Elizabeth's disapproval of the marriage suit. Cecil spent the whole of 1 May in the Privy Council looking for a way to stop it. On 3 May, Mary received a letter from Maitland warning of Elizabeth's anger. She immediately replied to him that he should tell her sister queen that 'she did mind to use her own choice in marriage'.[20] By the time he received it, he was at Newark on his way north and thought better of returning to London, realising that her attitude would threaten the amity. Throckmorton was shown the letter after Maitland caught up with him at Alnwick, and reported that it 'wanted neither eloquence, despite [contempt], anger love nor passion'.[21] He had never seen Maitland so irate, although it can be surmised that much of this was caused by 'his loss of personal control over the direction of Mary's policy'.[22] Her decision to marry Darnley was a catastrophe for him. Although he remained nominally in office, his authority was significantly weakened.

Mary, who was at Stirling, asked Maitland to delay Throckmorton's arrival, hoping to present him with a fait accompli, but he did not do so. On receiving Elizabeth's letter, she was distraught but retorted that she would marry Darnley. Although she tried to win over Moray by saying that Darnley, as a minor, would not be granted the Crown Matrimonial, both Moray and Argyll remained 'indignant at [his] overwhelming insolence' and refused their support. Nevertheless, on 15 May, she formally asked the Lords of Parliament at Stirling for support in the face of Elizabeth's opposition. Despite their lack of enthusiasm, they were affronted at England's blatant interference in a Scottish matter and closed ranks behind Mary. 'Many consented on condition that no change was made to the established state of religion.'[23]

Mary believed that Maitland had let her down by failing to return to London with her letter. He remained at court but was out of favour and was completely diverted by Mary Fleming. He told Cecil that his passion brought him at least one 'merry hour' in the day, despite the difficulties of state matters. Their age disparity (he was thirty-six and Mary Fleming twenty-two) caused some ribaldry and Kirkcaldy considered her about as suitable for him 'as I am to be pope'.[24] Randolph reported that 'wise as he is, he will show himself a fool'. It was Maitland's assistant, John Hay, Commendator of Balmerino and Master of Requests, who was sent back to London in Maitland's place. On 22 May, Mary asked the Cardinal of Lorraine to seek a papal dispensation in view of her kinship with Darnley. The cardinal seems to have reacted slowly, as she later sent William Chisholm, Bishop of Dunblane, to seek it in Rome and to request a subsidy to restore Catholicism. Maitland was not going to accept being sidelined like this without a fight. He would resort to every subterfuge to return to favour, even masterminding Riccio's and Darnley's murders. This left him mistrusted on all sides.

If anyone believed that the marriage would founder out of lack of support, they bargained without Lady Margaret's scheming from imprisonment in the Tower. In November 1564, she had negotiated her cousin Morton's important backing by ceding her claim to the earldom of Angus to his nephew, over whom he acted as ward (see Endnote 7). Mary gained Ruthven's support and, despite her concerns at his use of sorcery, made him her chief councillor to promote the marriage. Erskine was persuaded that it was a true love match by his wife, Annabella, who had become Mary's close confidante. On 23 June 1565, Mary fulfilled his family's long-held claim for restoration to the earldom of Mar. Alexander, 5th Lord Home, confirmed his loyalty, despite facing threats from Bedford at Berwick. Even Glencairn, who disliked Darnley and supported Moray, attended the marriage ceremony. It would not take long for Darnley to undo all this goodwill.

Mary was popular, and most Scots did not consider Darnley a bad match. Of the lords at Stirling, only Ochiltree, Knox's father-in-law, now opposed it on religious grounds, but Moray left before the vote and Argyll refused to attend. On 21 May, Moray began to muster support at Lochleven, and, as he was now shunning council meetings, Atholl was given formal control. With Maitland having been dismissed, he was left with more time to woo Mary Fleming. He wrote to assure Cecil that 'their private friendship should not be violated', despite the amity being endangered.[25] With Moray and Maitland now out of the picture, Mary's government was in the hands of her private servants – Italian and French – of whom 'Riccio was the chief'.[26] Being independent of the nobility, they could, at least, be relied upon to be discreet.

Throckmorton concluded that the marriage was 'irrevocable otherwise than by violence'.[27] He told Leicester that Mary was 'seized with love in ferventer passions than is comely in any mean personage ... I cannot assure myself that such qualities will bring forth such fruit as the love and usage bestowed on Darnley shows'.[28] Randolph reported: 'Shame is laid aside, and all regard of that which chiefly pertaineth to princely honour removed out of sight.'[29] They were rumoured to be in bed together, but this was later denied by Randolph, who would have been only too keen to report such a scurrilous titbit. He noted pessimistically:

> [Mary] was so altered with affection towards the Lord Darnley that she hath brought her honour in question,

her estate in hazard, her country to be torn in pieces … The queen in her love is so transported, and he is grown so proud, that to all honest men he is intolerable, and almost forgetful of his duty to her already, that hath ventured so much for his sake. What shall become of her, or what life with him she shall lead, that taketh so much upon him to control and to command her, I leave to others to think.[30]

Despite their daily exchange of love tokens, Darnley became progressively more objectionable and hot-headed. 'He spareth not, in token of his manhood, to let blows fly.'[31] On 23 May, when Châtelherault came to make his peace, Darnley threatened to 'knock his pate'. 'His pride was intolerable, and his words could not be borne except where no man speak again.'[32] After the vote by the lords at Stirling, he was knighted and created Earl of Ross. When the grant was delivered, he threatened Bellenden, the Justice-Clerk, with his dagger, because he was not made Duke of Albany as he expected. Mary had held this back while awaiting Elizabeth's reaction. Darnley, who was soon frequenting Edinburgh bars and brothels with fellow court reprobates and unable keep his mouth shut, leaked the marriage terms before their approval by the council. Maitland and Moray saw this as calamitous.

Mary was distraught at her failure 'to frame and fashion [Darnley] to the nature of her subjects'. He remained 'proud, disdainful and suspicious'.[33] On hearing of his behaviour, the Cardinal of Lorraine cautioned Mary against the marriage, but she would not be diverted. Even the four Maries caused a rift by expressing concerns.[34] Randolph wrote prophetically: 'What shall become of him I know not, but it is greatly to be feared that he can have no long life among these people.'[35]

Mary summoned a convention of the nobility to meet at Perth on 22 June to gain formal approval for the Catholic marriage ceremony, but Moray excused attendance by claiming illness with diarrhoea. Leslie dissuaded her from using the meeting as the opportunity 'to take the final order of religion'. Randolph attended to provide Elizabeth's formal offer of financial support for anyone seeking to prevent the marriage. Civil war seemed inevitable. Argyll supported Moray and moved to Castle Campbell to be within reach of Lochleven. Their envoy met Randolph in Edinburgh before proceeding to London to establish Elizabeth's support. There were rumours that the Lennoxes were planning Moray's assassination. It was also claimed that Moray planned to kidnap Darnley and Lennox to return them to England. Other stories suggested that he planned to arrest Mary and Darnley. There is no firm evidence for any of this, but it caused sufficient alarm for Atholl and Ruthven to escort Mary from Perth to Callendar with 300 horse at 5 o'clock in the morning. They arrived an hour before they had been expected to leave Perth after completing their thirty-mile journey without a break. It was not just Moray trying to kidnap Mary and Darnley. Mary arrested the four leaders of a Protestant citizens' army opposing her in Edinburgh.[36]

On 2 July, Elizabeth recalled Lennox and Darnley to London, causing Mary to retire to her rooms in tears. If she defied Elizabeth, she risked her hopes of the English succession. If she capitulated, Darnley would be charged with treason. After delaying her reply for a fortnight, she defiantly instructed them to stay. She told Randolph that Elizabeth had sent Darnley north believing him unworthy of her, but she would choose her own husband and would 'snap her fingers at all who opposed' their marriage. When Randolph suggested that she should become Protestant, she was furious at being asked to barter her religion to gain approval. She warned that if the amity were lost, it would be just as much an 'incommodity' for Elizabeth.[37]

Although Cecil threatened war, he shared Maitland's secret conclusion that the marriage would destroy Mary's credibility. Randolph now understood their objective, recognising that it would jeopardise support for her from English Catholics. In June, the English Privy Council secretly agreed to finance Moray 'to uphold the true religion and to support their queen with good advice'. He had hoped for English troops and artillery, but, as always, Elizabeth would not be seen to provide overt support against an anointed queen. Realising that he was outnumbered, he offered to back the marriage if Mary abandoned the Mass and undertook to maintain the Scottish Reformation. He was convinced that her adherence to papacy was 'political rather than religious'.[38] She was certainly preferable to the Hamiltons or Lennoxes. When she refused, Knox and other Reformist ministers condemned her from the pulpit. She diffused their opposition by confirming religious freedom and denying 'the existence of any danger to the established religion'.[39]

On 9 July, Mary and Darnley spent two nights at Seton, away from prying eyes at court, while Seton himself was in France. Randolph reported to Elizabeth that they had been secretly married (probably a betrothal ceremony) beforehand in Riccio's apartments at Holyrood 'with not above seven persons present'. This was a normal step to allow couples to consummate their union.

On 12 July, Mary also sought Catholic support from the Continent. This made civil war inevitable. Three days later she summoned her subjects to Edinburgh in arms with provision for fifteen days. She had quietly pledged jewellery to fund a royal army of between 6,000 and 7,000 men. With Mar holding the castle on her behalf, she controlled the capital. Moray was summoned to answer for his alleged kidnap attempts, but he remained with Argyll at Stirling, leaving himself open to charges of treason. Three days later, at a meeting with Argyll, Châtelherault, Kirkcaldy and William Leslie, the pretended Earl of Rothes, they sent another plea to Elizabeth for military support. Mary would need to act fast. On 24 July, she wrote to the Pope of her intention to restore Catholicism in Scotland, hoping for a subsidy.

On 22 July, the wedding banns were read at St Giles', and Darnley was at last made Duke of Albany. On 29 July, Mary confirmed that he would be crowned as King Henry. Although this needed parliamentary approval, she later attended the vote to assure agreement. As a minor, Darnley was refused the Crown Matrimonial, which would have promoted him ahead of the Hamiltons as her successor, if she died childless. As Francis II had received this honour, it remained a bone of future contention.

The Catholic wedding ceremony took place on 30 July at between 5 and 6 o'clock in the morning. Mary wore 'a great mourning gown of black with the great white mourning hood' and was escorted by Lennox and Atholl. Darnley was dressed in a magnificent jewelled outfit. Other than Moray, Châtelherault and Argyll, almost all the nobles including Maitland attended. After the marriage Mary celebrated nuptial Mass to symbolise her replacement of widow's weeds for wedding finery. Darnley remained in his chamber, not wishing to offend the Protestant lords. Although Randolph did not attend, he reported that they did not immediately retire to bed 'to signify unto the world that it was not lust moved them to marry, but only the necessity of the country, if she will not leave it destitute of an heir'.[40] Following a magnificent reception, the couple returned to Seton for their honeymoon.

Mary seemed blind to Darnley's shortcomings, having 'given over unto him her whole will to be ruled and guided as himself best likes, but she can as little prevail with him in anything that is against his will'. He was again proclaimed king, and on her instruction, his name received precedence over hers on state documents and coinage struck to mark the occasion.[41] She asked Melville 'to wait upon the King, who was but young, and give him my best counsel, which might help him to shun many inconveniences, desiring me also to befriend Riccio, who was hated without cause'.[42] Melville seems to have gained Darnley's respect.

After returning to Edinburgh, Darnley attended St Giles' for the next two months after installing an ostentatious throne above the rest of the congregation to listen to Knox's sermons. Never one to mince his words, Knox referred to Mary as 'that harlot Jezebel,' and claimed that God had set boys and women to rule over them. Darnley stormed out, refusing dinner, and went hawking. Despite being suspended for fifteen days, Knox published his sermon.

Through her envoy, John Thomworth, Elizabeth challenged Mary over her 'unkind and undutiful' behaviour in marrying without English consent and for heeding 'evil advisers'.[43] She worried that the restoration of Catholicism in Scotland was the prelude to Mary seeking the English throne. Knowing that Moray was about to start the rebellion she had financed, she told Mary to be reconciled to him as he had 'served her with truth, love and ability'.[44] Mary would have none of it and speedily isolated Moray and his fellow rebels. She refused to call Parliament to avoid making it a platform for opposition. Marriage gave her the confidence to stand up to Elizabeth. She warned her 'to meddle no further with private causes concerning [Moray] or any other subjects of Scotland'.[45] This bravado made Elizabeth worry that she had more foreign support than was the case. Mary told Castelnau, the French ambassador, that if Elizabeth supported Moray, there would be no order in the world, and that she would interfere on behalf of her mother-in-law, Lady Margaret, who had been unjustly imprisoned. She offered a deal: she and Darnley would do nothing to enforce their immediate dynastic claim to the English throne and would not assist English rebels against her or seek to change the religion, laws or liberties of England. In return, they expected Elizabeth not to support the Scottish rebels against her rule and to settle the English succession in her favour by Act of Parliament. Mary threatened 'to resort to foreign assistance, should the English Queen furnish supplies to her rebellious subjects'.[46] Elizabeth was in an awkward position. France was threatening to support Mary if Elizabeth helped the Huguenots. Catherine de Medici told her that Mary's marriage was insufficient reason to go to war.[47] She wanted to prevent Mary from allying with the Guise family and Spanish interests, but, like the Spanish, wanted a peaceful end to the quarrel.

Mary's continued religious tolerance gained her support. She reconfirmed her 1561 proclamation to maintain the religious status quo in both Darnley's and her name. When the General Assembly tried to abolish the Mass, she refused to risk 'losing the friendship of the King of France, the ancient ally of this realm, and of the other great princes, her friends and confederates, who would take it in evil part, of whom she may look for support in all her necessities'.[48] She demanded freedom of Catholic worship, and Randolph estimated that papists now outnumbered Reformers in Edinburgh.

Chapter 9

Moray's rebellion

On 1 August 1565, Moray was again summoned to appear before the queen within six days. On his non-appearance, he was 'put to the horn' (attainted with his estates being sequestered) and Mary portrayed him as petulant at losing power. By 14 August, the estates of Rothes and Kirkcaldy had also been seized and Mary began converting court members to Catholicism. Moray was supported by Argyll, Glencairn and other Protestant lords, who mistrusted Darnley's Catholicism, and initially by the Hamiltons, who believed that the Lennoxes threatened their position as heirs to the throne.

Mary had significant backing. Her allies were open-minded about Darnley, but many were quickly alienated. Support was for Mary alone, although after Darnley's murder even this almost evaporated until her imprisonment at Lochleven. As the senior Catholic noble and head of government, Atholl supervised her 'Marian' supporters. They were not all Catholic and were not close-knit. Despite their greater numbers, their forces lacked training and Lennox was their only experienced commander. Being in need of military skills, she recalled Bothwell from France.

Moray sent a second envoy to Elizabeth, urgently requesting her promised assistance, while his allies retired to their homes to await her reply. She still wanted to avoid providing overt support so that she could deny having done so. Although she had provided money, Moray was left irretrievably weakened. Despite his obvious qualities, he was nonetheless illegitimate and would require greater backing in order to force Mary and Darnley off their throne. Mary was popular. She isolated him politically by exposing the flaws in his propaganda. On hearing that Mass was being celebrated in northern Scotland, she gave instructions to avoid action 'as was feared by the Protestants'. She attended the Protestant baptism of Alexander, Master of Livingston, and heard sermons from approved Reformist preachers. Few Reformers believed their religion was under threat, and even Knox did not support Moray's hopes for the Crown. If he could not be king, Moray hoped to remain the power behind the throne, but the intolerable Darnley would undo all his good work.

Moray resorted to inciting the Scottish nobility's traditional divisions – which he had spent so long in trying to heal – and attacked the Lennoxes by cultivating their feudal enemies. He allowed self-interest to override more realistic objectives, not realising that his challenge was doomed to failure. On 15 August, he left Edinburgh for Ayr with Châtelherault and Argyll, after summoning Glencairn, Rothes, Boyd, Ochiltree and Kirkcaldy to join them in arms within five days. From Ayr he called 'all good subjects to join them in resisting tyranny, for a king had been imposed on them without the assent of parliament'.[1] Although Maxwell supported him, he remained in the south-west, leaving Moray with only 600 horse, although probably more than double that number arrived in Edinburgh. Maitland maintained his cover by remaining at court but was regarded with suspicion. He undoubtedly supported Moray, but 'was not the sort to commit himself prematurely to a hazardous course while other options remained open'.[2]

Mary told Castelnau that, if Elizabeth supported Moray, there would be no order in the world. Before leaving Edinburgh, she appointed the Catholic Sir Simon Preston of Craigmillar as provost to assure her continued control of the capital and he joined the Privy Council. On 28 August, she set out wearing a steel cap and carrying a pistol in a saddle holster with between 8,000 and 10,000 men, although they were untrained for battle. Knox could only admire her, writing: 'Albeit the most part waxed weary, yet the Queen's courage increased man-like, so much that she was ever at the foremost.'[3] Darnley was resplendent in gilt armour, spoiling for a fight, with his earlier grandeur turned to defiance. Atholl was appointed lieutenant of the north to deal with Argyll, while Lennox became lieutenant of the west, and later of the south-west. She branded Moray's followers as republican, set on destroying both Darnley and herself, just as they had deposed her mother. Although she sought French help, Castelnau had instructions to avoid conflict and told her to be reconciled with Moray. She ignored his advice that 'utility, prudence and expediency' obliged her to make concessions. Although the papacy offered a subsidy, it delayed making payment.

In what became known as the 'Chaseabout' or 'Roundabout Raid', the two opposing armies never met. Mary set out towards Ayr through wind and driving rain, with her hackbutters pushing Moray's troops ahead of her and giving them no time to rest. Despite being hopelessly outnumbered, Moray managed to bypass her army and reached Edinburgh on 31 August to await Argyll who was seeking troops in the north. A drumbeat was used to muster recruits in Edinburgh, but few joined him.[4] Despite Châtelherault, Glencairn and Rothes being with him, the combination of the townsfolk under Preston and Mar at the castle held Edinburgh for Mary. Moray's army was forced to leave on the following day. Although Bedford had troops readied at Berwick, he needed Elizabeth's authority to send them.

Mary remained in Glasgow until the end of September, waiting for her northern levies to muster at Stirling. On arrival, she doubled back to Edinburgh to face Moray in battle, but he again avoided her by heading south-west to Lanark and Dumfries. She knew that he was likely to gain English support. On 7 September, she sent Elizabeth a strongly worded warning through Randolph not to help him. Elizabeth dithered, remaining fearful of French reaction, but promised Moray asylum. Having negotiated more funding from her bankers, Mary wore down Moray's other allies. Lennox and Atholl pursued Argyll back to the Highlands and, on 6 September, captured Castle Campbell. With Lochleven being used as a store for munitions, Mary threatened to sequester Moray's half-brother, Sir William Douglas, if he failed to support her. When told to surrender, he feigned sickness, but agreed to hand the castle over at twenty-four hours' notice.

Mary now had the support of Moray's traditional enemies. When she called Elizabeth's bluff by calling on her to provide her with 3,000 troops, Elizabeth proposed a truce, if Mary would pardon Moray and his fellow rebels. With Bothwell reaching Edinburgh in September, a negotiated settlement was out of the question. He was restored to the Privy Council and became Lieutenant-General of the Borders, where his military skills proved effective against English incursions. He brought many Border lairds into Mary's camp, but remained mistrusted. Randolph reported: 'His power is to do more mischief than ever he was minded to do good in all his life.'[5] His arrival caused Mary's first public row with Darnley, who was furious at Bothwell being given command of the royal army ahead of Lennox. Although she believed that Bothwell's deep-seated hatred of Moray made him the more determined, she was forced to compromise. Bothwell retained command, but Lennox was to lead the van in battle. Although Lennox remained a powerful ally, he was now promoting Darnley to her detriment.

George Gordon was released from Dunbar and was restored as Lord Gordon. Although he was soon affirmed as Earl of Huntly and joined the Privy Council, Mary did not immediately restore his estates. As another enemy of Moray, he was soon closely allied with Bothwell and hurried north, returning with troops on 4 October. He had made a show of becoming a Reformer at Dunbar and refused Mass with Mary in the Chapel Royal but was soon back in the Catholic camp. On 8 October, his principal estates were restored but were left sufficiently dissipated to prevent him becoming a magnate on his father's former scale. Both the Dowager Lady Huntly and her daughter, Jean, returned to court, and were soon on remarkably good terms with Mary. With Bothwell, Huntly and Atholl now being Mary's principal advisers, Maitland retired to Lethington, leaving the post of Secretary of State vacant, but they lacked his statecraft and Moray's ability to coordinate the nobility.

Mary now set out to challenge Moray at Dumfries, but when Lennox and Darnley delayed their departure for a week to go hunting, Moray slipped across the border to Carlisle, which gained them Bothwell's lasting antagonism. All he could do was garrison Dumfries with 1,500 men to prevent Moray's return. Although Moray received further English funds, he was powerless without military support. Mary ignored Elizabeth's pleas to offer him clemency and brazened it out. Unknown to the English, she had disbanded her remaining troops as she was unable to pay them. As both Randolph and Bedford realised, 'the expenditure of a few thousand pounds of English money, and a small contingent of English troops, seemed all that was needed to bring to the ground the crazy edifice of her power'.[6]

Elizabeth was 'not only defeated but disgraced'.[7] Despite having a force at Berwick to support Moray, she had felt it more important to avoid provoking the French. When at last she brought Moray to London, 'in a piece of refined deceit', she forced him onto his knees before the French and Spanish ambassadors to tell him that she would never support him against Mary (though she secretly granted him a further £3,000 to re-establish himself in her favour). Although forced to leave London, Moray was permitted to return to Newcastle. When Robert Melville was sent north to intercede on his behalf, Mary would not barter his pardon for Lady Margaret's release from the Tower. Both Mary and Maitland were taken in by Moray's public humiliation. With Argyll in hiding in the western Highlands, Châtelherault took the opportunity of Darnley's absence on another hunting trip to submit to Mary. On 2 January 1566, she pardoned him, but exiled him to France for five years. The Lennoxes disapproved of her leniency, but she already mistrusted their motives and needed the Hamiltons in reserve. On 12 March, Moray and his allies were summoned to the Scottish Parliament 'to hear and see the doom of forfeiture orderly led against them', but they remained south of the border.[8]

With Bothwell now dominating Scottish government, Mary agreed to negotiate a new English treaty, but when she appointed him as one of her commissioners, the English withdrew in pique. She also signed a contract for him to marry Huntly's sister, Jean. As third cousins, they needed papal dispensation and the necessary documentation was signed by Archbishop Hamilton. With Huntly providing £8,000 as a dowry, Bothwell could redeem Crichton from his creditors, but Jean astutely retained a jointure over it. She lacked beauty and softness and it was no love match, but she was 'a cool detached character,' with 'masculine intelligence'. Bothwell insisted on a Protestant wedding ceremony, which took place on 24 February at the Canongate Church, attended by Mary, who paid for the celebration at Holyrood afterwards. Their honeymoon at Seton was far from idyllic. Within a week, Bothwell had returned alone to Edinburgh after Jean wore black in mourning for the loss of her sweetheart, Alexander Ogilvy of Boyne. Two months later, Mary arranged Ogilvy's marriage to Mary Bethune, who had broken off her long-running attachment to Randolph (see Endnote 8). Although Bothwell and Jean eventually lived 'friendly and quietly' together, they had no children.

Moray's allies were greatly disturbed by the new axis developing between Bothwell and Huntly. They shared Maitland's concern that Mary was bent on weakening Reformist power. Morton, Ruthven and Lindsay realigned with Moray, but needed Cecil to arrange his rehabilitation. With Riccio 'daily mounting into power and fortune by [Mary's] lavish favour', Maitland was 'biding his time'.[9] He could only look on with silent contempt, working out what to do.

PART III

MAITLAND RE-ESTABLISHES HIS STANDING

Chapter 10

Riccio's murder

Mary soon became disillusioned at Darnley's shortcomings, but by September she was pregnant. This was of huge dynastic importance. The child would provide immeasurable support for her claim to the English Crown and would stand ahead of Darnley, with or without the Crown Matrimonial, as her heir. She was still suffering from a recurring pain in her side, probably the symptoms of a duodenal ulcer, and forwent normal Catholic practices by eating meat during Lent. Darnley paid her little attention and spent much of his time away hunting. This may have been a cover for Catholic scheming with his father. He was never devoutly Catholic but was encouraged by his parents to parade his faith to promote his personal claim to the Scottish and English Crowns. He cultivated European Catholic heads of state by pushing the Scottish court into open celebrations of Mass. The Chapel Royal was like a Catholic parish church, and he used Castelnau to seek for him the Order of St Michel, the highest badge of French chivalry.

Mary and Darnley increasingly appointed middle-class Catholics to the Council, upsetting the nobility, who saw government roles as their right. These new appointees were generally Darnley's friends. They included Sir James Balfour, Riccio, Leslie, David Chalmers – a lawyer closely associated with the Admiralty Court, over which Bothwell presided – and Francis Yaxley – a protégé of Lady Margaret Lennox – who provided a link to English and overseas Catholics. Yaxley led Mary to believe that her support among English Catholics was 'never so great', and Darnley was soon using him on diplomatic missions to Continental Catholic powers to promote a coup for Mary, with Darnley at her side, to replace Elizabeth. Although Yaxley returned from Philip II with the long-awaited 20,000 crowns to support a Scottish Counter-Reformation, he was shipwrecked and drowned off the Northumbrian coast. Elizabeth promptly scooped up the bounty as treasure trove.

Mary, meanwhile, needed a Secretary of State to replace Maitland. The two obvious candidates were Balfour and Leslie, both trained in canon law. Balfour had proved a successful Lord of Session and joined the Privy Council in July 1565. He had become Darnley's right-hand man, but was treacherous and corrupt, always trying to further his own ends. Darnley considered Leslie more suitable. He was a good Catholic, conscientious and hard-working, but lacked sound judgement. Mary countermanded his appointment but made him Bishop of Ross. She preferred Riccio; he was also close to Darnley and had done much to clear the obstacles to their marriage. Although he took Maitland's place, he was a foreigner and was never formally confirmed as Secretary.

In a desperate attempt to regain rehabilitation to Scotland, Moray wrote to Riccio from Newcastle, offering £5,000 if he would arrange it. As Riccio was seeking Parliament's agreement to prosecute Argyll for treason and to sequester all the dissident nobles' estates, he demanded £20,000. Moray then approached Darnley, who was never his friend, sending a fine diamond and signing an obligation to be 'his loyal servant'. Again, his overtures failed. Although Mary's attitude towards the rebels was softening, she was being encouraged to proceed against them by the newly elected Pope Pius V and by Archbishop Bethune, now her ambassador in Paris. Darnley was determined to prevent their return and arranged for their moveable possessions, confiscated by the Crown, to be auctioned off. On 1 December, when Glencairn, Ochiltree and Boyd were found guilty of treason in their absence, they contemplated kidnapping the couple.

Darnley was soon persuading Mary that the religious status quo was not equitable. At Parliament in the spring, he demanded 'liberty of conscience', saying that 'she will have the mass free for all men that will hear it'.[1] This might have seemed reasonable, but, after masterminding the Scottish Reformation, Knox feared all his hard work being undone, and the Kirk refused to give ground.

Mary's stance changed very rapidly. As late as 10 December, she had reconfirmed freedom of Reformist worship and, at Christmas, deliberately sat up at cards to avoid attending Mass with Darnley. This enabled him to prick her Catholic conscience by implying that his faith was the more devout. Pushed by her papist advisers, Mary forgot her agreement only to attend Mass in private and stopped at nothing in attempts to charm her most intractable advisers to become Catholic. Randolph reported that she was 'bent in the overthrow of religion'.[2]

On 7 February 1566, Darnley was invested with the Order of St Michel, which Castelnau had obtained to acknowledge his pro-Catholic leanings. He celebrated with a Catholic festival over Candlemas, which had begun on 2 February. Praise flooded in from abroad. The cardinal sent a letter from Pius V, congratulating the couple in glowing terms on the 'brilliant proof of your zeal by restoring the due worship of God throughout your realm'.[3] This was, of course, premature, but the Pope was encouraging Mary to weed out the 'thorns and tares of heretical depravity'. With so many foreign dignitaries watching for progress, Mary had to be seen to support her husband, and her pregnancy provided a greater sense of security. She wanted to diffuse any perception that he was taking the lead. On 31 January, she wrote to the Pope, buoyantly promising to restore 'religion in splendour' in Scotland and later in England.

When Reformers shunned Darnley's investiture, he locked Bothwell and Huntly in a room and threatened to throw away the key, but they refused to attend and went to hear Knox at St Giles'. Despite this, there were 300 attendees. Insensitive as ever, Darnley threatened to restore the Mass at St Giles' and in the Council. Randolph reported Mary's preparations to renew her immediate Catholic claim to the English throne (see Endnote 9). At the banquet for the foreign ambassadors, she pointed to a conveniently positioned portrait of Elizabeth and announced that 'there was no other Queen of England but herself'.

Despite Mary's public support for her husband, their relationship was not harmonious. Darnley was not playing his part in government and failed to assist her with royal papers. He reduced her to tears when she tried to temper his debauchery at parties with members of the French ambassador's suite, and again denied him the Crown Matrimonial until he showed himself to be worthy of it. During Christmas, there were spats in their apartments, and she cancelled the understanding that they ruled jointly. State documents that had placed Darnley's name as king ahead of hers now referred to 'the Queen's husband'.[4] Coinage struck at the time of their marriage, which showed 'Henry and Marie by the Grace of God King and Queen of Scotland', was changed on the issue to celebrate victory over Moray to show 'Marie and Henry, Queen and King'. And at his investiture of the Order of St Michel, he was not permitted to bear royal arms.

Darnley showed Mary no affection, preferring liaisons in male brothels in Edinburgh or with ladies of the court but continued his ostentatious displays of devotion to imply that he was the stronger Catholic. She may have become aware of his underhand diplomacy in Europe, on which she was not being consulted. She began to feel threatened, and Randolph was aware of a scheme by Lennox and Darnley 'to come to the crown against her will'.[5] They were growing apart. Her pregnancy was another factor. Having sired her child, she no longer required him to sleep with her. As he showed no enthusiasm for visiting her bedroom, she saw no reason to go to his, and by all accounts they lived separately.

Scottish nobles of all religious persuasions ganged up against the new government of 'foreign minions'. The prospect of Moray and the other rebels in exile being attainted at the forthcoming Parliament on 13 March seemed to pressage further forfeitures. With every reason to fear a Counter-Reformation, the Reformers needed a solution. Maitland was determined to find a way to be restored to his former role and to gain Moray's rehabilitation, recognising that the amity upon which union with England would depend was in jeopardy. Darnley's arrival in Scotland 'had turned out badly for both realms. It had paralysed and humiliated England, and it had temporarily submerged the Protestant party in Scotland.'[6] Cecil rekindled his former warm association with Maitland, who responded that he would 'do all that may tend to quiet the realms and unite the Queens'.[7] Maitland had long feared a Catholic circle of ministers surrounding Mary and knew his own rehabilitation was dependent upon breaking it. That would require Moray's reinstatement, but he despaired at how to achieve it.

Mary had been extremely imprudent to show Riccio favour. With the Reformers needing a scapegoat for the move towards Catholicism, he was their obvious target. The deterioration in the Protestant nobility's power made his removal essential. He was blocking Moray's recall and keeping Maitland sidelined. Melville was not alone in believing that he 'had secret intelligence with the Vatican'. But Mary's isolation made her totally reliant on him. He had 'the whole guiding of the queen and country'.[8] On 9 February 1566, Maitland wrote to Cecil: 'All may be reduced to the former estate if the right way be taken ... I see no certain way unless we chop at the very root – you know where that lieth, and so far as my judgement can reach, the sooner all things be packed up the less danger there is of any inconveniences.'[9] He was seeking Cecil's blessing to arrange Riccio's murder.

There has been much debate on precisely what Maitland meant by chopping 'at the very root'. E. Russell concludes that it was Mary's Catholic government, in which Riccio played a key part. Despite his affection for Mary Fleming, Maitland may have been contemplating her mistress's removal from her throne. More certainly, Darnley had his father's support to use Riccio's murder as his means of bringing down the queen. With the plot already arranged, Randolph wrote to Cecil: 'I know that there are practices in hand contrived between father and son to come by the Crown against her will. I know that if that take effect which is intended, David, with the consent of the King, shall have his throat cut within these ten days. Many things grievouser and worse than these are brought to my ears, yea, of things intended against her own person.'[10] With Châtelherault in exile, it was, of course, an ideal moment for the Lennoxes to remove Mary and her unborn child, and to claim the Crown for themselves. The conspirators' later actions show that the queen's downfall was an objective. It was almost certainly Maitland who encouraged Lennox to propose to Argyll that Darnley would arrange for Moray and the other exiled lords to be recalled and pardoned, and he would reconfirm the religious status quo if offered the Crown Matrimonial. Moray would be required to support the person against whom he had rebelled only five months before. With everyone benefiting at Mary's expense, Moray cynically agreed. Maitland implied to Darnley that his elevation was being blocked by Riccio, whose close friendship with Mary raised doubts about the paternity of the child in her womb.

Randolph and Bedford fanned the scandal by claiming 'that David had more company of her body than [Darnley], for the space of two months'. Rumours reached Catherine de Medici that Darnley had returned to Mary's apartment late one evening to find the door locked. After shouting to gain entry he had found Riccio in a nightshirt quailing in a cupboard. This seems highly unlikely as Riccio would never have survived such an encounter, and Darnley never reported it, even when needing to justify Riccio's murder. Although a sexual liaison with Riccio seems unrealistic, Darnley was undoubtedly jealous of Mary's close friendship with him. It is probable that, being pregnant, she wanted to avoid Darnley's sexual overtures and chose to sit up late with Riccio playing cards. This left Darnley believing that Riccio had usurped her affections.

With Darnley now hooked into the plan for Riccio's removal, he turned to Morton and Ruthven, his Douglas kinsmen, to manage it. Morton was personally aggrieved, as Mary had handed the Great Seal, for which he was responsible as Lord Chancellor, to Riccio. He saw the murder as his opportunity to re-establish his status after Maitland persuaded him that Mary's friendship with Riccio demeaned Douglas honour. He seems to have upset Riccio by refusing to sell him a piece of land between Lasswade and Dalkeith so that he 'might have a fair house within three miles of Edinburgh'.[11]

Maitland knew that the conspirators would need Moray's rehabilitation to garner the nobility's more general support. Both Randolph and Bedford were kept informed and Cecil was also closely briefed. With Mary having learned of Randolph's involvement in funding Moray's revolt, although he hotly denied it, he was instructed to leave Scotland with a safe conduct. Even so, he remained in Edinburgh until 2 March to keep Cecil abreast of the detail. By then he was able to advise that Moray and the exiled lords would leave Newcastle for Berwick on the next day with plans to reach Edinburgh on the day following the murder. Elizabeth wrote to Mary complaining of Randolph's dismissal, still angry at Moray's exile, despite his all-too-obvious treasonable activities financed by herself, and she now sent him a further £1,000.

Most people seemed to know of the plan for Riccio's murder. Other than Mary, the few exceptions included Bothwell and Huntly, who were bound up in arrangements for Bothwell's marriage to Jean Gordon on 24 February, and, who would never have welcomed Moray's return. As a Catholic, Atholl was also kept in the dark, despite his close association with Maitland, but he too mistrusted Riccio and was not averse to his death. Cecil knew every detail. This was not simply a plan to remove Riccio, but to discredit Darnley and restore Moray and Maitland. It might even fulfil the objective of toppling the queen. The main objective was to bring down Mary's Catholic advisers, thereby regaining liberty of religion and the return of the conspirators' estates. They needed to have Darnley involved to provide immunity from prosecution, but he would never be allowed to govern.

Failing to see his own shortcomings and 'infatuated by his own arrogance', Darnley blamed Riccio for freezing him out of government. He wanted revenge and the Crown for himself. He believed that, with the Crown Matrimonial, he could dominate Mary. The disaffected nobility was only too willing to encourage him to plan the murder by appearing to indulge his ambitions. 'His youth and inexperience would render him as wax in the hands of the ruthless, power-hungry men who were closing in on him, and as such he would prove their most dangerous weapon.'[12]

Having supported Darnley's marriage, Morton could claim to be affronted at Mary's infatuation with Riccio, but his principal motive was to restore Moray. He was one of many nobles who, like Moray, faced the sequestration of parts of his estates on Riccio's recommendation at the forthcoming Parliament. They needed him murdered beforehand. Although Maitland orchestrated the plan, his involvement evaporated. On the evening of the murder, he made a point of dining at Holyrood with Mary's supporters, including Atholl, Huntly, Caithness, Bothwell and Sir James Balfour, in an attempt to keep them out of the way. Afterwards, the other conspirators, particularly Darnley, all confirmed his intimate involvement, leading to his attainder.

Morton formulated the murder plan during January and February 1566. With Ruthven and George Douglas 'the Postulate', he gathered together other Douglas connections bent on family advancement (see Endnote 10). Most of them had supported Darnley, as their kinsman, to marry Mary. Others included Ruthven's son, William, later to become Earl of Gowrie, and Sir William Douglas of Lochleven, no doubt out of loyalty to Moray, his half-brother. He had made a miraculous recovery from his apparent sickness during November when threatened with the sequestration of Lochleven and its store of munitions. Lindsay of the Byres, who had supported the marriage and was close to Morton, also joined them. There was also a group of henchmen, including Andrew Ker of Fawdonside, Patrick Bellenden, brother of the Justice-Clerk, and two Ruthven retainers, Thomas Scott, under-sheriff of Perth, and Henry Yair, a former priest. In all there were about eighty conspirators.

Lady Antonia Fraser has pointed out that if the conspirators' only objective was to murder Riccio, there were ample opportunities away from Edinburgh, and Morton originally planned to seize him more clandestinely in his quarters at Holyrood. It was Darnley who arranged for the murder to take place during a private supper party held by the queen at Holyrood, in expectation of her consequential death and that of her unborn child. He remained convinced that Riccio had taken his place in Mary's affections, notwithstanding that she was six months pregnant.

By murdering Riccio in her presence, there was a realistic expectation of shock causing a miscarriage in mid-pregnancy, which invariably led to a mother's death. Even Randolph had heard this. Given Maitland's close association with Mary Fleming, it has often been assumed that he was unaware of the objective to bring about Mary's death. However, as he certainly knew that the murder was to take place at a dinner party in Mary's presence, he must have understood what was intended. Mary herself came to believe that she had been an intended victim and some of the conspirators undoubtedly terrified her. They played along with Darnley's treasonable plan to provide grounds for his future deposition, thus allowing Moray to be swept to power.

As the conspirators did not trust Darnley, they insisted on a bond to prevent him denying knowledge of the plot afterwards or to 'allege that others persuaded him to the same'.[13] On 1 March, he signed a deed acknowledging that he was the chief author of a plan to murder the 'wicked, ungodly' Riccio, even though 'the deed may chance to take place in the presence of the Queen's majesty'.[14] He assumed full responsibility for this, despite Morton's and Ruthven's apparent concerns. The deed was signed by all those actively involved. They were not to 'spare life or limb in setting forward all that may bend to the advancement of his [Darnley's] honour'. It confirmed that Darnley would be offered the Crown Matrimonial in return for pardoning and protecting the other signatories and permitting the exiles' return to their estates. It also confirmed that Protestantism would be maintained, despite Darnley's very public show of Catholicism at Candlemas only a month earlier. Although Maitland supported the plot, he avoided signing the deed. A copy was sent by Lennox to Newcastle for signature by the other exiled lords, but this may not have been known to the conspirators at Holyrood. Moray, despite confirming his approval, was permitted to keep his hands clean and to avoid having to sign it.

Though he had opposed Moray's rebellion, Morton knew that only Moray commanded a sufficient following to assume control. On 8 March, the day before the murder, Darnley granted Moray a passport to return to Scotland, not realising his real objective. Home was detailed to escort him and to time their arrival in Edinburgh so that it immediately followed the murder. On 13 February, Randolph sent Leicester full details, mentioning the rumoured plan to engineer Mary's death, but told him to keep it to himself for fear of word reaching Elizabeth, who might warn her. Cecil learned of Darnley's involvement from Randolph and Bedford four days beforehand, and Elizabeth was advised of the political necessity to remove Riccio. The plan fitted well with Cecil's hopes of bringing down both Darnley and Mary. Darnley could then be charged with treason and Mary might die from a miscarriage. If she survived, the conspirators agreed to imprison her at Stirling with Darnley to await her child's birth. Moray would then become regent for her unborn child. If she died, he could aspire to be king.

It can be no surprise that rumours of the plan leaked and, though Mary told Sir James Melville that she had heard them, she dismissed them, claiming 'our countrymen were well-wordy,' and asking: 'What can they do? What dare they do?'[15] Melville even warned Riccio, 'but he distained all danger and despised counsel', claiming: 'They are but ducks, strike one of them and the rest will fly.'[16] Mary much later recorded a wider plan, which miscarried, to murder her close advisers, including Bothwell, Huntly, William 6th Lord Livingston, John 5th Lord Fleming and Sir James Balfour, but there is no further evidence for this. Although Bothwell, Huntly and Balfour dined with Maitland that evening and tried to reach the queen, they were told that Riccio was the only intended victim. Balfour's inclusion in Mary's list is surprising as he was still Darnley's close associate. His loyalty may have been in doubt, however, as he was threatened with being 'hanged in cords' if he revealed Darnley's involvement.

The plot was brought to a head by the opening of Parliament on 7 March. Still piqued at not being granted the Crown Matrimonial, Darnley did not attend. Despite being nearly six months pregnant, Mary arrived to propose the dissident nobles' attainder, setting the hearing for 12 March.

Details of the murder are well known. After appearing at Mary's dinner, Darnley and Ruthven provided access to the remaining conspirators, led by Morton, resulting in Riccio being stabbed to death in what appears to have been a ritual killing. Maitland avoided involvement, but his dinner party guests in another part of Holyrood were disturbed by the noise. Bothwell, Huntly and Argyll went to investigate, and Maitland kept up appearances by following. When Morton told them of Riccio's murder, though no harm was intended to the queen, they thought it wiser to escape. Bothwell and Huntly went to Dunbar to plan Mary's rescue, and Atholl retired to Dunblane. The indomitable Lady Huntly remained at Holyrood to assist in a rescue attempt. Maitland may also have left but was at Holyrood the next day when Mary appealed to him to have her guard removed.[17]

The conspirators now awaited Moray's arrival in expectation of his return to power. They still planned to send Mary to Stirling 'under safe keeping' for her confinement and to retain her there afterwards.[18] Darnley was assured that he would receive the Crown Matrimonial and would share government with the nobles, so long as liberty of religion was confirmed. Ruthven, however, warned him: 'If you wish to obtain what we have promised you, you must needs follow our advice, as well for your own safety as for ours. If you do otherwise, we will take care of ourselves, cost what it may.'[19] He was told not to talk to the queen without other conspirators being present. Ruthven further warned that if any of them tried to assist her escape, they would 'throw her to them piecemeal'.[20] Lennox and Darnley suddenly feared for their lives.

Mary knew that Darnley was the conspirators' weak link. She needed to separate him from them to establish who was behind the plot and for him to assist her escape. The story of this is also well known, and Maitland was not involved. On Moray's arrival he tried to broker a pardon for the conspirators, and Mary called for documentation to be provided for her signature. With this incriminating evidence prepared, she arranged for her guards to be removed by feigning a miscarriage. She then gained the assistance of Sir John Stewart of Traquair, the captain of her guard, to provide horses for her escape with Darnley to Seton late that night. On arrival, she met up with Bothwell and his allies, who escorted her to Dunbar. Atholl and others of her allies soon arrived with a strong force. Despite her exhaustion after five hours in the saddle, Mary was cock-a-hoop. Atholl and others of her allies arrived with a strong force. There were soon 4,000 men pledged to restore her to the throne, and she consulted Leslie on how to deal with her mutinous nobility and the despicable Darnley. She told both Bethune in Paris and Charles IX that she was not 'in robust health after the bodily indisposition of our person'.[21]

Despite being wary that Elizabeth was behind the plot, she dictated a graphic letter to explain her ordeal: 'Some of our subjects and council by their proceedings have declared manifestly what they are … having slain our most special servant in our own presence and thereafter held our proper person captive treasonably.'[22] She warned that it could happen to Elizabeth but apologised for being too tired to write herself.

Darnley was now regarded with ill-concealed contempt, shunned by most of Mary's supporters. Fearing for his life, Mary forced him to name the conspirators. His list included Maitland, but not Moray, Argyll or Glencairn. As Moray had not signed the bond sent to Newcastle, it is possible that Darnley could not verify his complicity. On 15 March, Mary rewarded Bothwell with the wardship of Dunbar. Five days later, Huntly replaced Morton as Chancellor, and Balfour took over from MacGill as Clerk-Register. She also confirmed Sir John Maxwell to his wife's inheritance at Terregles. She thanked Melville for his loyalty after he delivered a letter from Moray who was desperately seeking rehabilitation. Darnley asked whether Moray had sent him a similar letter, but Melville answered diplomatically that he considered Darnley and the queen to be as one. Darnley was relieved to learn that his fellow conspirators had fled.

Mary mustered troops to escort her back to Edinburgh. On reaching Haddington on 17 March, she confided in Melville of her bitterness at Darnley's behaviour. Melville blamed his youth and the bad counsel he kept with George Douglas, among others, but could see the 'great grudges which she held in her heart'.[23] On the next day, she made a triumphant return to Edinburgh which was acclaimed on all sides. She was supported by Bothwell, Huntly, Home, Seton, Marischal and Archbishop Hamilton with 8,000 men. She refused to return to Holyrood, fearing that conspirators might still be there, lodging instead at Sir John Maxwell's home in the High Street, where cannon were positioned outside, and later at the Bishop of Dunkeld's larger house in the Cowgate. Bothwell received support from the Hamiltons to police the streets with trained bands.

Morton and the others involved in the murder headed for England, and in their absence were denounced as rebels by the Privy Council. Maitland was not among them. He had 'acted so warily that no proof of his complicity was available', except for Darnley having informed on him.[24] On 29 March, the conspirators were attainted, with their homes being stripped of chattels. Mary particularly blamed Morton, as his adherent, Ker of Fawdonside, had levelled a pistol at her. Atholl replaced him as the young Angus's guardian and took control of Tantallon. Morton moved to Alnwick, while Ruthven, who was gravely ill, was escorted to Newcastle by his son. On arrival, they sent a grovelling letter to Cecil protesting that they had acted on Darnley's orders and 'for the preservation of the state and the Protestant religion'.

Embarrassed at their failure to detain Mary, Elizabeth witheringly advised Morton to find 'some place out of this realm' where he might hide.[25] Although he tried to go to the Low Countries, Mary had already called for his entry to be prohibited, and he returned into hiding in England. In May, Elizabeth again told him to leave, but as so often, this was for public consumption and he remained unmolested with his colleagues in the north. On 21 March, Knox, who had supported the murder, left for Ayrshire, where he wrote his history of the Reformation in Scotland, beseeching God to 'destroy that whore in her whoredom'.[26]

Mary had always warned Maitland that he would be blamed first.[27] He was warded at Inverness but remained with Atholl at Dunkeld. His lands at Haddington Abbey, received two years previously, were attainted and granted to Bothwell. He would need help from Moray and Atholl to recover them. Although Atholl tried to intercede, Bothwell blocked his rehabilitation. He was ordered into exile in Flanders, but, fearing capture by Bothwell at sea, stayed where he was. He hoped to buy a pardon, but Randolph did not think he would succeed.

Although Moray assured Mary that he had not been a party to the murder conspiracy, he was not sure that she was convinced. He retired with Argyll to Linlithgow, where they worked with Cecil to gain the conspirators' rehabilitation. Mary had to be pragmatic; most of the nobility was implicated, and she needed a government. She absolved those who did not appear to have played an active part in Riccio's murder, sending Balfour to Linlithgow with a pardon for Moray and the former exiles. She even undertook to restore their estates if they returned home and did not intercede on the conspirators' behalf. Argyll and Glencairn were back at court within ten days.

Although Randolph spread rumours that Mary had approached the papacy for a divorce from Darnley, she would not have considered this before her child's birth. She had to confirm Darnley's innocence, as a divorce or his conviction for treason would prejudice the child's legitimacy. On 20 March, Darnley signed a declaration before the Privy Council 'upon his honour, fidelity and the word of a prince,' that he 'never counselled, commanded, consented, assisted nor approved' Riccio's murder. When this was publicly proclaimed at the Mercat Cross on the following day, it was 'not without laughter'.[28] Mary was contemptuous of his disloyalty to his fellow conspirators but needed to deflect rumours that he had acted out of revenge, particularly after arranging for Riccio's body to be reinterred in 'a fair tomb' at Holyrood Abbey Church.

Darnley continued to deny any part in the 'conspiracy whereof he is slanderously and sakelessly traduced', admitting only to have rehabilitated the exiled lords from England without authority. He gave orders for the henchmen's arrest, resulting in Henry Yair, Thomas Scott, Sir John Mowbray of Barnbougle and William Harlaw being condemned to be hanged, drawn and quartered. As Mowbray and Harlaw were Lothian lairds, Bothwell stepped in to reprieve them at the scaffold. Darnley's fellow conspirators sent Mary the bond he had signed authorising the murder in her presence. If they should return, he would face a blood feud for failing to protect them. Moray provided Mary with the bond signed in Newcastle, which disclosed Darnley's offers to pardon the exiles and to maintain the religious status quo in return for the grant of the Crown Matrimonial. She now knew he had betrayed Riccio, his fellow conspirators, her unborn child and herself. To maintain appearances, she kept him with her in the High Street, where he could be watched, but away from her bed and state affairs. When he attempted to go to Stirling to rebuild bridges with Moray and Argyll, they were on their way to Edinburgh to see Mary. Randolph reported that he planned a visit to Flanders 'to move his case to any prince' who would listen. Although Lennox was banned from court, he remained 'sore troubled in mind' and still ill at Holyrood, but Darnley visited him only once.[29]

Bothwell 'now began to be in great favour', becoming Mary's de facto chief adviser and the most influential member of the Privy Council.[30] He had always supported Mary and her mother, despite his lengthy imprisonment in both Edinburgh Castle and the Tower. She praised his administrative 'dexterity', which was 'so acceptable to us that we could never to this hour forget it', particularly during her escape after Riccio's murder.[31] As a soldier, he combined resource, dependability and leadership. The captaincy of Dunbar provided him with income from its surrounding estates, in addition to the fertile lands of Haddington Abbey. He even seized the Maitland family's lands at Lethington.

As a committed Reformer, Bothwell ended the swing towards Catholicism. He arranged a further £10,000 from the Catholic Church to supplement Kirk revenues. This increased ministers' stipends to a level well above that previously received by the priesthood. By an

Act of Council, benefices worth less than 300 marks annually were automatically offered to Presbyterian incumbents, and some were taken up. Despite showing administrative efficiency, Bothwell was hated by the English and lacked political finesse. He had none of Moray's and Maitland's diplomacy and was out of his depth with Cecil's subtleties. He was impatient, preferring differences to be settled with a duel rather than by persuasion. In Mary's memoirs, written in England, Nau recorded: 'He was a man whose natural disposition made him anything but agreeable or inclined to put himself to much trouble or inconvenience to gain the goodwill of those with whom he was associated.'[32] Nevertheless, at her confinement in June, his influence, according to Killigrew – now Cecil's brother-in-law – who had replaced Randolph as English ambassador, was greater than all the other lords together, making him 'the most hated man in Scotland'.

Bothwell was aged thirty and, despite a string of female conquests, was not handsome. In May 1566, while visiting Haddington with his wife, he enjoyed a fifteen-minute liaison in the steeple of the abbey with her serving maid, twenty-year-old Bessie Crawford, a blacksmith's daughter. On a second occasion, Bessie's black hair was in disarray after a tryst in a chamber within the cloister, and he needed help to rebutton his trousers. Jean dismissed Bessie and appears to have been granted the lands of Nether Hailes by him as a peace offering. Mary was not immune to his appeal, as Sir John Maxwell (later Lord Herries) explained: 'He was high in his own conceit, proud, vicious and vainglorious above measure, who would attempt anything out of ambition. His reckless daring appealed to her romantic sentiments, while his strong character and resolute purpose contrasted forcibly with the weakness of her husband Darnley, and his inability to control or protect her.'[33] That said, there is no plausible evidence of any impropriety prior to them contemplating marriage at Dunbar. Historians have been swayed by the flawed evidence, provided in 1568 for the Conferences at York and Westminster, aimed at blackening Mary's name.

Despite the return to Reformist government, Mary depended on papal funding and could not let the Catholic powers think that she was abandoning them. She sent the Bishop of Dunblane to Rome to report Riccio's murder and asked her uncle, the Cardinal of Lorraine, to request further Vatican aid. She hoped that the Pope would understand her need for a careful balancing act, but he sent the fanatical Nicholas de Gouda as Nuncio, accompanied by Father Edmund Hay, Rector of the Jesuit College in Paris, to assess her difficulties. Philip II was shocked, not only at Mary's rapidly changing religious stance, but at the fervently Catholic king joining with heretics in a murder conspiracy.

Riccio's death brought a renewal of Elizabeth's correspondence with Mary. She had been genuinely shocked at the manner of his murder, sending warnings to both Darnley and Moray for betraying her. Fearing reprisals on his mother in the Tower, Darnley wrote to confirm that she was not involved. Elizabeth refused to receive his letter. She told de Silva, 'Had I been in Queen Mary's place, I would have taken my husband's dagger and stabbed him with it!'[34] Robert Melville was sent to assure Mary of her support, and to Darnley's chagrin, on 4 April Mary invited her to stand as godmother to their unborn child. When Melville delivered the message, he suggested to Elizabeth that it was an opportunity for them to meet, 'whereat she smiled'. Darnley chose Charles IX as a godfather but ignored Philip II, perhaps because of his recent coolness, although Mary invited his close ally, the Duke of Savoy.

Chapter 11

Restored as Secretary of State

With Mary about to move to the royal apartments at Edinburgh Castle to await her child's birth, she was under the protection of Mar, its hereditary Keeper. She could not face Holyrood, with the nightmare of Riccio's murder fresh in her mind. As Maitland was banished from court, she regularly presided over a Council consisting of Bothwell, Huntly, Atholl, Seton, Livingston and Fleming. Although she wanted sound government during her confinement, Bothwell was proving politically inept. Though she did not trust Moray, Mary realised it was expedient to remain socially on good terms with him. She needed the reasoned leadership and close English ties that only he could provide. On 21 April, he was recalled with Argyll to Edinburgh for a formal reconciliation with Bothwell and Huntly brokered by Castelnau, who was doing much to appease rivalries.

On 29 April, Moray, Argyll and Glencairn were restored to the Council, but Mary kept them at the castle to keep her eye on them. She held a feast to underline the reconciliation and required everyone to join hands to symbolise that they would work together. With Maitland still sidelined at Dunkeld, Moray prevented Bothwell from hunting him down for his part in Riccio's murder. Despite its lack of cohesion, the Council was united in its disaffection with Darnley, whose plotting was carefully watched. His one influential supporter was Balfour, who had fallen out with the queen, but even he was soon of doubtful loyalty. Mary told Moray to reprove Melville for associating with Darnley when he attempted to mediate between them. Only Atholl and Lennox would talk to him, and Lennox, who was at Dunbar and banned from court, was much offended with him. Darnley seemed oblivious of his precarious standing but, like Bothwell, wanted Maitland kept away from court lest he should reveal his part in the murder. He again suggested the appointment of the Bishop of Ross as Secretary of State and was furious when Mary disagreed.

Darnley did not 'seem bad personally, or in his habits'. He passed his time 'mostly in warlike exercises', being commended for his horsemanship.[1] Mary made a show of marital harmony, and they were reported to be living as husband and wife again, although this is uncertain. With Mary conciliating the Reformers, Darnley tried to improve his flagging image with foreign heads of state and English Catholics by sending letters to show that he was the more ardent papist and a more suitable Catholic pretender for the English Crown. He denied any involvement in Riccio's murder, telling Charles IX and Catherine de Medici that he had been 'greatly wronged by a rumour that makes me guilty of such a horrible crime'.[2] He signed himself as king of Scotland, sealed with the royal arms, and was encouraged when Philip acknowledged his letter.

Cecil had heard that Darnley claimed to have at least forty English supporters involved in a hare-brained plan to gain control of both the Scilly Isles and Scarborough Castle as bridgeheads for a Spanish invasion. There is no evidence that this was supported by Philip, who was reliant on Guise backing for his military objectives in the Low Countries. It was Mary who remained the focus of Catholic intrigue to replace Elizabeth. Just as Cecil had feared, her pregnancy caused her stock to rise. On 12 May, the Pope promised her 150,000 crowns to restore Catholicism. He sent the hardline Jesuit Vincenzo Laureo as Nuncio to investigate. Laureo, the recently appointed Bishop of Mondovi, left Rome on 6 June to visit his new see, before travelling to Savoy and on to Scotland. Mary wrote to the Pope to welcome the visit, although this strained her relationship with Moray.

Although Mary was warned of Moray's part in Riccio's murder, she refused Bothwell's and Huntly's request to imprison him during her confinement, and though they remained her most influential advisers, she gave Moray charge of her government. He promptly refused them lodgings in Edinburgh Castle, until Mary barred all of them from dining with her. She then riled everyone by appointing Riccio's eighteen-year-old nephew, Joseph (Giuseppe), who had arrived in Castelnau's train, as her new French Secretary.

Before her confinement, Mary asked the Bishop of Ross to prepare a new will in triplicate, one for her Guise relations, one for herself and one for her chosen regents. Although the regents' document has not survived, she is known to have appointed a committee of three, consisting of Argyll, Mar and probably Darnley. The latter resented the others' inclusion, but she wanted conciliatory government with absolute loyalty to the Stewarts. Neither Bothwell nor Moray would have been acceptable. The lords all signed an undertaking to be bound by it, but she no doubt avoided divulging its content. Much of it was taken up with bequests of her jewellery, often to family members in France, but the principal pieces were added in perpetuity to the Scottish crown jewels. The remainder was designated for her unborn child. Darnley was to receive twenty-six bequests, which returned gifts he had made to her. She remembered members of her household and the nobility, but Maitland and the Hamiltons, who were out of favour, were excluded.

By 3 June, Mary had withdrawn for her confinement, still depressed by Darnley's failings. It took another fifteen days before she began a difficult and protracted labour. After twenty hours, James, Duke of Rothesay, was born, on the morning of 19 June. Despite her exhaustion, his abundant health caused great rejoicing. A male heir greatly strengthened her claim to the English throne, and James now stood ahead of his father, with or without the Crown Matrimonial. Darnley, who had 'vagabondised every night' during her lying in, was treated with disdain.[3] When he visited her to see their child in a cradle by her bed, she demanded a solemn oath that he was 'begotten by none but you'. She reportedly said: 'He is so much your son that I fear it will be the worse for him hereafter.'[4] She still feared him attempting a kidnap to rule on the child's behalf.

The pain in Mary's side left her depressed, and she recovered only slowly. In late July, with her doctors advising a change of air, Moray and Mar escorted her down the Firth of Forth to Alloa Tower, Mar's home near Stirling. She was accompanied by her intimate friends, the Countesses of Mar, Argyll and Moray. As Lord High Admiral, Bothwell arranged the trip but did not go with them. Castelnau joined Mary at Alloa, hoping to reconcile her with Darnley, who was not told of the trip in advance. On learning of her whereabouts, he rode to join them, but she could not abide his company. After a massive row, he left a few hours later, and Castelnau barely saw him. Bedford reported: 'The Queen and her husband agree after the old manner, or rather worse. She eateth but very seldom with him, but lieth not nor keepeth no company with him, nor loveth any such as love him … It cannot for modesty nor the honour of a Queen be reported what she said to him.'[5]

After several days of dancing, masques and sports with the court ladies, Mary received Maitland, but his rehabilitation was barred by Bothwell. Kirkcaldy reported that Bothwell 'hath now of all men greatest access and familiarity with the Queen, so that nothing of importance is done without him'. This made him 'the most hated man among the noblemen of this realm, and it is said that his insolence is such that David was never more abhorred than he is now disliked on every side'.[6]

While in Alloa, Mary heard that Mondovi was waiting in Paris for her call to allow him to visit, but a Counter-Reformation was no longer a realistic prospect, and Moray persuaded the nobility to refuse him entry. John Bethune, Master of the Household, carried Mary's apologies to Paris, but Mondovi sternly rebuked her for not restoring the Catholic faith. Bethune returned with part of the promised subsidy as an inducement. On 21 August, Mondovi wrote to the Cardinal of Alessandria in Rome that her difficulties 'might be obviated if the King of Spain should come, as it is hoped, with a strong force to Flanders … If justice were executed against the six rebels, who were leaders and originators of the late treason against the Queen, [their] deaths would effectually restore peace and obedience in the kingdom.' He named the rebels as Moray, Argyll, Morton, Maitland, Justice-Clerk Bellenden and former Clerk-Register MacGill, 'a man of no family and contriver of all evil'.

This indicates a general acceptance that Moray had been behind Riccio's murder. Mondovi described Darnley as 'an ambitious and inconstant youth, [who] would like to rule the realm'.[7] As Mary was proving unhelpful, Darnley offered the only means of restoring Catholicism and of bringing Riccio's murderers to book. Not being in Scotland, Mondovi could not see what was going on for himself, but the Pope naïvely approved his approach.

Despite no longer trusting Moray, Mary lacked other able advisers to re-establish her authority and could not manage without him. When Darnley threatened to kill him, she warned Moray and, on her return to Edinburgh, humiliated her husband before the court by telling him that 'she would not be content that either he or any other should be unfriendly to Moray'. She forced him to admit that his hatred arose from hearsay 'that Moray was not his friend, which made him speak that which he repented'.[8] Darnley continued plotting and complained to his father of Mary's lack of respect and refusal to sleep with him.

Bothwell also wanted Moray sidelined. He suggested that George Douglas should be offered a pardon in return for providing evidence of Moray's and Maitland's part in Riccio's murder. Mary would have none of it, knowing their importance in government. Meanwhile, Moray incited border lairds, who were receiving English backing, into a confederacy against Bothwell, forcing him to leave Edinburgh to deal with it.

On 3 August, Mary, who was still no better, paid a second five-day visit to Alloa. She wanted religious tolerance and, although Bothwell tried to keep the Catholic nobility marginalised, she was increasingly taking advice from Atholl, who was guided behind the scenes by Maitland. It was on this second visit that Atholl and Moray again requested Maitland's rehabilitation, and, on 4 August, he formally submitted to her at Stirling. The only evidence for his involvement in Riccio's murder was Darnley's increasingly unreliable word for it. After dining with him alone, she reappointed him as Secretary of State, showing that Bothwell did not always have his own way. Maitland immediately advised Cecil and, by 11 August, was officially reconciled to Bothwell at Craigmillar. Bothwell was forced to relinquish Haddington Abbey, but remained for a considerable period in occupation, leaving them at daggers drawn. There were even rumours of Maitland attempting to poison him. His reappointment heralded Atholl's growing prominence, which left his long-term enemy, Argyll, in the wilderness. Despite Moray's efforts, Mary would still not agree the exiles' rehabilitation, which was opposed by Bothwell, causing Maitland and Moray to combine against him.

After Maitland's reappointment, Darnley went off hunting and was increasingly shunned. He remained in touch with Philip II, now in the final stages of his planned invasion of the Low Countries. When, on the rare occasions that he was seen conversing with members of the nobility, Mary assumed he was plotting against her. It was probably her need to keep tabs on him that persuaded her to resume sexual relations with him. On 13 August, she made a large payment to him from her Treasury and provided a magnificent upholstered bed that had belonged to the queen regent, and cloth of gold to furnish caparisons for his horse. Although she may have hoped for a reconciliation, he was still frequenting Edinburgh brothels. In mid-August, she joined him for stag-hunting at Meggetland, south of Peebles, accompanied by Bothwell, Huntly, Moray, Atholl and Mar. This does not suggest harmonious company, and Buchanan claimed that she treated Darnley 'capriciously, arrogantly and disdainfully'.

On 19 August, Mary visited Traquair on the Tweed, where Darnley joined them unexpectedly.[9] The hunting had been disappointing, and, although she remained unwell, he asked her at supper to ride out with him again on the following day. She later told Nau: 'Knowing that if she did so, she would be required to gallop her horse at a great pace, she whispered in his ear that she suspected that she was pregnant.' As it was only two months since James's birth, she could not have known this by then. Darnley's infamously callous response was: 'Never mind, if we lose this one, we will make another.' Although Traquair had been knighted at their wedding and was a close ally, he 'rebuked him sharply', saying: 'He did not speak like a Christian.' Darnley retorted: 'What! Ought we not to work a mare well when she is in foal?'[10] It is no surprise that their rapprochement failed.

On 22 August, Mary returned to Holyrood for two days after hearing that Darnley planned to kidnap James to gain the Crown Matrimonial. Although the prince was in Mar's care at Edinburgh Castle, Mary decided to move him to Stirling, the traditional childhood home for royal children. She took no chances, and, on 31 August, Lady Forbes of Reres set out with the prince in a litter escorted by four or five hundred hackbutters. Bothwell was appointed captain of the guard to supervise the royal nursery's security arrangements. Mary then maintained appearances by rejoining Darnley to hunt at Glenartney, near Loch Earn, and at Drummond Castle, near Crieff. Although her health was not improved, she was not pregnant.

On 6 September, Mary returned to Edinburgh to plan James's christening celebration, but Darnley, who was apparently in a foul mood at Maitland's reappointment, did not accompany her. Lennox wrote to her of his son's humiliation and intention to go abroad as he felt unsafe in Scotland. Scheming from overseas would be even more dangerous, and his departure might raise questions over James's paternity. Mary came to Stirling to have it out with him, but he refused to return with her to Holyrood. Having shown Lennox's letter to the Privy Council, they resolved to talk to Darnley. When he made an unexpected reappearance in Edinburgh, the new French ambassador, Philibert du Croc, who had replaced Castelnau, witnessed '*une forte belle harangue* [a big slanging match]' between the couple.[11] She 'took him by the hand, and besought

Right: Sir John Maitland of Thirlestane was continuously loyal to his elder brother, ultimately becoming James VI's all-powerful chief minister. (*Bridgeman Images 1155874*)

Below: Lethington House (later renamed Lennoxlove and substantially extended), the Maitland family home in East Lothian (*scran.ac.uk / SC1031177*)

Above left: Mary Queen of Scots in her *deuil blanc,* which she wore when first back in Scotland as the widow of Francis II. (*Oil on Panel / Bridgeman Images 67973*)

Above right: Mary of Guise, the mother of Mary Queen of Scots. She appointed Maitland as her Secretary while Mary was living in France. (*Oil on Panel / Corneille de Lyon/Scottish National Portrait Gallery / Bridgeman images 68380*)

Left: Lord James Stewart, later Earl of Moray, who controlled Mary's Government working with Maitland, and became Regent of Scotland after Mary's deposition. (*National Galleries of Scotland / scran.ac.uk 000-000-483-747-C*)

Right: David Riccio, whose murder was arranged by Maitland after he threatened his role as Secretary. (*Bridgeman Images 3764527*)

Below: Palace of Holyrood House, Edinburgh, where Riccio was murdered while attending a dinner party with Mary Queen of Scots. (*Bridgeman Images / 3153826*)

Left: Henry Stuart, Lord Darnley, Mary Queen of Scots' second husband, whose murder was masterminded by Maitland. (*Oil on panel / Hardwick Hall / National Trust Photographic Library / Bridgeman Images 1161843*)

Below: Craigmillar Castle, Edinburgh, where Maitland approached the other senior Scottish Lords to arrange Darnley's murder. (*Bridgeman images 646723*)

Right: James Douglas, 4th Earl of Morton, who gained the Scottish Lords' approval to imprison Mary Queen of Scots at Lochleven Castle. (*Arnold Bronckorst/Scottish National Portrait Gallery PG1857*)

Below: Lochleven Castle, where Mary Queen of Scots was imprisoned while in Scotland. (*Bridgeman Images 5977520*)

Left: Matthew Stuart, 4th Earl of Lennox, the father of Henry Lord Darnley, and later Regent of Scotland, who was assassinated at Stirling Castle by Marian supporters. (*Oil on Panel / Bridgeman Images 1161874*)

Below: Stirling Castle, Mary Queen of Scots' principal stronghold outside Edinburgh. (*Bridgeman Images 4530637*)

Above left: James Hepburn, 4th Earl Bothwell, who was manipulated by Maitland into organising Darnley's murder and subsequently to marry Mary Queen of Scots. (*Miniature, Scottish National Portrait Gallery/Bridgeman Images 772800 (1)*)

Above right: Robert Dudley, Earl of Leicester, who was put forward by Elizabeth I as a prospective husband for Mary Queen of Scots. (*Oil on panel / Bridgeman Images 2597267*)

Thomas Howard, 4th Duke of Norfolk, who was encouraged by Maitland to become betrothed to Mary Queen of Scots after her imprisonment in England, resulting in his execution. (*His Grace the Duke of Norfolk, Arundel Castle / Bridgeman Images, 279033*)

Elizabeth I, who respected Maitland's intellect, but came to mistrust him after Darnley's murder. The sieve symbolised her virginity. (*Oil on canvas / Zuccaro / Pinacoteca Nazionale, Siena / Bridgeman Images 183354*)

William Cecil, 1st Lord Burghley, who worked behind the scenes with Maitland to support the murders of Riccio and Darnley but became suspicious of his later support for Mary Queen of Scots. (*Oil on panel / National Portrait Gallery / Bridgeman Images 106907*)

him for God's sake to declare if she had given him reason [to go abroad]; and entreated he might deal plainly, and not spare her'. '[She had] a clear conscience, and that all her life she had done no action which could anywise prejudice either his or her honour.'[12]

He admitted that he was not leaving on account of any waywardness on her part but complained at being inadequately recognised as king. As he left, he whispered theatrically: 'Adieu, Madame. You shall not see my face for a long space.'[13] She was visibly upset, but both the Council and du Croc advised her to continue her wise and virtuous existence. Du Croc told Catherine de Medici that the Scots were 'so well reconciled with the Queen as a result of her own prudent behaviour, that nowadays there was not a single division to be seen between them'.[14]

With Mary's blessing, the Council sent Catherine a full account of Darnley's behaviour to prevent him attempting to set up a royal court in exile. Despite his threats, he remained in Scotland hunting and fishing. Du Croc reported: 'It is vain to imagine that he should be able to raise any disturbance, for there is not one person in all the kingdom, from the highest to the lowest, that regards him any further than is agreeable to the Queen. And I never saw her majesty so much beloved, esteemed and honoured.'[15] If there had been any hint of an affair between Mary and Bothwell at this time, as Buchanan later claimed, Darnley would surely have raised it. She told Lennox that he had no cause for complaint. Melville told Archbishop Bethune in Paris that Darnley was seeking the dismissal of Maitland, MacGill and Bellenden.

Mondovi had remained in Paris awaiting a call to visit Scotland. By now, Pius V believed that it would take the threat of Philip II's delayed invasion of Flanders for his mission to succeed. The Cardinal of Lorraine was in no hurry to intercede on his behalf and discouraged him from doing 'something signal for the service of God in Scotland'.[16] By mid-October, Mondovi had been recalled to his see.

Chapter 12

Ending Mary's marriage to Darnley

Notwithstanding continued discomfort from the pain in her side, Mary was determined to demonstrate greater involvement in government and agreed to attend assizes in Jedburgh to deal with petty offences postponed during her pregnancy. Before leaving Edinburgh, she called on leading Council members to subscribe to a bond for mutual support, but to ignore the king 'when his orders conflicted with the queen's wishes'. On 1 October, she ordered Border lairds to meet her at Melrose. Although Darnley was invited, he was still threatening to go abroad and did not appear. On 7 October, she left for Jedburgh with an entourage of forty men, including Moray, Maitland and other principal advisers, together with judges and court officials. As Lieutenant of the Borders, Bothwell had left for Liddesdale three days earlier, taking 300 horse to round up offenders for trial. During this process, he was severely wounded in a skirmish and had to be carried to Hermitage unconscious from loss of blood.

On arrival at Jedburgh on 9 October, Mary was greeted by the news of Bothwell's injuries. With fewer cases for trial than expected, the assize ended in six days. On 16 October, she rode with Moray, Maitland and her party to visit Bothwell at Hermitage, a round trip of fifty miles. After a two-hour meeting, she set off back to Jedburgh. As she was returning, she fell from her horse when it slipped in a bog. The next day she was feverish and the pain in her side was so acute that she vomited blood 'more than sixty times'. This led to convulsions, with a loss of vision and ability to speak, until she became unconscious. With her gastric ulcer having haemorrhaged, her entourage feared for her life. Despite his injuries, Bothwell arrived on a horse litter from Hermitage to hear her final wishes if the worst should happen, determined to prevent Moray from usurping authority.

Mary's life was saved by her French doctor, Charles Nau, who treated her by 'extreme rubbing' and wrapping her limbs in bandages. She made a will to ensure that Darnley did not inherit the throne and, to Bothwell's chagrin, gave Moray 'the principal part of the government'.[1] As Mary was on friendlier terms with Elizabeth, who was concerned at Darnley's underhand dealing with the Spanish, she entrusted her sister-queen with 'the special care of the protection of our son'.[2] Darnley, who had been hunting in the west of Scotland, only arrived when the worst was over, and being unwelcome, he soon departed. Mary had already told Maitland that she wanted to be freed from her marriage. He believed: 'The occasion of the Queen's sickness is thought and displeasure ... and the root of it is the king. For she has done him so great honour, contrary to the advice of her subjects, and he, on the other part, has recompensed her with such ingratitude and misuses himself so far towards her that it is a heartbreak for her to think he should be her husband, and how to be free of him she sees no outgait.' Mary recovered quickly and, on 9 November, moved back by easy stages in a litter towards Edinburgh. After three weeks, she reached Sir Simon Preston's home at Craigmillar. Although Darnley appeared there, Mary would have nothing to do with him, and he again threatened to leave Scotland.

While at Craigmillar, Maitland took the lead in discussing with those present how to arrange a separation between Mary and Darnley. Although divorce seemed preferable, Maitland knew that the only acceptable grounds for a Catholic divorce were adultery or an annulment. Although there was ample cause for separation on grounds of Darnley's adultery, neither party would be permitted to remarry, and Mary wanted more heirs to protect her succession. An annulment would result in James being deemed illegitimate. In cases where a marriage was annulled because the couple were within the fourth degree of consanguinity (third cousins or closer), there was precedent for children to remain legitimate, if the couple were unaware of their consanguinity at the time of the marriage. However, Mary had received a papal dispensation for this, so the only hope was to argue that it was invalid as it had arrived after the marriage had taken place. A second problem was in controlling Darnley afterwards. Far from improving the realm's security, he would become the focus of every Catholic scheme against Mary. Lennox heard that the lords at Craigmillar planned to imprison Darnley after the prince's baptism, but there is no evidence of this, and it would only alienate English Catholics, some of whom preferred his claim to the English throne to Mary's.

The more certain solution was to bring about Darnley's death, and Maitland considered a prosecution for treason. Although under Scottish law a king could not be charged with treason, the Bishop of Ross believed that this could be overcome as he was a consort. However, a treason trial for his part in Riccio's murder would implicate Morton and his fellow exiles and bring to light Moray's and Maitland's involvement. With so many foreign dignitaries due to arrive shortly for James's baptism at Stirling, a trial involving Darnley and the principal Scottish lords could not be contemplated. Furthermore, if Darnley were found guilty, James's legitimacy would again be in doubt. This left murder as the only clear solution, although Mary would never sanction it and could not be told but achieving it might be more straightforward. If the conspirators in exile were repatriated, they were sure to arrange his death in a Douglas blood feud.

Maitland thus glossed over divorce difficulties and focused on gaining the exiles' rehabilitation. He and Moray approached Argyll, Huntly and Bothwell for help in gaining Mary's agreement. They offered to help, if it did not offend her, but Bothwell's and Huntly's only motive for supporting the return of Moray's allies was to achieve Darnley's murder. Although Bothwell did not initiate the plan, as Buchanan later claimed, he was outraged at Darnley's behaviour and supported it. Maitland suggested that Mary could be persuaded to agree to the exiles' repatriation in return for an offer to arrange her divorce. When Argyll, who had long wanted a divorce for himself, said that he 'knew not how that might be done', Maitland assured him that a way could be found 'to make her quit of him, so that you and my Lord of Huntly will only behold the matter, and not be offended thereat'.[3] This careful reply does not necessarily imply that divorce was the intention.

As their spokesman, Maitland now approached the queen, offering to arrange matters 'as well for her own easement as for the realm', in return for her agreeing to pardon the exiles and to restore their attainted estates.[4] Despite mistrusting Morton, Mary agreed to his rehabilitation on two conditions: 'One that the divorcement were made lawfully; the other that it was not prejudicial to her son; otherwise Her Highness would rather endure all torments and abide the perils that might chance her.'[5] With the English succession in mind, she would not countenance an impediment to James's legitimacy and did not know how this could be overcome.

Although Maitland assured Mary that their means to be rid of Darnley would be legal, he stated rather obliquely that Moray was as scrupulous a Protestant as she was a Catholic, adding: 'I am assured he will look through his fingers thereto, and will behold our doings, saying nothing of the same.'[6] This has to mean that Moray would be allowed to keep his hands clean while some underhand plot took place. He was still seen by the nobility – other than Bothwell and Huntly – as their natural leader. Mary was given similar assurance that nothing would tarnish her reputation. However, she later realised that, in removing Darnley, Maitland persuaded the Protestant lords to sully her honour and even to make her son illegitimate to allow Moray to take the Crown.

In 1569, Moray was challenged over reports of his part in the discussions at Craigmillar but denied any involvement 'tending to any unlawful or dishonourable end'. This, of course, was not a denial of his knowledge of the murder plan, only that he had not implemented it. If he were allowed to 'look through his fingers', his personal agenda was clearly to regain control of government. Mary was in a similar position. The lords knew she would not agree to Darnley's murder and kept her unaware of the plan. Two of the depositions made for her defence in England show that she knew that means other than divorce had been contemplated and that she vetoed them. In the *Protestation of Huntly and Argyll,* prepared by Mary in January 1569, but intercepted by Cecil before being sent for their signature, she claimed to have told them: 'I will that you do nothing by which any spot may be laid to my honour or conscience, and therefore I pray you rather let the matter be in the estate as it is, abiding till God in his goodness put remedy thereto, than you, believing to do me service, may possibly turn to my hurt and displeasure.'[7] Maitland had smoothly replied: 'Madam, let us guide the matter among us, and Your Grace shall see nothing but good and approved by parliament.'[8] The second deposition was prepared in 1568 by her Scottish supporters, including Huntly and Argyll. It implied that she knew that they had considered 'other ways [from divorce and treason] to dispatch him; which altogether Her Grace refused, as is manifestly known'.[9] She knew that murder was contemplated and that the exiles would want revenge on their return, but she wanted to prevent it. As she would need to conduct a proper investigation afterwards, she had to be kept in the dark over the detail. Her passionate behaviour with Darnley at Kirk o' Field makes it highly unlikely that she was aware of his imminent death.

To confirm their agreement, the lords at Craigmillar will have signed a bond similar to that for Riccio's murder, but with the precise objective left ambiguous. Although no such document has survived, it is evidenced from several sources. Mary told Nau that when Bothwell left her at Carberry Hill, he gave her a paper and told her to guard it well, as it was the evidence of the other lords' complicity in the murder. If this were the bond, as seems likely, it was quickly removed from her and destroyed. If Casket Letter II is to be believed (and it is the one part of them that appears plausible), Darnley told her in Glasgow that he was aware that a bond for his murder had been prepared at Craigmillar. In the admittedly suspect deposition of Bothwell's henchman, James 'Black' Ormiston, before his execution in 1573, he recalled: 'It was thought expedient and most profitable for the Commonwealth, by the whole nobility and Lords underscribed, that such a young fool and proud tyrant should not reign or bear rule over them: and that for divers causes therefore, that these all had concluded that he should be put off by one way or another: and whosoever should take the deed in hand, or do it, they should defend and fortify as themselves.' It is, of course, unlikely that the bond would so openly have contemplated Darnley's murder, but the signatories' names have a ring of authenticity, particularly as Moray, by then deceased, is not mentioned. These were Huntly, Argyll, Bothwell, Maitland and Balfour, who was said to have drafted it. As Darnley's ally, Balfour's involvement may seem surprising, but as a lawyer he was closely associated with Bothwell, then sheriff of Edinburgh. His signature denotes one of his many changes in loyalty during his political career. With Darnley isolated, he now hoped for advantage by backing his enemies. Just as Morton retained the bond for Riccio's murder, so Bothwell, the soldier among them, retained this bond as security and agreed to brief and assist the returning exiles. It is unlikely that Mary saw it until Carberry Hill.

On 7 December 1566, the queen left Craigmillar for Holyrood to finalise arrangements for the prince's baptism at Stirling ten days later. This was to be a celebration, not only for the heir to the Scottish throne, but for a future king of England. Three days later, she travelled to Stirling. Although Darnley was already there, she gave Bothwell responsibility for the arrangements and for greeting visiting dignitaries. Sir John Forster reported to Cecil: 'All things for the christening are at his appointment and the same scarcely well liked of with the rest of the nobility as it is said.'[10] By giving him such prominence, Mary again showed a lack of tact with so many English being present, and Sir James Melville reported afterwards that he 'had a mark of his own that he shot at', strutting about full of self-importance.[11]

Mary remained so concerned at rumours of Darnley's scheming that the Privy Council issued an edict to prevent firearms being brought into the castle. She dismissed most of his servants but remained concerned at their number when he replaced them with Lennox dependants. Du Croc reported that she was wary of 'further contrivances' and forbade him from meeting foreign dignitaries unless she were present. According to Melville, she was 'still sad and pensive', fearing that the exiles' rehabilitation would inevitably lead to a blood feud. He tried to console her by saying that 'her friends in England would soon help her to forget her enemies in Scotland'. He too commended a grant of clemency for the exiles 'to best gain the hearts of the whole people, both here and in England'.[12]

Mary had obtained support from both Catholic and Protestant Council members to make the prince's christening a spectacular a three-day fête. She borrowed £12,000 from Edinburgh merchants, raising taxes to repay it. This was not just a celebration of his baptism, but of Moray's and Argyll's reconciliation with Bothwell. Although they would not attend the Catholic ceremony, she provided new clothing for them to attend the celebration afterwards. Moray wore green, Argyll red and Bothwell blue, while many others were magnificently attired, 'some in cloth of silver, some in cloth of gold, some in cloth of tissue, every man rather above than under his degree'.[13] Banquets with fine wines matched the magnificence of the costumes. A stage was built for Buchanan's masques, which extolled Mary's virtues (hardly in accord with his later *Detectio*). Mary's valet, the witty Sebastian Pagez, an accomplished musician from Auverne, prepared entertainments including a ballet, which caused the English great offence by depicting them as satyrs holding their tails in their hands to make obscene gestures. The Scots roared with laughter, but Bedford had to restore order when an Englishman threatened to stab Pagez through the heart. The Comptroller of the Royal Artillery prepared a spectacular firework display as a finale, with cannon from the arsenals at Edinburgh and Dundee being hauled up the sides of the castle rock to maximise its effect.

Darnley wanted to avoid foreign dignitaries present seeing his fall in status. Even Catholics were disillusioned with him. Du Croc had already reported that he was unlikely to be at the baptism, 'as his pride could not brook the insulting neglect'.[14] He was shunned both by Bedford, who had instructions from Elizabeth not to recognise him as king, and by du Croc, who was advised from France not to allow him an interview as he was not 'in good correspondence' with Mary. On the day before the ceremony, Bedford presented Mary with Elizabeth's gift of an opulent enamelled gold font, but Darnley did not attend the presentation, piqued at Elizabeth telling him to be obedient to Mary in all matters. The Catholic service was conducted by Archbishop Hamilton, but Mary would not let him spit into the child's mouth, as was the custom, knowing that he suffered from syphilis. The prince was christened Charles James, taking his first name from the king of France.

Though the queen put aside her problems and presided in style over the three days of celebration, she was privately 'pensive and melancholy'. Du Croc found her weeping on her bed, after Bedford had at last persuaded her to repatriate the exiles. On Christmas Eve, she formally pardoned Morton and seventy-six other conspirators, but banned them from court for two years. She saw this as another step towards gaining recognition as Elizabeth's heir and was encouraged when Bedford confirmed that Elizabeth wanted a conference to discuss her claim to the English throne. For Elizabeth to reopen this 'vexatious question' was a major coup for Mary. The birth of a son had tipped the balance of power between the two queens in Mary's favour. She immediately involved Maitland in these new proposals, hoping to eliminate both Henry VIII's will and her Scottish birth as valid grounds for overlooking her claim. Maitland argued that the English throne was Mary's birthright, as sanctioned by the principle of English law, but seems to have avoided the thorny difficulty of Mary's Catholic faith. (His personal attitude to the reopening of these negotiations is discussed in Chapter 13.) Mary could not resist writing to mimic Elizabeth's earlier stance over Mary's choice of husband. She 'expressed hope that Elizabeth would marry soon and that: "For our part, the personage chosen, next to her own contentment, should benefit the utility of both countries and assist our amity and intelligence."'[15] She concluded by saying that 'there is no one who we would like better [than the Archduke Charles]'.[16]

Darnley caused great embarrassment at Stirling by remaining in his apartments. Although his absence implied doubt over the prince's paternity, he did not want the lesions and suppurating pustules over his face and body to be seen, following another outbreak of his secondary syphilis. Du Croc reported that he was being treated with salivation of mercury and medicinal baths, the standard remedy at the time. He told Archbishop Bethune: 'His bad deportment is incurable, nor can there be ever any good expected from him for several reasons which I might tell was I present with you. I can't pretend to foretell how all may turn; but I will say that matters can't subsist long as they are without being accompanied by several bad consequences.'[17] Darnley was being cold-shouldered and was in mortal fear of the returning exiles, who saw him as the direct cause of their banishment and the loss of their estates.

Even now, Mary still hoped to arrange a divorce from Darnley. On 23 December, she temporarily restored Archbishop Hamilton so that he could find a way to achieve it without prejudicing her son's legitimacy, but, by 9 January, he had advised that a Catholic divorce could not be achieved on acceptable terms. On 13 December, with unfortunate timing, Father Edmund Hay reached Edinburgh with William Chisholm, Bishop of Dunblane, on the Pope's behalf. Although they immediately went to Stirling, Mary was tied up with the christening arrangements and probably did not meet them. She knew that their demand for her to execute the senior Protestant lords would be politically disastrous, if not practically impossible.

Thoroughly disaffected, Darnley crept away to Glasgow before Christmas without taking his leave, intending yet again to go abroad. His affliction only gradually became public knowledge. It was initially reported that he had been poisoned, and later that he had 'the Pox', which was assumed to mean smallpox. Once on the road, a white taffeta mask was needed to cover his disfigured face. Buchanan reported: 'Hardly a mile out of Stirling, a violent disorder struck every part of his body. Livid pustules broke out accompanied by much pain and vexation in his whole body. [He had] black pimples all over his body, grievous sweat in all his limbs, and intolerable stink.'[18] By 2 January 1567, he was too ill to travel abroad and needed proper treatment. He wrote to Mary asking to see her. Although she did not go immediately, she sent her physician to continue an eight-week course of salivation of mercury. This involved sweating the patient and applying mercury both orally and to anoint the gums. This loosened the teeth as the gum tissue died, causing bad breath and copious flows of saliva. The treatment was completed with a series of sulphurous baths. Despite Darnley's predicament, he continued scheming to replace Mary on the throne, demanding the dismissal of her closest Protestant advisers, particularly Maitland.

On 6 January, Mary attended Maitland's marriage to Mary Fleming in the Chapel Royal at Holyrood. This provided him with 'a new and extensive kinship base'.[19] The newly-weds had little time for a honeymoon and Maitland remained at court. Four days later, he accompanied Mary to Stirling to assist in escorting the prince back to Edinburgh, so as to lessen the risk of a kidnap attempt being launched from Glasgow. He remained with her until about 12 January, when they returned with the prince to Holyrood after spending a night with the Livingstons at Callendar on the way. As late as 20 January, Mary wrote to Bethune in Paris that she knew of Darnley's plotting, 'but God moderates their forces well enough, and takes the means of execution of their intentions from them'. It can be no surprise that she deferred going to him, despite his continued requests.

With divorce no longer an acceptable option, Mary decided to make a new start with Darnley while supervising his movements to limit any further plotting against her. This was in keeping with her rehabilitation of Moray after the Chaseabout Raid and of the exiles involved in Riccio's murder, despite their all too obvious treasonable actions. His assassination would only prejudice her hopes of recognition as Elizabeth's heir. She set out to Glasgow intending to bring him back to Edinburgh where he could be watched. Once the symptoms of his syphilis had subsided, his restoration to her bed could provide more heirs. It also assured her son's legitimacy and enhanced her claim to the English throne. Yet it was a blow to those who wanted to use her disillusionment with her husband to justify his removal with the prospect of immunity from prosecution.

To gain assurance that the returning exiles would not contemplate Darnley's assassination on their return, Mary sent Bothwell to Dunbar to see Morton. As Bothwell was organising them to arrange it, he was not the ideal messenger. The returning exiles saw Darnley as a political embarrassment and feared for their lives if he should regain authority. On arrival at Dunbar, Bothwell suffered a haemorrhage, a legacy from his wounds received in Liddesdale, and was laid low for a week.

By then, Morton was with Archibald Douglas at his brother Sir William's home at Whittinghame, six miles nearer to Edinburgh. By 19 January, Bothwell was sufficiently recovered to meet them. Despite ostensibly being on honeymoon at Lethington six miles further on, Maitland, who was Sir William's brother-in-law, joined them after having returned from Stirling two days earlier.

Bothwell saw Darnley's murder as a political necessity and knew that the exiles would want their revenge for his failure to protect them following Riccio's murder. He privately asked Morton to arrange it, 'seeing it was in the Queen's mind that the King should be taken away'.[20] Morton later claimed that he asked to see Mary's warrant approving it, but they became evasive. He testified that, even with the queen's sanction, he would have preferred to return to exile. This, of course, was a blatant attempt to demonstrate his innocence. Although he claimed that Archibald Douglas and Maitland added their persuasion, it is more likely that he and Maitland encouraged Bothwell to take it in hand. Although Morton wanted Darnley dead, he was in no position to arrange his murder as the terms of his rehabilitation prohibited him coming within seven miles of court. Despite having refused to be involved, after being so recently pardoned, he undoubtedly provided henchmen. It is often suggested that Morton persuaded his 'cousin' Archibald Douglas to take his place, but he was only a remote connection. Archibald took part because he was associated with Bothwell in the Admiralty Courts as a Lord of Session. He was also a minister of the Kirk, but a devious character nonetheless. He had been on the fringes of Riccio's murder plot and provided the communication link between the Craigmillar bond signatories and the exiles in England. He later married Bothwell's sister, Jean, the widow of Lord John Stewart.

As Bothwell had to organise the murder himself, he needed to cover his tracks. The plausible evidence shows that he was not at Kirk o' Field at the time of the explosion, despite falsified depositions to the contrary. He was residing at Holyrood with his wife, where any movements would have been noted by the guard. He remained in the queen's company for the whole of the day of the murder, much of it attired in fancy dress. He was also at the palace shortly beforehand, holding a late meeting with Mary and Stewart of Traquair, captain of the guard, almost certainly to discuss the prince's future protection, and was in his bed at Holyrood with his wife when he was woken to be told.

There is no reliable evidence that he left Holyrood after meeting the queen, and the guard was never asked to verify his movements. Nevertheless, he was deluded to think that he would avoid being implicated. Too many of his enemies knew of his involvement. The falsified depositions attempted to demonstrate that he and his henchmen had undertaken every stage of the murder without the assistance of others. Moray's allies could plant rumours without infringing their bond, and they fanned them to good effect. Within a week the public learned from placards posted in Edinburgh that Bothwell had not only organised the murder but was also implicated with the queen in a crime of passion, despite there being no hint of impropriety between them beforehand.

PART IV

DEVELOPING THE TALE OF A CRIME OF PASSION

Chapter 13

The Chameleon

At the beginning of 1567, Maitland's motives were become more puzzling. Not for the first time, this indisputably able politician displayed apparently conflicting objectives. Despite having held office as Secretary of State for the Catholic Mary of Guise, he had become a Reformer and supported the Lords of the Congregation against her government with its French and Catholic loyalties. He had wanted to replace Scotland's Auld Alliance with Catholic France by amity with Protestant England. His initial hope was to cement this by Elizabeth's marriage to Arran. But Elizabeth was at the height of her romance with Dudley and turned Arran down. Maitland had little alternative but to support the widowed Mary Queen of Scots' return to Scotland and hope that amity could be achieved by her being recognised as Elizabeth's successor. For this to serve his purpose of unifying the two kingdoms and to be acceptable to the English, Mary would need to become Protestant, but it was not a step she would consider. Moray and Maitland later hoped that if Mary made a Protestant marriage acceptable to the English and maintained a politically Protestant policy, the English might approve her claim, but Cecil was adamant that she needed to become personally Protestant. With Mary refusing to abandon her Catholic faith, Maitland and Moray, working in close alliance, concluded that she was unacceptable as the catalyst for the amity, and that Moray should replace her as Scotland's head of state, either as king or as leader of a Scottish republic.

The issue for both Maitland and Moray was to find a means to demonstrate Mary's shortcomings as monarch of Protestant Scotland, particularly when she was exuding great charisma and religious tolerance. It was on her instruction that Maitland conducted negotiations with de Quadra, the Spanish ambassador in London, for her to marry Don Carlos, heir to the Spanish throne. Despite giving every impression of strongly supporting the suit, it can be certain that Maitland's objective was to demonstrate that if Mary remained as the Scottish queen, she would seek to restore Catholicism. His negotiation seemed to incur both Cecil's and Moray's wrath, but they quickly understood his purpose and were soon back on cordial terms with him. Elizabeth then stepped in to propose that Mary should marry her former paramour, Leicester. As a Puritan, Leicester met with Moray's and Maitland's approval, and Elizabeth intended that it would lead to Mary's nomination as her successor. Yet a Catholic heir remained unacceptable to Cecil, who was also averse to promoting his political rival to the Scottish and English thrones. Furthermore, Leicester had no enthusiasm for marrying Mary while the greater prize of Elizabeth was still seemingly available.

To deflect interest away from his suit, Leicester promoted Darnley, with his Tudor pedigree, as an alternative. With Darnley being seen as morally degenerate, Cecil encouraged his overtures, hoping that they would delay Mary from considering a more threatening candidate. Maitland concluded that Darnley's shortcomings might even tarnish Mary's impeccable reputation, as no one believed that she would tolerate his boorish personality for long. Although Moray rapidly fell out with Darnley and openly opposed the marriage, Maitland was more circumspect and gave the appearance of encouraging it. When Mary eventually married Darnley out of unbridled passion, Moray took up arms against them, expecting to gain English support, while Maitland maintained a neutral stance to avoid them being implicated together in a treasonable revolt. With Elizabeth fearing recrimination from France, she failed to provide military support, leaving Moray hopelessly outnumbered. He was forced into exile, thereby enabling Mary and Darnley to install a Catholic government. When Maitland was replaced in his former role by Riccio, he hinted to Darnley that Riccio was paying Mary improper attention and incited him to arrange his murder. Although he expected that Mary and Darnley would be imprisoned afterwards, they escaped, but by then Darnley had agreed Moray's repatriation. Although Mary believed that Maitland was involved in the murder plot, she had no plausible evidence to confirm this, and Moray was able to arrange his rehabilitation.

Once back in office, Maitland was asked by Mary to arrange her divorce from Darnley, but he eventually concluded that this could not be achieved on acceptable terms. Although Darnley was plotting to gain both the Scottish and English thrones to Mary's detriment, she contemplated making a fresh start with him. Despite his scheming, Elizabeth concluded that she should recognise Mary as her heir, particularly as she now had a son. Newly restored as Secretary of State, Maitland was tasked with handling the discussions. As Mary's most able diplomat, he made a strong case to support her right to the English succession. Nevertheless, he knew that Cecil would only support her if she became Protestant as it otherwise conflicted with the objectives for amity. He told him: 'Her conversion is one of the things that I most desire on earth: I have even dared to suggest it to her majesty, trusting that she will not like me any the less for stating an opinion that is in her best interest. And I do not despair that, although she will not yield at first, over time she will be won over.'[1] He cited her recent financial support for the Kirk, and her coolness to Mondovi. Whether he genuinely believed that Mary might at last convert may seem unlikely, but he was about to marry Mary Fleming, Mary's closest confidante, and it has been suggested that his love for her encouraged a more benevolent attitude towards her mistress. Yet there is no evidence, at this time, that Maitland was veering away from his plan, shared with Moray and Cecil, to cause Mary's undoing. Moray would make a much more appropriate head of state to cement a Protestant union with England.

By this stage plans for Darnley's murder were well advanced. It has been suggested that Maitland hoped its impact would force Mary to rethink her religious affiliation. This seems unlikely. Once murder was committed, Maitland's private agenda was to persuade Mary to marry Bothwell, his archenemy, despite knowing that this would make her unacceptable to Elizabeth as her heir. If she agreed, it would make the crime of passion story seem plausible. Maitland remained at her side to ensure that she did not falter. He also manipulated their correspondence to provide the Casket Letters as evidence against her.

Maitland has to be seen as the root cause of Mary's downfall, despite later doing what he could to support her in captivity. This change of heart would cause him to fall out with his erstwhile allies, but for now he remained at the forefront of the underhand plotting against her.

Chapter 14

The plot to murder Darnley unfolds

The most important issue for those planning Darnley's murder was to persuade him to return to Edinburgh from Glasgow, where he was recuperating. As we have seen, Mary also wanted him back under her control to curtail his plotting against her. She set off for Glasgow, hoping to make a new start to their marriage once the symptoms of his disease had subsided. On 19 January, the day after his meeting at Whittinghame, Bothwell joined up with Huntly and a company of mounted hackbutters to escort Mary to Callendar, where she spent the night with the Livingstons. From here, he returned with Huntly to Edinburgh to deal with pressing business in the Borders, leaving a party of about forty Hamiltons, including Archbishop Hamilton, to escort her to Glasgow. As long-standing Lennox opponents, the Hamiltons were not the most conciliatory group with which to enter Glasgow on 22 January, but Mary needed protection.

Mary used all her guile to persuade Darnley to return with her. She wrote a long report of their conversation, which she sent from Glasgow to her senior advisers, including Bothwell and Moray, in which Bothwell is referred to in the third person. The report was found in a silver casket among Bothwell's possessions at Edinburgh Castle, after his escape from Carberry Hill. The only remaining version of it forms letter II of the so-called 'Casket Letters'. These formed part of Mary's and Bothwell's correspondence, manipulated with falsified additions designed to incriminate them in a crime of passion (as Maitland wanted to imply). There is general consensus that only Maitland, among the Scottish Lords, had access to Mary's papers, and a sufficient understanding of court etiquette and French vernacular poetry to make the amendments seem plausible. The letters would then have needed redrafting to incorporate his changes and he admitted his ability to forge her handwriting. Presenting a coherent and plausible story was a difficult task. Detailed examination reveals numerous inconsistencies when compared with other evidence, particularly with the depositions made by henchmen under torture. Maitland was not directly involved in obtaining these depositions but may have provided initial guidance on their content. They were put together over a two-year period, by the end of which Maitland was out of favour, having fallen out with Moray for seeking Mary's restoration. This explains why some of the later depositions contain evidence against him.

For the conferences in England, Thomas Crawford of Jordanhill, a gentleman of Darnley's bedchamber, provided an almost identical version of Mary's report included in Casket Letter II. According to this, Darnley claimed to have been cruelly treated by Mary after she refused to accept his repentance for having 'failed in some things, even though such like greater faults have been made to you sundry times, which you have forgiven. I am but young.' He blamed this on them not living as man and wife, which 'bringeth me in such melancholy as you see I am in'. When she asked why he had a ship waiting to take him abroad, he blamed his lack of money. He told her that he was aware of a bond prepared at Craigmillar that she had refused to sign. He again asked her to 'bear him company', but she remained 'very pensive, whereat he found fault'.[1] The conversation then moved onto safer territory. She wanted him to return with her to Edinburgh and had arranged for him to convalesce at Craigmillar, 'where she might be with him and not far from her son'. He agreed to come, if 'he and she might be together at bed and board as husband and wife, and that she should leave him no more'. Realising that his principal objective was to renew sexual relations, she confirmed that this was why she had come, but insisted that, 'before they could get together, he must be purged and cleansed of his sickness, which she trusted would be shortly, for she minded to give him the bath [for his cure] at Craigmillar'. She told him not to divulge their discussion, as 'the Lords would not think good of their sudden agreement considering he and they were at some words' before.[2] While this confirms her intention to be rehabilitated with Darnley, she remained disillusioned with him and probably intended keeping him under house arrest in Edinburgh to curtail his plotting. There is no hint that she was bringing him to Edinburgh to facilitate his murder, as the Casket Letters later implied, and she was trying to gain Morton's assurance that he would be protected. Although she persuaded him to return with her, he did not divulge the details of his scheming, which might more easily be put into effect in Edinburgh.

Both Darnley's father and Crawford warned him not to go with Mary. Crawford objected to Craigmillar being used for his recuperation, seeing it as better suited as a prison or a murder location. If Mary genuinely sought her husband's rehabilitation, he believed that she should have brought him to Holyrood. Nevertheless, on 27 January, the royal party left Glasgow with Darnley in Mary's litter. They spent a night at Callendar, followed by one or two nights at Linlithgow, where they were joined by Bothwell who returned from the Borders to provide an escort to Craigmillar. Shortly before leaving, Darnley announced that he would not stay there, perhaps heeding Crawford's concerns. With Darnley not wanting to be seen with his taffeta mask at Holyrood, it was suggested by Balfour that the Old Provost's Lodging, just within the Town Wall at Kirk o' Field, was available for lease from his brother. One of Darnley's servants recorded: 'It was devised in Glasgow that the King should have lain first at Craigmillar, but because he had no will thereof, the purpose was altered and the conclusion taken that he should lie beside the Kirk o' Field.'[3]

There is no plausible evidence that Kirk o' Field was chosen because it was a suitable place for Darnley's murder, though this was to be alleged by Buchanan. Neither Bothwell nor Morton was involved in choosing it, although they could only have approved of its layout and location. It could be accessed almost unnoticed through a postern gate from the far side of the town wall. Although its accommodation was adequate, Darnley was disappointed at its lack of grandeur, and 'in no wise liked of'. It took all Mary's persuasion for him to agree to occupy its rooms, which were 'more easy and handsome'.

Darnley agreed to sleep in the upper bedroom where he made a rapid recovery. His own bed, previously belonging to the queen regent, hung with violet-brown velvet and richly decorated with cloth of gold, was brought in, with a bath placed beside it for his medicinal treatment. Mary occupied the bedroom on the floor below, from where she could nurse him and keep a watchful eye on what he was up to. She slept at Kirk o' Field on 5 and 7 February after administering Darnley's medicinal baths. She also considered staying there on the night of the murder, again demonstrating that she was unaware of the plot to blow it up. She visited him daily and, by all accounts, good relations were restored. To regain his confidence, she would sit up with him until midnight, playing cards or listening to music. She tried to arrange his reconciliation with the nobility, but they would have none of it, warning her that he would put a knife to her throat and theirs. Yet Darnley used the friendlier atmosphere to discuss Maitland privately with Mary, warning that he 'was planning the ruin of the one by the means of the other and meant in the end to ruin both of them'.[4] Despite Maitland's recent marriage to Mary Fleming, Darnley still feared his plotting.

Although Darnley had at least four personal servants at Kirk o' Field, in addition to the six lodging staff, there were no guards, indicating that he was oblivious to the rumours of plotting against him. Maitland had arranged for Bothwell, a man whom he hated, to manage the murder, but Bothwell had assistance from a number of Douglas and Hepburn henchmen. Moray left Edinburgh beforehand to avoid being implicated but wanted Morton to organise the nobility and to ingratiate himself with Bothwell so that they could share the government afterwards. He was to follow Maitland's plan of enticing Bothwell into setting his cap at the queen, hoping to implicate her in a crime of passion. To return to power, Moray would need Bothwell out of the way and the queen discredited. He could then arrange for Morton's, Maitland's and Balfour's involvement in the murder plot to be airbrushed out, although Maitland had sidestepped the detailed arrangements.

It was Archibald Douglas who coordinated the plan, relying on Moray's and Cecil's protection in return for his silence. He was ultimately found innocent of a crime for which several others were executed. Without realising it, Bothwell was now isolated as the sole perpetrator with his henchmen, allowing Moray and Maitland, who had always hated him, to imply that he had acted alone. Morton told the truth in 1581, when he admitted under oath that he knew of the plot but had played no part in it. Yet, he is thought to have signed the Craigmillar bond with Douglas at Whittinghame and took no steps to warn his kinsman, Darnley, of his impending murder.

Bothwell soon had enough assistance to 'take the deid in hand'. As he was 'ruling all at court', there is evidence of him recruiting help by claiming that the murder had the queen's approval.[5] There is a report that, after meeting at Whittinghame, Bothwell and Maitland went with Archibald Douglas to Holyrood to seek her sanction, which she refused. This seems to be another attempt to suggest that Mary was aware of the murder plan, even if she did not approve it. As she failed to arrange a full investigation afterwards, any foreknowledge would have implicated her. In all probability, no such meeting took place. If the conspirators wanted her kept in the dark, they would hardly have sought her approval.

On the morning of Sunday, 9 February, with the murder imminent, Moray sought Mary's consent to leave Edinburgh to see his wife, who had suffered a miscarriage at St Andrews. As he later admitted, he knew that Darnley was to be murdered that night. On the same morning, Darnley attended Mass before taking his last medicinal bath. Mary attended the Chapel Royal for the marriage of her French valet, Sebastian Pagez, to another favourite servant, Christily Hogg. The guests wore carnival clothes with masks, and Pagez had prepared a masque for the evening, which the queen promised to attend. As a Reformer, Bothwell would not have attended the Catholic marriage service, but was at the wedding lunch in carnival clothes. At four o'clock, and without changing, he was with the queen at a dinner for the Duke of Savoy's ambassador in the Canongate, where most of the nobility, other than Moray and Maitland, were in attendance. Maitland's absence has not been explained, but he joined the royal party at Kirk o' Field later and was not involved in the murder plan.

At about seven o'clock, with the dinner over, court members, still in costume, rode with the queen to Kirk o' Field, where she was joined by 'the most part of nobles then in this town,' including Bothwell, Huntly, Argyll, Cassillis and Maitland. Darnley tried to persuade her to spend the night there on the last day of his convalescence, but she had always promised to attend the wedding masque and her horses were waiting at Kirk o' Field for the purpose. Darnley entertained her with music, and they chatted 'more cheerfully than usual for a few hours' and 'often kissed'. Before leaving, she gave him a ring as a token of her promise to be permanently reunited by sleeping with him on the following night. The guests showed no apparent concern at the royal embraces, with Bothwell, Huntly, Argyll and Cassillis playing dice.

It was after eleven o'clock when the queen was reminded that she needed to leave for the masque. To Darnley's disappointment, she immediately set out for Holyrood with her entourage, telling him she would remain there for the night. Bothwell had reminded her that she was going to Seton the next morning and would want an early start. It is alleged that Maitland also discouraged her return (but this may not be true). As she mounted her horse to leave, she saw her French servant, Paris, who also worked for Bothwell, with his face all blackened, saying: 'Jesu, Paris, how begrimed you are!' He did not respond, but she would hardly have drawn attention to him, if she knew that he had been moving gunpowder into the cellar under cover of the babble above. Before retiring, Darnley ordered wine and sat up playing the lute for about an hour with his remaining servants. They had no forewarning of what was to happen.

After arriving at Holyrood, Mary saw the end of the masque, but around midnight, held a private conference with Bothwell and Traquair, who left after fifteen minutes. Bothwell stayed with her 'for a considerable time'.[6] It has been argued that he needed Mary's blessing to light the fuse, but this is unrealistic as his henchmen were already committed to the plan. Given the late hour, they may have been making arrangements for the prince's security while she was at Seton, but it gave Bothwell a convenient alibi. Apart from some extraordinarily dubious depositions taken from his henchmen under torture, there is no evidence of him leaving Holyrood that evening to supervise the explosion, and the guard was never asked to confirm his movements. When he went to investigate on the next day, he did not seem to know what had happened.

Although Maitland had initiated the murder objective, the detailed plan was put together by Bothwell, Morton, Balfour and Douglas (though neither Bothwell nor Morton were there on the night). Bothwell provided at least eight henchmen, some of whom were employed at the lodging as downstairs staff. Archibald Douglas, Bothwell's close associate, came with a dozen or so Douglas adherents provided by Morton and himself. Morton's follower, Ker of Fawdonside, was outside with a detachment of mounted men. There were probably about thirty men involved. Their plan was to blow up the lodging at night after encircling the building to prevent Darnley's escape.

It was Bothwell who had devised the plan to use gunpowder to destroy the evidence. With Darnley having several loyal servants on the premises, he did not believe that secrecy could be maintained if he were stabbed or poisoned. While in captivity in England, even Mary came to accept (if she did not already know it) that Bothwell was 'one of the murderers of the King'. Balfour's name was also linked with Bothwell's on billboards in Edinburgh shortly after the murder. He had purchased and supervised the movement and packing of the gunpowder, and presumably arranged its storage close to Kirk o' Field, possibly at the New Provost's Lodging. He may not have been involved thereafter as there were enough servants to heave it into position, but his movements on the day of the murder are unknown. An almost complete absence of evidence against him is explained by his part in putting the official story together. Morton, Maitland and Balfour later admitted becoming aware of the detailed plan on about 7 February, as did Moray. It could not have been developed until Darnley's arrival at Kirk o' Field on 1 February, and it was probably not finalised until a week later. It is known that the gunpowder was moved into position only on the evening of 9 February, shortly before the explosion. Yet, they all knew well before this that murder was contemplated.

Darnley must have been disturbed, probably by those lighting the fuse, and with his valet, Taylor, tried to escape by scrambling over the Town Wall, only to be accosted in the south garden and orchard by Archibald Douglas and his henchmen. Darnley pleaded for his life before both he and Taylor were suffocated.

At about two o'clock in the morning, there was a huge explosion, like a volley from twenty-five or thirty cannon, which woke people all over Edinburgh. It was followed by 'the confused cries of the people'.[7] The Old Provost's Lodging and adjacent Prebendaries' Chamber were destroyed 'not only the roof and floors, but also the walls to the foundation, so that no one stone rests on another'.[8] A large crowd gathered, and people started digging frantically, knowing that Darnley was staying there. At Holyrood, Mary was also woken by the explosion and sent messengers to establish the cause. They returned to report that Kirk o' Field was destroyed. Bothwell, as sheriff of Edinburgh, was woken to be told that Darnley was believed to have been killed. He shot up shouting: 'Fie! Treason!'[9] He sent men to investigate before returning to bed to await news.

At about five o'clock, a search of the south garden and orchard revealed the nearly naked, but unmarked, bodies of Darnley and Taylor more than fifty yards from the lodging. All the plausible evidence shows that Archibald Douglas and about a dozen followers had been hiding in the cottages nearby. In 1581, Douglas's servant testified under torture that his master was 'art and part' of the murder and 'did actually devise and perpetrate it'. Although Douglas was eventually charged, his trial was so arranged that he was exonerated.

A message was sent to Mary at Holyrood to confirm Darnley's death, and Bothwell, who was still in bed there, was woken by Huntly. He dressed quickly and, with Huntly, Argyll, Atholl, Maitland and the Countesses of Atholl and Mar, went to console the Queen. He reported that she was 'greatly afflicted by it all'.[10] She seemed unable to deal with her correspondence but sent Bothwell with men to make a diligent search. The court was ordered into mourning and, in accordance with French custom, she retired into forty days' seclusion. Huntly called on the Privy Council to 'deliberate about the means of apprehending the traitors who committed the deed'. With many of its members being parties to the conspiracy, they offered a reward of 2,000 crowns for information but professed their own ignorance. They also prepared a detailed account for Catherine de Medici, reporting Mary's belief that it was only good fortune that prevented her being killed with Darnley.

Chapter 15

Providing the evidence of a crime of passion

Moray and Maitland knew that Mary's Catholicism alone did not provide acceptable grounds for her deposition. Their efforts to wrest control from her in the Chaseabout Raid had been a dismal failure. Moreover, there was little genuine grief at Darnley's passing,[1] and its 'impact was insufficient to act as a brake on the progressive prosecution of Mary's claim to the English throne'.[2] It was Mary's disastrous handling of subsequent events that caused her undoing.

It was Maitland who devised the scheme, which was developed with Moray and Cecil, to implicate Mary in Darnley's murder as a means of replacing her on the throne. If Bothwell could be persuaded to arrange it, rumours of his involvement could be spread without infringing the bond signed at Craigmillar. Maitland went further. If they hinted that Mary had been conducting an affair with Bothwell beforehand, they could claim that the couple were involved in a crime of passion to kill Darnley, thus enabling them to be together. This involved engineering a tale of a romance between them, where none existed. To make the story credible, they would need to persuade them to marry. They had three goals: Moray would be restored as regent of Scotland; Cecil would remove two unacceptable claimants to the English throne; and England's northern border would be protected by amity with an anglophile Protestant government in Scotland. It was indisputably pre-planned. Even Mary came to accept this. In Nau's *Memorials*, written on her instruction while in captivity in England, he records that her enemies 'having used [Bothwell] to rid themselves of the King, designed to make [him] their instrument to ruin the Queen'. They thus signed a bond to induce her to marry Bothwell, 'so that they might charge her with being in the plot against her late husband and a consenting party to his death'.

A romance between Mary and Bothwell was not completely unrealistic. Bothwell detested Darnley, but also seems to have developed an infatuation for Mary in the weeks before the murder. This was mentioned by both Melville and Livingston, not people with reason to falsify it. He was certainly not averse to marriage when encouraged by Morton, but it is highly unlikely that he arranged the murder in the hope of marrying Mary as he was already committed to Jean Gordon.

The first evidence of Maitland's scheme arose less than a week after the murder, too short a time for communication with Cecil in London, which means that it was indisputably pre-planned. On 16 February, a series of accusatory placards began to appear in Edinburgh. The first of them named Bothwell, Balfour, Chalmers and 'Black' John Spens, the Queen's Advocate, who was described as 'the principal deviser of the murder, the Queen assenting thereto'. All were recent appointees to government made by either Darnley or Bothwell, so it is reasonable to assume that Maitland was trying to demean his rivals for office. More importantly, they diverted suspicion away from Moray.

Although Spens was later arrested, it is unlikely that either he or Chalmers played any part in the murder. Balfour kept his head down and, on 26 February, returned home by a secret way with an escort of thirty armed men. On the following night the placards accused Mary's foreign servants, Pagez, Joseph Riccio and Francisco Busso, again suggesting an anti-Catholic slant to the propaganda. Bothwell threatened to wash his hands in the blood of the placards' creators, but they were not silenced and, after a few nights, voices in the streets were shouting out that he had murdered Darnley.

By a stroke of good luck for Maitland's plan, the Lennox faction believed the rumours that Bothwell had murdered Darnley and began to expand the placard campaign themselves. This was almost certainly initiated by William Murray of Tullibardine, with help from his brother, James Murray of Pardewis. Tullibardine had always remained loyal to Darnley and was one of the few seeking justice for him. Their campaign gathered pace. There were crude portraits of Bothwell with the words, 'Who is the king's murderer?' or 'Here is the murderer of the king'. Nevertheless, as Catholics, they made no attempt to implicate the queen in a crime of passion.

Very soon afterwards, there was a third, more sophisticated, source of propaganda. Both Maitland and Buchanan are plausible candidates for initiating it, but it was more realistically Cecil, who, at this time, was employing Sir Francis Walsingham in anti-papist publicity in England. This new campaign was meticulously planned, and as each placard appeared, those involved made sure that the content was fed to Lennox, while Sir William Drury at Berwick kept Cecil closely advised of its impact. On 1 March, Mary was depicted as a mermaid – a well-known symbol for a prostitute – next to a hare, which was the Bothwell crest. The image was full of scurrilous classical metaphor. In her right hand, she held a large sea anemone – the symbol for female genitalia – while in her left was a folded net with which to snare her prey. The hare was surrounded by swords to denote Bothwell's military standing, with one suggestively positioned as a phallic symbol. Mary and Bothwell were mortified and tried to establish who was behind it. On 14 March, when Bothwell asked the Council to silence it, a warrant accused Pardewis of having 'devised, invented and caused to be set up certain painted papers upon the Tolbooth door of Edinburgh, bending to her majesty's slander and defamation'. He fled to England but offered to return to defend himself. Being Catholic, he is most unlikely to have been behind the smutty innuendo of the mermaid.

On 19 June 1567, four days after Bothwell's escape from Carberry Hill, by which time Mary was already imprisoned, there is the first mention of a letter written by her being found in a silver casket among Bothwell's possessions left at Edinburgh Castle. Balfour apparently handed them over to two of Bothwell's servants, who had come to collect them, but Morton sent men to track them down. The casket caused no great initial interest, but, by the time of the Conferences at York and Westminster, its content had become the principal evidence to incriminate Mary in the murder of Darnley. It is generally believed that the casket originally contained a single document, probably Mary's official report of her meeting with Darnley at Glasgow, but with further manipulated letters being added to this single apparently innocent report which was also doctored. Documents were progressively added, with earlier, less plausible, attempts being removed when they failed to stand up to closer scrutiny. Nevertheless, the casket became the source of all the falsified correspondence used to justify Mary's detention in England.

There is also conflicting evidence for the timing of the casket's discovery. In November 1567, the lords confirmed in Parliament that they took up arms against the queen on 15 June, as a result of seeing 'divers her privy letters'. Yet in his sworn statement to Elizabeth and Cecil,

Morton said that the letters were found on 19 June, four days too late to justify their action at Carberry Hill. While Moray was returning to Scotland from France in early July, he told de Silva in London of a single letter written by Mary to Bothwell from Glasgow, which implicated her in the murder. De Silva was also aware from du Croc of the lords' assertion that Mary was an accomplice to her husband's murder which was 'proved by letters under her own hand'.

So long as Mary was held without trial at Lochleven, Moray and Maitland could avoid producing documentation against her on the apparent grounds of protecting her honour. When she escaped to England, an enquiry became inevitable and Maitland set to work to provide the necessary evidence. By the time of the Conferences at York and Westminster, the casket had become the repository for a total of eight letters, now numbered in rough chronological order, two versions of Mary's contract to marry Bothwell and twelve sonnets written in rather poor French; a total of twenty-two items. As no originals now exist, the casket's content is known only from French or English language transcripts made for the Conferences, or, in a few cases, from translations included as appendices to the Scottish edition of Buchanan's *Detectio*, in which only the first sentence is in the original French. Without having the originals, the handwriting cannot be authenticated. Most of them seem to have been constructed from genuine letters, either taken out of context or manipulated with false additions, though at least one may be a complete forgery. None of the transcripts is dated, addressed or signed. Mary's letters were always addressed and included a carefully constructed phrase before her signature. Each of the letters also has textual shortcomings, suggesting inexpert and hurried manipulation.

Taken together, the documents contain a common thread, incriminating Bothwell and Mary at every step of a premeditated plan to murder Darnley so that they could marry. They imply that they were involved in a passionate relationship before Darnley's death and that Mary was encouraging their marriage even before Bothwell was cleared of the murder and before her abduction to Dunbar. All this is too convenient. Murder conspiracies are not fully documented by the perpetrators in advance. Yet they have fooled generations of historians and, at the time, seemed sufficiently plausible to keep Mary under arrest.

The following brief summary outlines the gist of the documents (and their shortcomings). A far more detailed exposition is included in

The Challenge to the Crown published by the Book Guild in 2012, and in *Mary Queen of Scots' Downfall* (Pen and Sword, 2017).

Casket Letter I was almost certainly a genuine letter written from Mary to Bothwell on Saturday 11 January while she was visiting Prince James at Stirling before going to Glasgow. Nevertheless, its date has been changed to look as if it were written while she was with Darnley at Glasgow a fortnight later. In the original context, it is clear that Mary was unaware of Bothwell's haemorrhage at Dunbar and is rebuking him for failing to confirm Morton's undertaking not to seek revenge against Darnley. She plans to take 'the man' [the infant James] to Craigmillar on the following Wednesday. By changing the date, it is made to look as if she is writing from Glasgow to suggest that she will be taking Darnley to Craigmillar as part of the plan for his murder.

Casket Letter II, representing Mary's lengthy report to several recipients of her meeting with Darnley at Glasgow, is full of insertions at points where there may have been gaps in the text or at the end. These bear little relationship to the surrounding wording. There are references to: 'the lodging in Edinburgh', even though by then Kirk o' Field had not been chosen; to Mary wanting to lie in Bothwell's arms; and to Darnley being a 'pocky fellow', although his illness was not generally known. At one point, she encourages Bothwell to add poison to Darnley's medicines, but it seems unlikely that she would include this in a report sent to several recipients. Elsewhere, Bothwell is told to 'burn the letter for it is too dangerous', but this did not happen, and such wording if genuine would have been absurdly incriminating.

It was claimed that Casket Letter III was written by Mary when Darnley was recuperating at Kirk o' Field. It complains at Bothwell's absence and refers to a black jewel sent to him as a symbol of her love, but the letter is uncharacteristically submissive. It is far more likely that this is a letter to Bothwell from one of his lovers, which was found by Maitland among his papers.

Casket Letter IV was purportedly written by Mary to Bothwell on 7 February, two days before the murder. It may have been intended to corroborate the assertion of a missing letter shown to the Conference at York, in which Lord Robert Stewart was incited by Mary to murder Darnley. This objective is entirely conjectural as no one is mentioned by name. It is also completely implausible that she would have taken time to write so long a missive when she was seeing him every day.

It seems to amalgamate at least two letters with a forged addition. It contains an obscure metaphor from Greek mythology and a quotation from an early version of a sonnet from *Le Second Livre des Amours* by Ronsard to imply that she worries that Darnley might try to escape. While Mary, Darnley, Maitland, Buchanan and Cecil might reasonably be expected to have understood the analogy, it would surely have gone over Bothwell's head. As Darnley refers to this same sonnet in his own verses, it is more likely that Mary wrote it to him using wording with which he was familiar. The remainder of the letter is a rebuke by a loving writer to a wayward recipient. In that context, she seems jealous at some new mistress, and threatens a separation if he does not return to her.

Mary is reputed to have taken time out of an impossibly busy schedule on Sunday, 9 February to write Casket Letter V to Bothwell. This concerned the dismissal of an 'unthankful' servant known to have become pregnant out of wedlock. While this did not happen infrequently, it was much frowned upon by both the Kirk and Mary. The heading of the letter refers to Mary's favoured lady's maid, Margaret Carwood, who married immediately after the murder, but she was certainly not pregnant and was never called to explain its content. Again, this seems to be a letter to Darnley, who has blamed her for continuing to employ a servant who has gossiped about him being unfaithful to her. She responds that if he finds an alternative she will be rid of her as soon as she has been married off. The French transcript continues: 'And if ye do not send me word this night, what ye will that I shall do, I will unburden myself of it [i.e., dismiss her], at the risk of making her attempt [reveal] something that could be harmful to what we are both aiming at [the English throne].' In the English version this has been maliciously mistranslated as: 'And if ye do not send me word this night, what ye will that I shall do, I will rid myself of it [Darnley], and hazard to cause it [the murder] to be enterprised and taken in hand, which might be hurtful to that where unto both we do tend.' This implies that Mary is planning Darnley's murder, despite it being completely out of context and making no sense in a discussion about the servant. Bothwell would not have been concerned at her servant's dismissal, and as they were together all that day, writing to him would have been unnecessary.

Casket Letters VI, VII and VIII and the French love poem were produced as evidence of Mary's collusion in her abduction to Dunbar (described on pages 159–60). Casket Letter VI records a row between

Mary and Huntly and is endorsed 'From Stirling afore the ravissement – proves her mask [pretence] of ravishing.' In all probability this is a genuine letter written by Mary from Dunbar after her marriage, where she indisputably had a row with Huntly and was extremely uncertain of his continued loyalty at a time when Bothwell was trying to gather support. If written after her abduction and marriage, it loses all value as evidence of a crime of passion. By claiming that it was sent from Stirling it can be implied that Bothwell has not confirmed where the abduction will take place and people may realise that she is colluding in it. However, there is no other record of her having a row with Huntly at this time.

The transcript of Casket Letter VII shows that it was intended as the second in a sequence of letters written by Mary from Stirling, and in all probability was designed to cover up the shortcomings of Casket Letter VI. It confirms that Mary knew of her abduction in advance, and by proposing that Bothwell deserves to be pardoned, implicates her in the murder. Yet if Casket Letter VI was written after the abduction, as seems certain, but was manipulated so that it appeared to be beforehand, it can only be a complete forgery. It does not mention any row with Huntly. It suggests that Lethington should receive 'many fair words' to persuade him to support the marriage, implying that he wanted people to think that he was vigorously opposing it, when he was in fact encouraging it.

Casket Letter VIII was deemed to be the third in the same sequence of letters sent to Bothwell by Mary from Stirling, although she was not there long enough to write three times. It refers to Huntly as 'your brother-in-law that was', who has come to her 'very sad' and in fear that he is acting treasonably. Yet Bothwell had not by then divorced Jean Gordon. As it also mentions Sutherland being present, it fits as a genuine letter, written to Bothwell at Melrose while Mary was at Borthwick.

The long love poem was also reputedly written from Stirling. Its twelve verses each take the form of a sonnet on a separate page. They show infatuation for an unnamed recipient, undoubtedly intended as Bothwell, to whom she has pledged her son, her honour, her life, her country and her subjects. Buchanan claimed that it was composed 'while her husband lived, but certainly before [Bothwell's] divorce from his wife,' and he admired its 'tolerable elegance'.[3] Yet both Pierre de Bourdeille, Abbé de Brantôme and Ronsard, who both knew her well, felt that its French was too unpolished to have been written by Mary, who was well trained in courtly phrasing and analogy, and its scansion is faulty. Buchanan probably wrote it himself, and despite its shortcomings, would have been one of the few in Scotland capable of it.

On 5 April, a Privy Council meeting was held at Seton, where it is alleged that Mary and Bothwell signed marriage contracts. There were two differing versions among the Casket Letters, one in French and one in Scots. In all probability they were both fraudulent, and neither is dated. Their only relevance to a crime of passion is that they predate Bothwell's trial on 12 April, suggesting that Mary signed them before Bothwell was cleared. The one in French has been thought to be an original document in Maitland's hand, but Mary's signature is indisputably forged. The lords went further by saying: 'Although some words therein seem to the contrary, they suppose [the contract] to have been made and written by her before the death of her husband.' The words are certainly 'contrary' as they refer to her 'late husband Henry Stuart called Darnley', who had died on 10 February, and state that Bothwell was free to marry. This implies that it post-dated his divorce from Jean Gordon on 3 May.[4] This removes their relevance as incriminating evidence, and neither of them is the contract which they indisputably signed on 14 May, the day before their wedding.

It was nearly a year later, on 27 May 1568, more than fifteen months after Darnley's murder, that Buchanan, now aged sixty-two, was commissioned by Moray to prepare his *Detectio*, a highly fanciful but damning account written in Latin, designed to colour public opinion against Mary. This provides page after page of scurrilously readable tittle-tattle written in vitriolic style. As he had not been at court, he relied on 'closed writings' fed to him by Moray. His first version became available only in early June 1568, when he referred to its hasty preparation. It recounts numerous liaisons taking place between Mary and Bothwell before the murder, but none stand up to critical examination. The couple had both been at death's door, hardly an aphrodisiac for a romance. In a court full of rumour, the ambassadors' grapevine would have relished any juicy impropriety, but with Mary actively seeking recognition as Elizabeth's heir, she would have wanted to avoid any scandal that might prejudice her hopes. Furthermore, Darnley, with his close bloodline to both thrones, was a far more appropriate consort than Bothwell.

At first glance, Buchanan seems an unlikely choice as the author of such propaganda. He was a classical scholar, poet and Calvinist, educated in Paris. He had helped Mary with her Latin on her return to Scotland, assisting her composition of poetry as part of her correspondence with Elizabeth, and had written masques to entertain the court. Having eulogised on the beauty of the Maries, he had most recently written a masque for the celebrations of Prince James's christening, extolling Mary's virtues. He had been brought up near Glasgow by impoverished parents, owing his education to Lennox philanthropy. He would support Mary while she was married to a Lennox son, but Darnley's murder made her his deadly enemy. He also owed a favour to Moray, who had appointed him as Principal of St Leonard's College at St Andrews. He was now using his platform as Moderator of the General Assembly to back Moray and his adherents. As a political theorist, he advocated the classical ideals of a free state, linking them with Calvinist doctrine to develop a far more sophisticated thesis than Knox's *Monstrous Regimen* [Rule] *of Women* for opposing the divine right of monarchy. Rulers, he believed, were chosen to fulfil defined roles and were not above the law. If they transgressed, they could be replaced, even by tyrannicide.

Buchanan trusted Moray and may genuinely have believed that Bothwell had arranged Darnley's murder with Mary's connivance. He followed the line that it was her lust for Bothwell that led them to plot his murder, leaving them free to marry. In mid-1568, without detailed examination, people grasped at his *Detectio* as the evidence needed to incriminate her. Yet on publication, he described it only as 'an information of probable and infallible conjecture and presumptions'. He certainly did not know whether his story were true. He painted Darnley as a saintly paragon to match the Lennox image of him and cunningly blended fact with scurrilous gossip to create a tissue of lies. It would never stand up to scrutiny to find Mary guilty of conspiracy, and it offered no credible evidence of her foreknowledge of the murder plot. Bothwell had no reason to believe that she would agree to marry him if freed from Darnley, and, in any case, he was already married. If marriage were his motive, he would have sought assurances of support from the other signatories of the Craigmillar bond. They would not have promoted a man they hated to replace Darnley. It was Moray who they wanted as head of Scottish government. If Bothwell married the queen, Moray would be left out in the cold. Yet with Darnley dead, Morton cynically enticed Bothwell into a marriage for Scotland's security. It was only this that gave the crime of passion credibility.

Chapter 16

Enticement for Mary to marry Bothwell

With Bothwell positioned to supervise the investigation at Kirk o' Field, Darnley's body was brought back to Holyrood where it was embalmed before lying in state at the Abbey Kirk. Although Mary was extremely shocked and no doubt frightened at her husband's death, she was expected to face up to it cool-headedly. In her letters written immediately afterwards to Elizabeth and her French relations, she confirmed her belief that she had also been an intended victim to make way for a regency for her son. Only by complete chance had she not spent the night of the explosion at Kirk o' Field. This implied that she believed that Moray was seeking the regency or even planning to usurp the throne. Nau later recorded her belief that Moray had left Edinburgh after finalising his plan to gain the Crown by ruining her. Either he had arranged the murder himself, or it had been done on his behalf by the returning exiles as a blood feud.

Mary wrote to Elizabeth and her French relations: 'We hope to punish the same with such rigour as shall serve for example of this cruelty to all ages to come. Always who ever have taken this wicked enterprise in hand, we assure our self it was dressed always for us as for the King.'[1] Although she also wrote to Lennox promising justice, she took no immediate action to set up an enquiry. She seemed too distraught to take control and her correspondence dried up. Had she sought a proper investigation, Darnley's murder would have been seen as the necessity it was for her security. Instead, she retired to seclusion in darkened rooms. The Council was also half-hearted. A reward of £2,000 Scots was offered for information, but little more. On its advice, she was moved with Prince James to Edinburgh Castle. Believing that her health was endangered, her physicians advised her to seek fresh air. She once more chose 'Seton to repose there and take some purgations', arriving on 16 February with Maitland, Livingston, Archbishop Hamilton and about one hundred attendants. Although Bothwell, Huntly and Argyll escorted her, Bothwell and Huntly returned immediately to Holyrood to act as James's official guardians.

From Mary's viewpoint, the one person who could hardly have been involved in Darnley's murder was Bothwell. He had been with her for the whole of the day beforehand, and she had seen him until he assuredly went to bed with his wife at Holyrood shortly before the explosion. Yet his attitude was unexpected. While it would be thought that he too would want Moray and the returning exiles investigated, he was advising her, like everyone else, not to review matters too thoroughly. Despite Lennox warning her that Bothwell was the culprit, Mary placed Bothwell in charge of her government in Moray's absence. Only he had the necessary prestige to manage affairs, and despite being a loose cannon politically, he had been her saviour after Riccio's death. He also had an apparently close alliance with Morton and the availability of military support from the Gordons.

Mary's lacklustre demeanour was out of character, but Darnley's death weakened her prospect of being recognised as Elizabeth's heir. She may have realised that his murder did not just involve Moray, Morton and the returning exiles. Perhaps the lords at Craigmillar, including Argyll, Huntly, Bothwell and Maitland, had taken the law into their own hands. We can be sure that she never gave approval for his death, but the nobility would never accept their reconciliation. If they had acted collectively, none of them would want a detailed investigation, and Bothwell would have been best suited to organise it.

Although Bothwell's power was growing, he needed a guard to travel through the streets and 'held his hand on his dagger' when meeting opponents.[2] Yet he brazened it out and attended Darnley's funeral on 14 February. On 7 March, he arranged Morton's formal rehabilitation. After humbly apologising for his part in Riccio's murder, Morton was restored to his estates and reappointed Lord Chancellor. Bothwell tried to assure his loyalty by agreeing to share government with him.[3]

Suspicion of responsibility for the murder initially fell on Moray. Mondovi reported from Paris that he 'has always had the throne in view although he is a bastard'.[4] Nevertheless, rumours of Mary's involvement started to grow, perhaps fanned by the Edinburgh placards. Even the

Cardinal of Lorraine ignored her, believing what he had heard in France. He wrote secretly to Moray, suggesting that they should unite to restore order and decency in Scotland. On 24 February, unaware of Cecil's involvement in the scheming, Elizabeth wrote in the strongest terms to advise Mary to seek out the murderer, even 'if it be the nearest friend you have'.[5] She wanted to avoid the ugly precedent of a monarch facing deposition. Catherine de Medici told Mary, through her ambassador, to 'do such justice as to the whole world may declare your innocence', but privately believed her well rid of her foolish husband.[6] Even Archbishop Bethune told her 'to preserve that reputation in all godliness you have gained of long', by prosecuting those who committed the crime.[7] In the light of all this forthright advice, Mary's failure to arrange an independent investigation was inexcusable. She seemed to believe that she could be next and would be at personal risk if she probed too far.

Mary and Bothwell failed to appreciate that they were being manipulated in a far more sophisticated game being played out around them. Although Maitland initiated it as the means of achieving a union between Scotland and England, both Moray and Cecil had complete trust in him and did everything they could from a distance to support him. He was extremely circumspect. Mondovi concluded that Maitland played his part as 'the architect of Mary's downfall "without seeming to move his hand"'.[8]

Cecil urgently needed secure Protestant government restored in Scotland. Elizabeth was facing a build-up of Catholic hostility, and Mary was the focus of every Catholic plot against her, whether from home or abroad. The birth of Mary's son had reinforced her dynastic claim to the English throne if Elizabeth should die childless. Although Elizabeth had advised Parliament immediately before Darnley's murder that she would not recognise the Scottish queen, she was still dangling the succession before her, despite it being an anathema to Cecil. She had failed to resolve the succession by marrying and producing heirs of her own and was now unlikely to do so.

Cecil needed a more drastic solution. If Mary could be implicated in the plot that killed her husband, she would lose prestige as a Catholic icon, and Elizabeth would find her unacceptable as her heir. His task was to protect his mistress and to secure her government. She was unaware of his scheming and initially took steps that conflicted with his objectives. She wanted the appropriate dynastic succession, even if that meant a

Catholic monarch. It was only much later that she recognised the danger posed by Mary and began to back her astute and loyal Secretary. Bethune was well informed. '[He] affirmed that the assassination was controlled from England, where the intention had been to kill the queen as well.' With great prescience he wrote from Paris: 'I fear this to be only the beginning of the tragedy, and all to run from evil to worse, which I pray God of his infinite goodness to avoid.'[9]

By this stage, Morton, another confirmed anglophile, had been brought into the conspiracy. His role was to work with Bothwell in government and to encourage him to set his cap at the queen, despite Bothwell being married to Jean Gordon. It would not be realistic for Maitland, Bothwell's enemy, to attempt this. Morton also had the difficult task of marshalling the Scottish nobility to support Moray in turning against the queen once she was committed to marry Bothwell. After the murder, Maitland continued to guide the queen and was no doubt assisted in this by Mary Fleming. He allayed the queen's suspicion by continuing to follow his official brief to gain the English succession for her. (This, of course, did not interfere with his objective of achieving the long-sought union with England.) Nevertheless, his private agenda was to persuade her to marry Bothwell, despite knowing that this would make her unacceptable as Elizabeth's heir.

Argyll also remained at court helping Bothwell to stabilise government. He may have been instructed by Moray to squeeze out Atholl, with whom he remained at loggerheads. Argyll's loyalty was to Mary alone and when Bothwell sought to marry her, he temporarily joined those seeking to oust him. Once Bothwell was gone, Argyll alienated Moray and Morton by reverting to his support for Mary. Atholl is an enigma as the conspirators kept him in the dark and he was likely to seek a proper enquiry. Having initially backed her marriage to Darnley, he had fallen out with Lennox over his son's shortcomings. Yet, as a leading Catholic, he was distressed by the murder and left Holyrood with Tullibardine. Buchanan claimed that Bothwell thought they were probing too far, so 'it behoved them, for fear of their lives, to leave the court', only to find themselves recalled to Edinburgh under penalty of rebellion.

Morton and Maitland had two pieces of luck: firstly, Bothwell was enthusiastic about marrying the queen, after his loveless relationship with Jean Gordon, and made all the running to obtain a divorce; secondly, Lennox believed the crime of passion story being fed to him and did much to promote it. Yet the conspiracy still needed very careful handling, and Mary remained popular. Although most of the lords wanted Darnley removed, none of them would want her to marry Bothwell. Furthermore, the Hamiltons and the Catholics would not want Moray to replace her.

Given Bothwell's role in Darnley's murder, it might have seemed logical for Maitland to encourage a detailed enquiry. Yet the evidence would incriminate most of the signatories of the Craigmillar bond, which Bothwell held. Other than this, the evidence against Bothwell was sparse, and there was none against the queen. She would protect him if he were accused. It was Moray who she mistrusted.

Moray went to great lengths to clear his name. On 13 March, he advised Cecil that he had been in St Andrews when the blast occurred. Yet Mary became suspicious when he asked for a passport to visit England, apparently en route for France. If innocent, he had no reason to leave. He had to avoid taking part in the struggle for power that lay ahead and could not challenge Mary for the throne for a second time. As her half-brother, he could not make the perfect political alliance by marrying her. Yet he was of royal blood, had held the reins of power before and had English support. He had to wait to be called. He knew only too well that without general support the regency was a poisoned chalice. If his departure allowed Bothwell to gain control by marrying the queen, he had enough evidence of Bothwell's part in Darnley's murder to bring him down later.

Moray did not leave Scotland immediately, but kept away from Edinburgh, despite Mary's requests for assistance. He used the excuse of his wife's miscarriage to remain at St Andrews, but she was not too ill to prevent him, on 26 February, travelling to meet secretly with Morton, Lindsay of the Byres, Caithness and Atholl at Dunkeld, where they would have focused only on a mutual desire to bring down Bothwell. With Atholl present, Moray will have glossed over the Craigmillar bond and Mary's future. Morton's attendance demonstrates that his friendship with Bothwell was illusory. Herries confirmed that the attendees agreed to form a coalition of Protestant and Catholic 'Confederate' lords working for the good of Scotland.

Moray made one short visit to Edinburgh, principally to meet Killigrew, who had been reappointed as Elizabeth's ambassador. He had arrived in Edinburgh on 7 March and delivered Elizabeth's stinging letter of 24 February demanding a thorough investigation into the murder.

After returning from Seton, Mary received him at Holyrood in a darkened room. Yet his main purpose was to establish how the crime of passion story was developing. After dining with Moray, Maitland and Morton, he provided an official report, which indicated that every effort was being made to find the murderers, but admitted: 'Despite great suspicions, there was no proof.' In all probability, he brought Cecil's sanction for her deposition, but this could only be justified if she married Bothwell, England's enemy. This would be difficult to achieve. Until her abduction to Dunbar on 24 April, the only hint of an amorous relationship between them was in the placards. Nevertheless, their marriage would be the means of provoking the Scottish lords into rebelling against her. With Cecil maintaining such detailed records, the lack of a contemporary explanation for Killigrew's visit is suspicious, and Moray told Cecil that Killigrew 'hath heard or seen more than I can write'.

Jean Gordon had been so ill at the end of February that one ambassador reported her death, and Bothwell began to think that he might be free to marry Mary. By 20 March, Jean had recovered and took the first steps in seeking a divorce. It is not clear what prompted this, but she had never loved Bothwell. Whatever her motive, the documentation cited his adultery with Bessie Crawford in May 1566, ten months earlier. Her action only added to speculation. Drury could soon tell Cecil that 'the judgement of the people' was that Mary and Bothwell would marry.

As criticism of Mary grew, she became increasingly concerned. On 19 March, with Bothwell's agreement, she arranged for James to be escorted by Argyll and Huntly to Stirling, where Mar was confirmed as governor so that he could continue his role in supervising the prince. He was replaced as governor of Edinburgh Castle by Sir James Cockburn of Skirling, who was a client of Bothwell's. Mar was greatly upset to lose his Edinburgh role, and its residents, who saw him as 'ane guid man', opposed Cockburn's appointment. This influenced Mar's later defection to the Confederates. Mary had discussed with Killigrew the possibility of sending James to England for his upbringing, but Elizabeth believed that this would cause Mary 'anxiety, as any little illness it might have would distress her'.[10] Elizabeth's only concern was to avoid the potential heir to the English throne from being sent to France. Although Mary had considered returning there, Catherine de Medici wanted her to clear her name.

On 30 March, Drury reported: 'She has been for the most part either melancholy or sickly ever since [the murder], and … often swooned …

the Queen breaketh [weeps] very much.'[11] Her letters were written in Scots rather than French, which confirms that she had not drafted them. Her extraordinary grief continued. Accompanied by two of her Maries, she prayed for four hours on Good Friday. By Easter, however, she was back to her old self again, returning to Holyrood for dancing and banquets. It was now that Bothwell started to court her, and no one was discouraging him.

Although the public was being persuaded that Bothwell had murdered Darnley to marry Mary, there is no evidence that she even remotely considered marrying him until her abduction to Dunbar on 24 April. Nevertheless, he was the one person she trusted, and, without his help, she believed the Reformers would want her replaced by Moray. The lords' only motive for encouraging Bothwell to marry her was to make a crime of passion appear plausible. They had to avoid a murder trial, as Lennox was demanding. This risked implicating Moray's allies without incriminating the queen. Many of Bothwell's principal opponents were under oath after signing the Craigmillar bond to protect him. If he cited it in his defence, he would incriminate those who were trying to bring him down.

Moray had to avoid being called to give evidence. On 7 April, five days before Bothwell's trial, he received a safe conduct from Elizabeth and left Edinburgh. Before his departure, he appointed Mary as guardian to his infant daughter, hardly likely if he considered her guilty. On reaching London, he claimed that he had not wanted to remain where 'so strange and extraordinary a crime went unpunished'.[12] Bothwell was overjoyed at him leaving, but Maitland and Morton were positioned to look after Moray's interests.

Chapter 17

Bothwell is exonerated and marries Mary

Mary's close advisers all discouraged her from bringing Bothwell to trial, and if she pressed for it herself, she risked losing the one person who might protect her throne. When Lennox forced her into it, the Council, with Bothwell present, met on Good Friday, 27 March, to assure her that his acquittal would be a formality.

The trial was set for 12 April. In his memoirs, Bothwell claimed to have called for it to silence the innuendo in the placards. Although trials for treason required forty days' notice, Mary wanted it resolved before Parliament met, and the Council agreed that fifteen days provided adequate notice, despite it leaving Lennox insufficient time to gather evidence. Realising that without this there would be no prosecution, Lennox, on 4 April, asked Elizabeth for help in seeking a delay while such evidence 'as the truth shall be known' was gathered.[1] His request to grant immunity from prosecution for Pardewis, so that he could be recalled from England, was refused. On 10 April, Lennox left Glasgow for Edinburgh with 3,000 men for protection. On reaching Linlithgow, he was advised that he would be limited by law to six supporters, and, with Bothwell having 4,000 men in the capital, Lennox was frightened off, and Mary was not insisting on a reduction to the four Bothwell was permitted. When Mary again refused Lennox his request for more time, he returned to Glasgow.

Realising Lennox's predicament, Elizabeth wrote to seek a postponement, advising Mary to 'use such sincerity and prudence in this case, which touches you so closely, that all the world shall have reason to pronounce you innocent of a crime of such enormity, a thing which, if you do it not, you would deserve to fall from the ranks of princesses'.[2] She did not understand and would not have approved of

Maitland's objective to encourage the marriage. She wanted Bothwell brought to book to prevent Mary from marrying him, fearing a renewal of the Auld Alliance with France.

Although Elizabeth's letter arrived in Edinburgh at six o'clock on the morning of the trial, those at the gate 'saw no likelihood of any convenient time to serve his turn until after the assize'.[3] After ten o'clock, Maitland and Bothwell came to demand the letter, but Maitland explained that, as Mary was sleeping, she would not see it until after the trial, but was caught out when she appeared at a window with Mary Fleming. His only motive for this breach of diplomatic etiquette was to ensure that Bothwell was exonerated and was able to marry Mary. As Cecil was in on the game plan, Maitland was probably not too worried. They both knew that Mary would be irretrievably damaged by marriage to Bothwell after a dubious acquittal.

The Queen gave Bothwell a friendly toss of the head as he set out for his trial. He was riding Darnley's horse, flanked by Morton and Maitland, his two traditional enemies, followed by 200 hackbutters. With Argyll, the Lord Justice General, and Huntly presiding, his acquittal was assured.

The trial started at noon and lasted seven hours. Lennox was represented by the capable Robert Cunningham, whose request for a forty-day adjournment was again refused. With no evidence being offered, the result was a formality. The jury retired and, after a decent interval, returned to acquit Bothwell of being 'art and part of the slaughter of the king'. Melville later stated that they had acted 'some for fear, some for favour, and the greatest part in expectation of advantage'.[4] The Court Recorder wrote: 'Bothwell was made clean of the said slaughter, albeit that it was heavily murmured that he was guilty thereof.'[5] The only concession was permission for a retrial, if evidence should come forward in future. The mud, though, continued to fly and Buchanan recorded that after 'this jolly acquittal ... suspicion was increased and retribution seemed only to be postponed'.[6] This made Balfour nervous; his house was guarded day and night, but his request for a similar trial was refused.

With the case settled, Mary added salt to the wound by showering Bothwell with benefits. On 14 April, he carried the sceptre at the opening of Parliament to endorse his innocence and was granted Dunbar Castle to reward his 'great and manifold services'.[7] Having had to sell land to Home to resolve his financial commitments undertaken on the

Crown's behalf, he was also recompensed with the principal estates of the Earldom of March. Nevertheless, there was no hint that Mary was contemplating marriage to him.

Bothwell immediately took control of government. An Act concerning Religion provided the Kirk with Crown protection. In a step that she had previously avoided, Mary confirmed Protestantism as her official religion, despite continuing to attend Catholic services in private. Her more hostile advisers in government were now replaced by Bothwell's supporters. Huntly was secretly promised the Lord Chancellorship in thanks for assuring Bothwell's acquittal. He was to replace Morton, who was starting to be mistrusted, despite continuing to encourage Bothwell's marriage to Mary. On 19 April, Huntly and his allies were officially restored to their estates. To smooth the divorce from Jean Gordon, Huntly received other parts of the March estates. Eleven forfeitures on dissident Protestants, including Morton and Argyll, were reduced. It all seemed like a pay-off.

Most Scots, particularly Catholics, believed that Mary's marriage to a fellow countryman would assure Scottish independence. With a Catholic consort being unacceptable to the Reformers, Maitland persuaded them that the Anglophobic Bothwell was the next best thing. On 19 April, Bothwell entertained twenty-eight members of the nobility for dinner at Ainslie's Tavern near Holyrood, ostensibly to celebrate his acquittal. With his guests well wined and dined, he produced a bond for their consideration. In addition to confirming his innocence, it suggested that the queen was 'now destitute of a husband, in which solitary state the commonwealth of this realm may not permit Her Highness to continue and endure'. It proposed that she should marry him, given his 'affectionate and hearty service ... and his other good qualities', particularly as she might prefer 'one of her native-born subjects unto all foreign subjects'.[8] He will have received tacit encouragement to make this proposal from Morton and Maitland (and probably even from Moray, who was still in Scotland despite his non-attendance). By falling into their trap, he also helped to ensnare Mary. Guests were asked to confirm their agreement for the sake of the realm. In return, they would be protected from prosecution for any past offences. It is known that the bond was signed by Morton, Huntly, and many other lords. These even included Archbishop Hamilton and six bishops. Argyll and Hugh Montgomerie, 3rd Earl of Eglinton, who were deeply offended at Bothwell's presumption, refused.

Maitland, Atholl and others avoided attendance at the dinner and did not sign it. (Maitland always avoided putting his name to anything conspiratorial.) Kirkcaldy was extremely shocked at the bond and wrote to Bedford that many acted in 'fear of their lives and against honour and conscience and that if Mary will pursue revenge for the murder, she will win the hearts of all honest Scotsmen again'. He went on to say: 'She cares not to lose France, England and her own country for him, and will go with him to the world's end in a white petticoat before she leaves him … Whatever is unhonest reigns presently in our court.'[9]

Armed with the bond and accompanied by Maitland and Patrick Bellenden, Bothwell visited Mary, who was back at Seton. Despite seeing the signatures in support of their marriage, she turned him down, telling the Bishop of Dunblane that 'our answer was in no degree correspondent with his desire'. She knew that rumours of his part in Darnley's murder were not silenced, and that the marriage would fatally prejudice her relationship with Elizabeth. Although he seemed to accept this with a good grace, the Council was still encouraging his suit. Mary told Nau that she was 'circumvented on all sides by persuasions, requests, and importunities; both by general memorials signed by their hands, and presented to her in full council, and by private letters'.[10]

On 20 April, Maitland was sent to speak privately to Mary to add his persuasion, despite knowing that it would destroy any hope of her being recognised as Elizabeth's heir. He also hated Bothwell for having kept him out of favour after Riccio's murder and for failing to restore his estates after their release from attainder. When they met, Maitland cited her recent lack of leadership, and advised that 'it had become absolutely necessary that some remedy should be provided for the disorder into which public affairs of the realm had fallen for want of a head'. He explained that the Council had been, 'unanimously resolved to press her to take Bothwell for her husband. They knew he was a man of resolution, adapted to rule, the very character needed to give weight to the decisions and actions of the Council. All of them therefore pleaded in his favour.' When she expressed concern at the continuing rumours of his part in Darnley's death, Maitland responded that 'Lord Bothwell had been legally acquitted by the Council. They who made this request to her did so for the public good of the realm'. This was persuasive and she 'began to give ear to their overtures, without letting it be openly seen'.[11] Bothwell had been loyal, was a brave leader, a good administrator and powerful personality. Their marriage would strengthen government, but contrary to the propaganda, it was not an insatiable love match. Despite his underhand objective, Maitland remained in high favour with Mary and continued in her service without apparently revealing his true feelings until the Confederates were ready to take up arms.

On 21 April, Mary returned to Edinburgh to sign papers. Later that day, she set out secretly for Stirling to visit James, now aged ten months, for what would be their last meeting. Maitland, Huntly and Sir James Melville escorted her with thirty armed horsemen. While there, in the only letter she wrote in the month before her marriage, she told Mondovi, who was back in Turin: 'I beg of you to speak well of me to His Holiness, and not to let anyone persuade him to the contrary concerning the devotion I have to die in the Catholic faith and for the good of his church.'[12] This implies that she had decided to marry Bothwell. Mondovi had already said that she would need a husband for protection and had suggested Bothwell as someone 'who has ever been the Queen's most trusty and obedient adherent'.[13]

Bothwell did not go to Stirling but remained in Edinburgh, where he raised a force on the pretext of going after Borderers who had recently despoiled Biggar. Nevertheless, both Kirkcaldy and Lennox had heard that he was planning the queen's abduction. On 29 April, Lennox left for England, not wanting to be in Scotland if they should marry.

After spending 22 April at Stirling, Mary left on the next morning. Maitland was with her. Although it has been suggested that Bothwell had asked her to bring Prince James back to Edinburgh to place him under his control, this did not happen. Mary wanted the Prince to remain in Mar's care, and she pressed him 'to be vigilant and wary that he was not robbed of her son'.[14] After leaving, she suffered a severe abdominal pain and had to rest at a cottage before reaching Linlithgow in the evening. Meanwhile, Bothwell had assembled 800 horse at Calder, south-west of Edinburgh, from where he rode to Linlithgow to seek Huntly's help in abducting her. Huntly's refusal to assist implies that Mary was unaware of the abduction plan. Had she colluded in her own abduction, as Maitland tried to suggest in Casket Letters VI, VII and VIII, it would make the crime of passion story seem more plausible.

On 24 April, the royal party left Linlithgow. On approaching the River Almond, six miles from Edinburgh, Bothwell appeared from Calder supported by his 800 men with swords drawn. The royal party halted and Bothwell rode forward to take the queen's bridle, telling her that an insurrection was threatened in Edinburgh, and he would escort her to Dunbar for safety. Neither Mary nor her entourage seemed to believe this, but she agreed to go with him 'rather than bloodshed and death should result'.[15] He was someone whom she trusted, and Maitland, Huntly and Melville went with her.

Mary's lack of resistance has fuelled speculation that she colluded in her own abduction, but there can be little doubt that she was not forewarned. Although Lennox and Kirkcaldy certainly knew in advance, and Paris claimed that Black Ormiston warned Maitland at Linlithgow, which seems probable, it is only the Casket Letters that suggest she was aware of what was happening. Though the Edinburgh town bell was rung to call the citizens 'to armour and weapons', little could be done on foot against Bothwell's mounted force. It was well after midnight when Mary's party arrived unchallenged at Dunbar, forty miles away.

Those seeking to exonerate Mary claim that she was raped by Bothwell at Dunbar and agreed to marriage only because of the resultant risk of pregnancy. She certainly wanted to give that impression. In two letters to France she claimed to have been taken by force. *The Diurnal of Occurrents* records that Bothwell 'ravished her and took her to his castle,' though the word 'ravish' at this time meant 'seize'. She was certainly seized, but he undoubtedly won her round to the idea of marriage, which would seem unlikely if he had raped her. Furthermore, Dunbar was full of people, including Maitland, so she could have screamed for help. She was there for twelve days with servants and advisers. On 26 April, Bothwell returned to Edinburgh with her encouragement to assist in his Protestant divorce petition from Jean Gordon. The guard at Holyrood were mutinous, and she seemed safer at Dunbar.

If it were not rape, Bothwell was certainly insistent in his suit, and persuaded Mary that he provided her only chance of retaining power. They agreed to consummate their relationship to prevent future attempts to separate them, and she became pregnant (but could not have known this at their wedding three weeks after her abduction, and rape would have been a good defence if she had wanted to back out of the marriage). She had fallen into Maitland's trap. It would take a lot of explaining to her Continental allies, and she did not bargain on the resultant damage to her prestige.

Although Maitland continued to show support, he remained fundamentally hostile to Bothwell and only wanted to escape from Dunbar. Matters came to a head when Bothwell threatened to murder him. Maitland told Cecil that it was only Mary's intervention that saved him, and both he and Melville were soon doubting whether the marriage would go ahead. When Bothwell heard this, he was furious at Maitland and Melville turning against him and had them both jailed overnight. Although Melville left with Huntly the following day, Maitland remained committed to seeing his plan through. He stayed behind to accompany Mary and Bothwell to Edinburgh for their wedding, waiting to see which way the wind blew.

At this stage, Kirkcaldy unquestionably believed that Mary had committed a crime of passion with his enemy, Bothwell, and wanted Moray to become regent. On 26 April, two days after Mary's abduction, he wrote to Bedford:

> Many would revenge it but they fear your mistress [Elizabeth]. I am so suited for to enterprise the revenge that I must either take it in hand or leave the country, which I am determined to do, if I get licence: but Bothwell minds to cut me off ere I obtain it. I pray you let me know what your mistress will do, for if we seek France, we may find favour; but I would rather persuade to lean to England. No honest man is safe in Scotland under the rule of a murderer and a murderess.[16]

Kirkcaldy, however, remained in Scotland, continuing to send increasingly vitriolic reports. He wrote to Moray in France, via Bedford, advising him to wait in Normandy for the Confederates' call.

Despite the rumblings of opposition, nothing would stop Bothwell from marrying Mary. He moved forward with all speed, believing that, as a queen's consort, he would be immune from prosecution. It took only three weeks from the abduction until their marriage. His biggest hurdle was to divorce Jean Gordon, but she willingly colluded in the civil proceedings put in motion within two days of the abduction. In the eyes of the Kirk, adultery with Bessie Crawford provided acceptable grounds, and the decree was confirmed on 3 May. This would not, however, allow a Catholic to remarry, and Bothwell asked Sir James

Balfour to fix it for him. The only acceptable form of Catholic divorce was an annulment on grounds that they were within the fourth degree of consanguinity. Archbishop Hamilton, who had conducted their marriage, was approached and, on 7 May, signed the papers (notwithstanding that his consistorial powers had already been revoked), conveniently forgetting that he had granted a dispensation on grounds of consanguinity before their wedding in the previous year. Mary knew the divorce was dubious, as she raised it with other bishops before marrying Bothwell.

While Bothwell was in Edinburgh resolving his divorce, Huntly stayed at Dunbar, where he argued with Mary over the marriage plan. This is mentioned in Casket Letter VI, which, as has been shown, was written by Mary from Dunbar and not prior to her abduction. Although he had agreed to the divorce and was formally restored to his estates, he felt he was becoming isolated in supporting the marriage and later failed to provide military support as promised. This was to be the nail in the coffin for Mary and Bothwell at Carberry Hill.

By now the Catholic lords were alienated and generally believed that Mary had connived in Darnley's murder. Bothwell kept her closely shielded from growing opposition. He picked ladies-in-waiting at Dunbar who would support his suit. These included his sister, Jean, widow of Lord John Stewart. Other than Mary Fleming, none of the Maries came to Dunbar and they all seem to have opposed the marriage.

On 27 April, Morton met at Stirling with Argyll, Atholl and Mar, who all believed that Mary was being held against her will. Morton's presence confirms that his support for the marriage at Ainslie's Tavern was a sham. With Bothwell and Mary now committed, he no longer needed to encourage it. A further gathering of rival factions met at Stirling on 6 May with the common goal of bringing down Bothwell. In Moray's absence, Morton was given the task to 'manage all', but they wrote to Moray seeking his return to Scotland.[17] The group also signed a bond as 'Confederate' lords to 'pursue the Queen's liberty, preserve the Prince from his enemies in Mar's keeping, and purge the realm of the detestable murderer of our king'.[18] They stopped short of accusing Mary of conspiring with Bothwell, despite a general belief that she had done so. Having been 'ravished and detained' against her will, they wanted her released from his cruel 'tyranny and thralldom'.[19] She found it hardly credible that his support had evaporated, given the signatures on the Ainslie's Tavern bond. Maitland failed to attend the meeting at

Stirling as he was still at Dunbar, and his non-appearance caused the Confederates to 'muse much'. Nevertheless, he followed through with his understanding with Moray to encourage Mary to go ahead with the marriage, even though both he and Mary Fleming were personally upset by it.

The Confederates were now a force to be reckoned with. They mustered 3,000 troops at short notice and, with their overwhelming public support, were positioned to make a stand against Bothwell and the queen. They included Argyll, militarily the most powerful of the Scottish magnates and traditionally a supporter of the queen, Atholl, head of the Catholic party, and Glencairn, in Moray's absence, the most powerful of the Lords of the Congregation. Morton, Argyll and Glencairn were not natural allies of Atholl, who had been kept in the dark about the plot to murder Darnley. It was perhaps as a result of Maitland's influence that Atholl was just as determined to bring down Bothwell. It was through him that the Catholic Tullibardine was attracted into the Confederate camp and he in turn enlisted his brother-in-law, Mar, who continued to supervise Prince James. It took a major change of heart for Mar to turn against Mary, but, with Bothwell having arranged his replacement as governor at Edinburgh Castle, he fell for the crime of passion story. The Catholics among them always remained loyal to the queen, believing that she was being held by Bothwell against her will. Moray's mainly Protestant supporters had the broader objective of deposing her to enable him to become regent.

Balfour seemed to be in Bothwell's camp after being installed at Edinburgh Castle with equal rank to the governor, Cockburn of Skirling. On 8 May, Bothwell tried to ensure his allegiance by appointing him sole governor, an unlikely role for a lawyer. Cockburn was compensated with the lucrative post of Comptroller of Customs. Yet Balfour's loyalty remained in doubt, and only six days later, Drury reported the governorship being offered to John Hepburn of Beanston. Melville later admitted to having persuaded Balfour to retain the keys to the castle, with its content of ordnance and royal treasure, so that it was held for the Confederates. By continuing to let Bothwell believe that he retained it on his behalf, Balfour was to be a principal factor in his undoing.

Cecil provided the Confederates with all the assistance he could without alerting Elizabeth to what he was doing. She would not back a rebellion against her sister queen, even though she was 'greatly scandalised' by events at Dunbar and would no longer accept Mary as a potential heir. She promised to help Lennox avenge his son's murder, hoping that James would be brought to England into his grandmother's care. This, of course, would assist Maitland in his hopes for the union.

With Bothwell raising troops in the Borders and having control of the munitions both at Dunbar and, as he thought, at Edinburgh Castle, his position seemed unassailable. On 6 May, he brought Mary to Edinburgh, accompanied by Huntly and Maitland. He arrived on foot, respectfully bareheaded, leading Mary's horse through the sullen crowds by its bridle. After taking up residence in the castle, he positioned his 200 hackbutters outside her rooms, hoping to shield her from the hostility they faced. Showing great personal loyalty, Herries [Sir John Maxwell] arrived to echo public concern at their intended marriage, but she told him 'there was no such thing in her mind'.[20] He apologised and withdrew, but she probably wanted to avoid him confronting Bothwell, who was in a volatile mood.

At this point, it probably did not matter too much to Maitland whether Mary and Bothwell actually married. It was their commitment to marry that made a crime of passion seem credible. He remained with Mary until the wedding, although she must have sensed his horror at it. Melville showed Mary a letter which claimed that marriage to 'a man commonly adjudged her husband's murderer would leave a tash [slur] upon her name and give too much ground for jealousy'.[21] Mary showed the letter to Maitland, complaining that it was part of his design 'tending to the wreck of the Earl of Bothwell'. Maitland was furious at Melville for producing it and warned him: 'So soon as Bothwell gets notice hereof, as I fear he will shortly, he will cause you to be killed.' Melville responded that someone needed to make her realise what people thought as it was 'a sore matter to see that good princess run to utter wreck'. Maitland told him 'he had done more honestly than wisely; and therefore I pray you, retire diligently before Bothwell comes up from his dinner'. Melville admitted keeping out of sight 'till his fury was slaked; because I was advertised there was nothing but slaughter in case I had been gotten'.[22]

Drury reported that Bothwell's efforts to keep Mary away from her traditional advisers caused a quarrel between them lasting half a day, and he concluded that they would not long agree after their marriage. Bothwell was ungovernably jealous at any favours she granted, and she 'much misliked' him writing to Jean Gordon, who remained at Crichton, although this was no doubt to settle their divorce proceedings. De Silva heard that he 'passes some days a week with the wife he has divorced'.[23] Once they were married, Maitland made efforts to turn Mary against Bothwell by claiming that he 'had written to Jean more than once, to tell her that he still regarded her as his true wife, and Mary as a mere concubine'.[24] This cannot have been true as Jean had always hated him. In the summer of 1567, when she eventually left Crichton to return to Strathbogie, she told Lady Moray, whom she visited, that 'she will never live with the Earl of Bothwell nor take him for her husband'.[25]

On 8 May, a proclamation was issued that Mary would marry Bothwell, with the banns to be read at both Holyrood and St Giles' on the next day. This was not well received. The minister at St Giles', John Craig, Knox's fearless assistant, denounced it and refused to read the banns without the Kirk's approval and until Mary provided a writ confirming that she had not been ravished nor kept in captivity against her will.

The Confederates made a last-ditch effort to prevent the marriage, but on the next day Mary and Bothwell signed their contract, which was witnessed by Maitland, still following his agreement with Moray, and by Huntly, who still supported Bothwell. There was a small group of other supporters at the signing including Herries, whose loyalty to Mary outshone his 'hatred of the newly created Duke. To appease Protestant opposition, Bothwell insisted on the wedding being held in the Great Hall at Holyrood with Protestant rites, rather than as a Catholic ceremony in the Chapel Royal. Mary's participation in a Protestant ceremony later caused her great distress and lost her the last vestige of papal support. She wore mourning clothes, but beneath these was a magnificent flowing black patterned velvet gown in the Italian style richly embroidered with gold strapwork and gold and silver thread. She later changed into a shimmering yellow silk gown.

The service was no better attended, despite some of the Confederate lords feeling duty bound to be there. Huntly was a witness and Maitland came with Mary's closest allies, including the four Maries, and the couple's servants. 'There was neither pleasure nor pastime used as is wont to be used when princesses are married, no masques, no rich presents, no elaborate gowns, no balling, dancing and banqueting.' There was no largesse, merely a wedding breakfast to which the public was invited, with the queen at the head of the table and Bothwell sitting at the foot eating in silence.[26] It was a pathetic little event compared to the glittering pageantry of her earlier celebrations. On the evening of the wedding, a further placard appeared in Edinburgh quoting from Ovid: 'Mense malas maio nubere vulgus ait [As is commonly said, wantons marry in the month of May].'[27] Cecil rubbed his hands in ill-disguised glee, writing that Scotland was 'in a quagmire; nobody seemeth to stand still; the most honest desire to go away; the worst tremble with the shaking of their conscience'.[28] His own conscience seemed unaffected.

PART V

MARY'S ARREST AND MAITLAND'S CONTRITION

Chapter 18

The Confederates challenge
Mary and Bothwell

Maitland could now sit back and watch the impact of his scheming. After her wedding, Mary sent Robert Melville to Elizabeth to explain why she had married Bothwell. Melville, who was Maitland's close ally, remained in London as her resident ambassador. Elizabeth was scandalised, and admonished Mary candidly:

> To be plain with you, our grief has not been small thereat: for how could a worse choice be made for your honour than in such haste to marry a subject who, besides other notorious lacks, public fame has charged with the murder of your late husband, besides touching yourself in some part, though we trust in that behalf, falsely. And with what peril you have married him, that hath another lawful wife, nor any children betwixt you legitimate. Thus you see our opinion plainly, and we are heartily sorry we can conceive no better. We are earnestly bent to do everything in our power to procure the punishment of that murder against any subject you have, how dear soever you should hold him, and next thereto to be careful how your son the Prince may be preserved to the comfort of you and the realm.[1]

On 4 June, Bothwell made a last-ditch effort to win over Elizabeth and Cecil, sending each a letter through Melville. The one to Cecil began: 'Seeing God has called me to this place, I heartily desire to persevere in all good offices.'[2]. Cecil had no desire to see Bothwell 'persevere'. To placate Elizabeth, he claimed that he did not deserve the evil reports circulating about him. Although men of greater birth might have been preferred, none could be more eager for her friendship. He assured her that he would be 'careful to see Your two Majesties' amity continued by all good offices'.[3] His approach was unsuccessful.

Bishop Chisholm was sent to the French court carrying letters from du Croc and to seek Catherine de Medici's and Charles IX's approval. Mary's letters confirmed that 'she had been very content to take him [Bothwell] for our husband. From his first entering into his estate, he dedicated his whole service to his sovereign'.[4] She cited her personal exhaustion and her need for a consort to share the burden of government, noting his long-standing loyalty to both the queen regent and her. She pointed out that he had been cleared by Parliament of all suspicion of murder, and that he had the support of the other lords, though with their factious nature, they were now trying to put him down. This lacked conviction when the other lords, speaking with one voice, were already seeking Elizabeth's help, but Mary also wrote to Cecil seeking his assistance in explaining her situation.

Immediately after the wedding, Mary seemed greatly distressed, and du Croc 'perceived a strange formality between her and her husband, which she begged me to excuse, saying that, if I saw her sad, it was because she could not rejoice nor ever should again, for she did nothing but wish for death', as she repeated on several occasions.[5] Du Croc 'counselled and comforted her' as best he could 'these three times I have seen her'.[6] She called in the Bishop of Ross and in floods of tears told him of her regret at both her marriage and the Protestant service, confirming that she would never again offend the Catholic Church.

Mary's rapid disaffection with Bothwell seems to have related to his frightening mood swings. Sometimes he was dour, distant and forbidding, sometimes embarrassingly over familiar and ribald. Although his display of Calvinistic demeanour seemed out of character, he now forbade all frivolity, including music, cards, hunting, hawking and golf. Yet his foul language and overbearing manner in private reduced her to 'an abundance of salt tears'. Drury reported that 'the opinion of divers is that she is the most changed woman of face that in so little time, without extremity of sickness, they have ever seen'.[7] After being able to do no wrong following her return from France, public opinion was suddenly against her. She now recognised that the rumours of Bothwell's part in Darnley's murder were likely to be true, and even Moray and Maitland appeared to be implicated and lined up against her. She had no shoulder to lean on.

As the Queen's consort, Bothwell made public displays of 'great reverence'. On 23 May, he belatedly organised a marriage celebration with a masque, a water pageant on the shores of the Firth of Forth and a tournament in Edinburgh, at which he ran at the rings. Although there was a mock skirmish acted out by soldiers, the event was sparsely attended. To show that her life continued as normal, Mary appeared in all her finery when she rode out in state with Bothwell. Drury reported that 'they now make outward show of great content'.[8] Du Croc was not taken in. On 18 May, he had again written to Charles IX and Catherine de Medici that 'all [is] amiss in the marriage, for it is very wretched and is already repented of'.[9] He reported that Mary had asked him to intercede with the Confederates on her behalf, but he considered this futile.

Any hopes of French sympathy for Mary's situation were ended when Chisholm admitted that she was no longer attending Mass, and that stories of large congregations attending Catholic services at Holyrood were fallacious. France and Spain turned their backs on her. It was Mary's remarriage, not Darnley's murder, which was now the focus of international scandal, and would prove her undoing. The broadsheets in Edinburgh had a field day, likening her to Delilah, Jezebel and Clytemnestra. In Catholic Europe, she was seen to have entered into a bigamous marriage with a heretic in an unlawful ceremony. Giovanni Correr, the Venetian ambassador in Paris, recognised that the Catholic cause in Scotland had been deprived of all hope of ever again raising its head. Catherine de Medici told Bethune that Mary had behaved so ill and made herself so hateful to her subjects that France could no longer support her. Her correspondence with her Guise relations evaporated.

The Pope had already recalled his Nuncio and stopped further contributions to her treasury. On 2 July, when made aware of the marriage, he broke off diplomatic relations. Unable to decide which of the two queens of Britain was worse, he announced that 'it was not his intention to have any further communication with Mary, unless in times to come he shall see some better sign of her life and religion than he has witnessed in the past'.[10] After having made her the focus for their Counter-Reformation, English Catholics could not believe that 'without fear of God, or respect for the world, [she] has allowed herself to be induced by sensuality, or else by the persuasion of others to take one who cannot be her husband and gives thereby a suspicion that she will go over by degrees to [Protestantism]'.[11]

At some point shortly after her wedding, Mary must have realised that she was pregnant. Although this was not generally known, it was an insuperable barrier to her ending her marriage and she stood firmly behind Bothwell. If he were found guilty of treason, their child's legitimacy would be questioned. The only matter of importance to her was providing a second heir. Despite James's robust health, life was unpredictable, and without her children, her death would cause anarchy.

Bothwell was now able to wield sovereign power. He wrote: 'They placed the government of the country in my hands with the wish that I should bring some order into the country.'[12] To his credit, he provided strong and intelligent leadership with 'a latent talent for diplomacy'.[13] To win over Reformist support, he blocked Catholic efforts to restore the Mass, annulling Mary's dispensation for Catholic nobles and her servants to worship with her in private. To ameliorate the nobility, he restored Morton to Tantallon. Fleming, who remained continuously loyal, was made governor of the seemingly impregnable Dumbarton Castle and would continue to hold it for Mary until 1571. Yet Bothwell lacked general support, and the Bishop of Ross prudently retired to join Balfour in Edinburgh Castle.

On 6 June 1567, Maitland had a furious row with Bothwell and, without taking his leave of the queen, left court with Mary Fleming. Mary was distraught. *The Diurnal of Occurrents* states that he feared for his life. More likely, he believed that he had done what was required of him and thought it was time to join the Confederates. They had become suspicious at him remaining with her for so long and feared that he was now operating as her agent. Yet it had always been Maitland's practice to try to influence 'the course of events from a position of strength on the inside rather than from the outside'.[14] As he explained to Cecil, *'il perd le jeu qui laisse la partie* [he, who deserts the side, loses the game].'[15] Before going to Stirling, he asked Atholl to assure the lords of his loyalty. There can be no doubt of his support for them. He continued to back Moray and was soon to manipulate the Casket Letters to provide evidence against Mary. His letter to Cecil, written a fortnight later, was probably for Elizabeth's consumption. He stated: 'The reverence and affection he had ever borne to the Queen had alone kept him so long in Court with Bothwell, from whom his life had been every day in danger ... [but] the Lords' call to him to join them in looking narrowly to his doings, made it impossible that he should decline so just and honourable a cause.'[16] Cecil, of course, was well aware of his objective.

Maitland's arrival proved a rallying point for the Confederates. Even the Hamiltons and Home, hitherto Mary's supporters, joined them, though Hamilton backing was conditional on them being recognised ahead of the Lennoxes as heirs to the throne after Prince James. Balfour also supported them, but as he controlled Edinburgh Castle, this was kept secret. He made his backing conditional on receiving immunity from prosecution 'by reason of his long familiarity with' Bothwell.

While the Confederates were united in their desire to bring down Bothwell, differences in their attitude to Mary strained loyalties between them. They signed another bond confirming, as common ground, their intention to free her from her husband. Many expected her to desert him when she realised the extent of adverse public opinion facing her, but most Protestants saw the marriage as their pretext for removing her as their Catholic monarch. If Bothwell should gain control of the prince, they feared he would proclaim himself king.

By 25 May, Bothwell already knew that he had a rebellion on his hands and prepared for action. He wanted to establish a standing army of 500 infantry and 200 cavalry. Mary could not believe that such a defensive step was needed, but with war inevitable, she raised 5,000 crowns and sent table silver and gold to the Mint for conversion to coin. Even Prince James's christening font was handed over, but the furnace generated insufficient heat to melt anything so large. The Privy Council, which Bothwell controlled, summoned the queen's lieges to Melrose on 15 June, ostensibly to raid Liddesdale, but in fact as protection against the Confederates. Mary was shocked at the level of opposition, but control of the prince was of paramount importance. She still trusted Mar to supervise James, saying: 'He hath assured me to be mine and faithfully ever.' By 1 June, it was strongly rumoured that Bothwell was planning the prince's kidnap at Stirling. Although he made repeated demands for the infant to be handed over, Mary sent the Bishop of Ross to forbid Mar from delivering him to anyone but herself. Melville reported: 'But my Lord of Mar was a trew nobleman, and would not delyuer him out of his custody, alleging that he could not without consent of [Parliament].'[17] Although Mary had wanted to go to Stirling herself, Bothwell feared that he could not provide her with protection. He was wise to forbid it.

With Holyrood lacking fortification, Bothwell decided to move with Mary into Edinburgh Castle. Balfour used masterly double bluff to discourage this, while assuring them of his continued loyalty. They now looked for a stronghold outside Edinburgh in which to await their levies being mustered at Melrose. On the day after Maitland's departure from court, they left for Borthwick Castle, twelve miles south-east of Edinburgh, where the Catholic William, 6th Lord Borthwick, was Bothwell's assured adherent. It was impregnable without cannon, but difficult to provision for a lengthy siege. After installing Mary there, Bothwell set out to link up with Home, not realising that he had defected to the Confederates. On learning this, he rejoined Mary, but their muster of her levies at Melrose was 'not so well obeyed, and so many as came had no heart to fight in that quarrel'. Bothwell urgently requested support from Balfour, Lord John Hamilton and Huntly.[18]

Casket Letter VIII was indisputably written by Mary from Borthwick on 8 June while Bothwell was trying to gather support, notwithstanding that it is annotated as being from Stirling before her abduction. As the letter refers to him as 'your brother-in-law that was', it can only have been written after Bothwell's divorce from Jean Gordon. Mary had had a furious row with Huntly and had refused to grant leave for him to visit his estates, believing that he was threatening to desert. She accused him 'with many bitter words' of plotting treason against her, as his father had done. Although Huntly returned from Edinburgh with 300 horse raised by Livingston and himself, his support seemed half-hearted. Being aware that the Confederates were planning to attack Borthwick on the following day (10 June) he disappeared north, apparently to raise more troops.

On the evening of 10 June, Home joined Morton and Mar at Liberton Park, four miles south of Edinburgh, from where between 700 and 800 mounted hackbutters with other Confederate troops that they had raised advanced on Borthwick. Drury had called on Cecil to send English troops from Berwick, but Elizabeth was still not prepared openly to oppose a fellow sovereign, despite the pleas of her advisers, who strongly disapproved of her dithering approach. Bothwell was still trying to gather support and dared not risk becoming holed up at Borthwick. Leaving Mary with a small garrison, he escaped by a postern gate to Haddington, trusting that the Confederates would not attack her on her own. Although Morton intercepted two of her messengers seeking Huntly's urgent help, he sent them on their way to avoid any accusations of treason. Although support for Bothwell was evaporating, he still trusted Balfour, but the Hamiltons were becoming ambivalent in the face of the substantial build-up of Confederate forces.

Unaware of Bothwell's departure, the Confederates lined out 2,000 men before Borthwick, taunting him with cries of 'Traitor! Murderer! Butcher!' Late in the summer evening light, Mary shouted out from the battlements that he had left. When she refused to return to Edinburgh to assist in finding Darnley's murderers, they continued to insult her, but having no artillery for an attack, they withdrew to Edinburgh. She was alone, and their acknowledged objective was to avenge the murder. On reaching Edinburgh, Morton's men plundered the gold collected at the Mint. He could now offer twenty shillings per month, a substantial rate, to anyone taking up arms to deliver the queen from Bothwell. When Argyll arrived with a substantial force, the Confederates boasted 3,000 men.

At midnight on the following evening, Mary escaped from Borthwick 'dressed in men's clothes, booted and spurred'. After being lowered by a rope from a window in the Great Hall, she made her getaway through the postern gate. Within a mile, she was met by Bothwell's servants who escorted her by a circuitous route to join him at Dunbar. Bothwell still had insufficient men to regain control of Edinburgh and returned to the Borders to raise more troops. Messages were again sent to Huntly and Lord John Hamilton to bring men with all speed, but they had lost any will to support him against the substantial build-up of Confederate forces and arrived too late to assist. (The Confederates already had 4,000 men and backing from the Reformist clergy.)

By 14 June, Bothwell had returned to Haddington with only 1,600 inexperienced men, after much of his hoped-for support had failed to materialise. Having left her clothing at Borthwick, Mary had to borrow garments from a countrywoman, 'a red petticoat' that barely covered her knees, 'sleeves tied with bows, a velvet hat and a muffler'. Despite lacking the trappings of royalty, she was burning with defiance and left Dunbar with 200 hackbutters, sixty cavalry and three field guns to link up with Bothwell at Haddington. She was joined by Seton, but, on arrival, still had only 600 cavalry and was dismayed at the small numbers coming to her aid.

With their numerical superiority, the Confederates were anxious to confront Mary and Bothwell before rumours of her pregnancy began to attract sympathy. Maitland interviewed Balfour for three hours to assure his loyalty and persuaded him to entice Bothwell and Mary to march on Edinburgh. Balfour told Bothwell that the Confederates would never hold their ground when he opened fire from the castle. Even though Bothwell and Mary were still awaiting more troops, they set out immediately. They billeted for the night at Prestonpans, from where they rode to Seton for what would be their last night together.

Early on 15 June, Bothwell advanced his men to Carberry Hill overlooking the River Esk, seven miles east of Edinburgh, positioning them inside an earthwork dug by Somerset prior to Pinkie Cleugh. After leaving Edinburgh at two o'clock in the morning, the Confederates mustered two miles to the south-east. They carried banners between two spears showing the infant James before his father's body praying: 'Judge and avenge my cause, O Lord.'[19] Maitland went with them. Morton and Home led the main body of cavalry, while Atholl, Mar, Glencairn, Lindsay, Robert 3rd Lord Sempill and Ruthven commanded the foot. Kirkcaldy was positioned with a smaller contingent of horse to block Mary from withdrawing to Dunbar.

Bothwell was facing unassailable odds and the day was taken up in fruitless negotiation. He offered to fight in single combat to defend his honour, but Mary intervened in tears to prevent the risk of losing him, knowing that she was pregnant. With the day hot, Bothwell's troops on the hill became dehydrated, but scouts sent in search of water were captured. Wine was brought in casks from Seton, but this caused even greater thirst. As the day progressed, raw Border troops slipped away to seek refreshment and others deserted to the Confederates. Mary would not surrender her throne lightly, but, with her army reduced to no more than 400 men, the outcome of military action was no longer in doubt. When she tried to leave, her way was blocked by Kirkcaldy. Although one of Bothwell's men took aim at him, she called on him not to shame her. She sought terms, but Maitland and Atholl were too embarrassed to negotiate. Kirkcaldy assured her that if she went with them, Bothwell could leave with a safe conduct until Parliament debated his guilt. Bothwell begged her to retreat with him to Dunbar: 'I told her they would take her prisoner and strip her of all authority.'[20]

As so often when faced with a crucial decision, Mary took the wrong one and overruled her husband. She wanted him free to regroup, after lying low, while she arranged a review of Darnley's murder. She made clear that she would investigate both her enemies and her husband. This implies that she was now fully aware of the Craigmillar bond. She told Bothwell that, if found innocent, 'nothing would prevent her from rendering to him all that a true and lawful wife ought to do, but, if guilty, it would be to her an endless source of regret that, by her marriage, she had ruined her good reputation, and from this she would endeavour to free herself by all possible means'.[21] By distancing herself from him, she hoped to demonstrate her own innocence.

Bothwell was granted a safe conduct to leave. This suited the Confederates, as it avoided his evidence being revealed in any investigation. Mary wept as they embraced, and he gave her what seems to have been the Craigmillar bond implicating many of their opponents, while telling her to 'take good care of the paper'.[22] Seton and Fleming then escorted him to Dunbar with between twelve and thirty horsemen. He never saw Mary again.

Always chivalrous, Kirkcaldy assured Mary of a safe conduct if she joined the Confederate lords, each of whom 'wanted no more than to accord her all honour and obedience in whatever way she wished to command them'.[23] She quickly learned that this was not their general intention, and Kirkcaldy considered her subsequent imprisonment to have breached his honour. He led her on horseback to join Morton, Home and the other lords, still in her clothes borrowed at Dunbar, begrimed from her day in the saddle. She held her head high, and Mary Seton, who had remained with her on her pony, attended her. Mary was received with 'all due reverence' by the lords, who assured her that she was now in her rightful place among her own true and faithful subjects.[24] Their deference, however, was short-lived. According to Drury, they produced the banner showing the dead king's body, which she later admitted 'she wished she had never seen'. Troops led by Atholl and Tullibardine jostled her, shouting: 'Burn the whore! Burn the murderess of her husband!'[25] She rounded on Morton: 'How is this, my Lord Morton? I am told that all this is done in order to get justice among Darnley's murderers. I am told that you are one of the chief of them.' He answered: 'Come, come, this is not the place to discuss such matters', but was sufficiently disconcerted to move out of earshot.[26]

She was escorted to Edinburgh under guard, with the banner showing Darnley's body carried ahead of her. They reached the gates after eight o'clock in the evening, but the streets were packed with people screaming: 'Burn the whore! Kill her! Drown her! She is not worthy to live!' 'All disfigured in dust and tears, she rode past amid execrations of the people from the windows and stairs.'[27]

At Maitland's suggestion Mary was not taken to Holyrood but to Turnpike House, a luxurious fortified house on the High Street and home of his brother-in-law, the provost Sir Simon Preston. It was eleven o'clock at night when she was placed under guard in a sparsely furnished upper chamber, with the banner depicting the dead king positioned opposite her window in the street below, where a hostile mob continued to shout abuse. With guards in her bedroom, and being without servants, she could not undress even when wanting to relieve herself. Although her captors invited her to join them for supper, she refused, perhaps in fear of poison. There was no chance of escape. If she were not already aware of its content, she had time to study the Craigmillar bond, which was signed by so many of those responsible for her detention. She realised that they would want her dead or removed from the throne. She was too exhausted to sleep, so lay down fully dressed for the night with the guards clattering outside her door.

The next morning, in a desperate bid for help, Mary appeared in hysterics at her window with her tangled hair hanging loose. She opened her bodice to expose her breasts, and with 'piteous lamentations', appealed to those below. Although some continued to shout insults, many were 'moved to compassion', until the guards pulled her out of view. Independent witnesses reported that the crowds were soon showing her support, and Home, with his cavalry, had to spend three hours clearing the streets to prevent an attempted rescue.

When Mary saw Maitland in the crowd below, she called on him to come to her. He was embarrassed and appeared not to notice. He was apparently too mortified 'to raise his eyes and look her in the face'. While imprisoned in England, Mary told Nau that he visited her privately, but refused her request for help to escape. He told her that she would be 'held in custody until everything had been done to authorise the investigation' of Darnley's death, as it was 'feared that she meant to thwart the execution of justice'. Nau reported that he 'discoursed with something more than freedom on Bothwell's habits, against whom he manifested an intensity of hatred'. She had replied that she was 'well aware … of the false pretexts that the Lords were employing [in] charging her with wishing to hinder justice done for the murder, which they themselves had committed. She was ready to refute these accusations by joining with the lords in the inquiry [knowing that it was the last thing they would want].' She told him that no one understood Bothwell's involvement better than he did. Morton, Balfour and he, 'more than any others, hindered the inquiry into the murder, to which they were the consenting and guilty parties'. Bothwell had 'acted entirely by their persuasion and advice and showed her their signatures'.[28] She warned Maitland that if he continued to support the Confederates, she would reveal everything Bothwell had told her of the part he had played. A furious Maitland 'went so far as to say that, if she did so, she would drive him to greater lengths than he yet had gone in order to save his own life. On the other hand, if she let matters tone down little by little, the day would come when he might do her good service.' He begged her not to ask to see him again as this caused him to be mistrusted and put his life at risk. If she left him alone, he might be able to protect her from being 'put out of the way'.[29]

Maitland's own version of this conversation, which he reported five years later while he was attempting to defend Edinburgh Castle with Kirkcaldy, was very different. He claimed that Mary had been arrested 'to punish chiefly my Lord Bothwell for the King's murder and to dissolve her "unhappy marriage" with him'. He recorded: 'I myself … that same night that the Queen was brought to Edinburgh, made the offer to her, if she would abandon my Lord Bothwell, she should have the thankful obedience as ever she had since she came to Scotland, but noways would she consent.'[30]

With the benefit of hindsight, Maitland could imply that Mary was determined to support Bothwell because she was pregnant and wanted another legitimate heir. However, neither he nor the Confederate lords were likely to have been aware of her pregnancy at the time. It was Maitland who focused them on holding Mary imprisoned, with a regency for her son to replace her on the throne. If their sole purpose were to punish Bothwell, they would not have permitted his departure unmolested from Carberry Hill. He was permitted to leave because, if he faced trial, he could confirm that he had been acting in concert with the rest of them and could provide evidence of their treasonable intent.

By 1572, Maitland had a very different objective and was feeling contrite. Mary Fleming's influence may have been wearing him down and the hated Bothwell was now out of the picture. He recognised that Mary's religion alone did not provide adequate grounds for her continued deposition, even if this meant deferring the union with England until her son, who was being brought up as a Protestant, took up the reins of government. By this time he was arguing that acknowledging James as king had been an 'ungodly' action and was merely a temporary ploy to hold the Confederates together, which he greatly regretted, saying that James 'can never justly be King so long as his mother lives'.[31] With Moray now dead, this change in approach left him out of tune with what Cecil and Morton wanted.

Chapter 19

Negotiations while Mary is held at Lochleven

Mary had understood that her surrender at Carberry Hill would lead to a parliamentary investigation into Darnley's murder, but, as she came to realise, that was exactly what Morton, Maitland and Balfour were most anxious to avoid. It was unlikely to incriminate her but would place at risk the signatories of the Craigmillar bond, which she now held. The Confederates had to decide what to do, but they were not a unified group. Mary's allies among them had achieved their objective of removing her from Bothwell's control and would have restored her to the throne. Most Reformers wanted Moray as regent and sought her immediate execution. John Spottiswood provided a letter, probably drafted by Knox, describing her as 'that wicked woman'. Morton, who needed to hold the Confederates together, gained a consensus to spare her life 'with provision of securitie of religion'.[1]

There was general agreement that Mary should be held securely to prevent Bothwell attempting a rescue. The island fortress of Lochleven was chosen as it would keep utterances about the Craigmillar bond out of earshot. The bond was taken from her and reputedly was later given by Argyll to Moray who destroyed it. It could not be used as evidence against Bothwell without implicating the remaining signatories. Her imprisonment presented a dilemma. If she were ever freed, the Confederates would need immunity from prosecution. Deposing her from the throne would require parliamentary approval, but calling parliament required royal assent, which would only become available after a regent's installation. Their solution was to avoid a trial on the grounds of protecting her honour. When Kirkcaldy argued that this contravened his undertaking to her, he was overruled.

As the Confederates' spokesman, Maitland provided du Croc with an official version of his conversation with Mary, supporting his theme of a crime of passion, first hinted at in the placards. He described her passionate love for Bothwell, claiming that she leaned out of the window at Turnpike House in tears to ask why she had been separated from the man 'with whom she had hoped to live and die with the full approval of the world'.[2] He again claimed to have warned her of a letter from Bothwell to Jean Gordon, in which Jean was treated as his true wife and Mary as his mistress. Mary had retorted that this was contradicted by his letters to her. According to Maitland, despite her misery since marrying Bothwell (which du Croc knew only too well), her desire to live and die with him remained as strong as ever. She would willingly take ship with him wheresoever the winds might take them. Maitland claimed to support her request for exile, but this seems unlikely.

Du Croc must have doubted Maitland's assertion of Mary's passionate love for Bothwell. Yet it provided the motive for her involvement in Darnley's murder and justified her arrest. As the Casket Letters also followed the theme of a passionate romance, it is further evidence that Maitland put them together. It was only much later that the story was fed to Buchanan to enable him to prepare his *Detectio*. It was Maitland's falsified evidence provided in the Casket Letters presented at the Conference at Westminster which would be used to justify Mary's continued detention. Despite his marriage to Mary Fleming, he falsely incriminated his queen. It was only after her imprisonment in England that he belatedly showed remorse, but by then her deposition had been achieved.

Mary Fleming's loyalty has also been questioned, sometimes being seen as a major influence on persuading Maitland to support Mary, but sometimes as the forger of Mary's handwriting in the Casket Letters, having learned similar calligraphy while in France. It is surprising, with her acknowledged hold over him, that Mary Fleming failed to curb his libels, but any disloyalty on her part is most unlikely. Her son, born at this time, was named James in the queen's honour and the Fleming family steadfastly backed their queen. Without the original Casket Letters, one can only speculate, but it is much more likely that Maitland made the manuscript changes himself. He later admitted to Norfolk that he had, from time to time, forged Mary's handwriting. There were of course able master forgers working for Walsingham in England, if Maitland was not personally responsible. His masterstroke was to employ parts of Mary's own writing and idiom, so that it would be difficult to brand the letters as complete forgeries.

By continuing to support Bothwell, Mary failed to contradict the innuendo of their passionate romance. Drury wrote: 'Though her body be restrained, yet her heart is not dismayed; she cannot be dissuaded from her affection to the Duke but seems to offer sooner to receive harm herself than he should.'[3] Even though she was aware of his signature on the Craigmillar bond, she did not denounce him until after her miscarriage. Treason, if proved, would make their child illegitimate.

Maitland's first task on the Confederates' behalf was to gauge French reaction. He needed to reach a deal with du Croc, who was advising that if Mary were sent to France, where her guilt was now accepted, she would be shut away in a convent, but if sent to England, they would feel obliged to take her side. They reached a secret pact. Du Croc agreed that France would not interfere so long as England did not assume control of Scottish government.

On 16 June, the day after Carberry Hill, Morton and Atholl moved Mary with an escort of 200 hackbutters from Turnpike House to Holyrood, still carrying the banner depicting Darnley's body, followed by 1,000 Confederate soldiers. The crowd was again packed. People shouted: 'Burn her, burn her! She is not worthy to live. Kill her. Drown her.' But she shouted back to confirm her innocence.[4] On arrival she was reunited with Mary Seton and Mary Sempill (her Marie, Mary née Livingston), but Morton stood behind her chair while they ate to prevent her from plotting an escape. During the meal he sent a messenger to establish if her horses were ready and abruptly told her to leave under cover of darkness. She set out in the clothes she stood up in – a silk nightgown and a coarse brown cloak – accompanied by two *femmes de chambre*. She believed that she would be taken to join Prince James at Stirling but was escorted by Ruthven and Lindsay to Lochleven. On arrival, she was treated courteously by Sir William Douglas, Moray's half-brother, but ate so little, that those around her feared for her life. With Sir William insisting on a warrant to confirm his authority to hold her, an order of the Council for her indefinite detention was signed by Morton, Glencairn, Home, Mar, Atholl, Lindsay, Ruthven and others. Its explanation that she had intended to 'fortify and maintain [Bothwell] in his crimes and was a woman of inordinate passion', shows Maitland's hand in its drafting.[5]

The Confederates were united in their determination to isolate Mary from Bothwell, but Moray's allies also planned her deposition. On 29 June, du Croc left Edinburgh with a letter from the Confederates to Charles IX, setting out 'the justice of our cause'.[6] It is not known what was said, but, in July, Throckmorton told Elizabeth that 'du Croc carries with him matter little to the Queen's advantage'.[7] He may also have carried early versions of the Casket Letters. Broadsheets emphasising her immorality incited public opinion against her, while, from the pulpit, Protestant ministers denounced her as a murderess. On 21 July, Knox returned to Edinburgh in triumph and thundered against 'the whore of Babylon and the scarlet adventuress'. According to Throckmorton, he warned: 'God would send a great plague on the whole nation if Mary was spared from punishment.'

There was some sympathy for Mary. Drury was soon reporting that she was 'better digesting' her captivity.[8] On 17 July, Bedford had heard that she was 'calmer and better quieted of late, and takes both rest and meat, and also some dancing and play at the cards, and much better than she was wont to do; and it is said that she is become fat [presumably as a result of her pregnancy]'.[9] Although Ruthven and Lindsay remained as her guards, Ruthven became smitten and proposed a night-time tryst. He burst into her bedroom at four o'clock in the morning and, on his knees, offered to free her if she became his lover. She was indignant and had him removed.

Moray's allies would not have dared to hold their anointed queen without Cecil's tacit approval. Cecil remained closely informed when any new evidence against her came to light. On 23 June, Bedford reported to him that the Confederates did not want to keep her imprisoned longer than necessary but would act on Elizabeth's instruction. This suggests that Cecil had approved her imprisonment. At the end of June, he wrote to Moray in Paris, sending packages thought to have contained transcripts of early versions of the Casket Letters. He also advised him to return to Scotland immediately.

Despite Cecil's concern for England's security, Elizabeth was not always harnessed to his views. She had watched the political changes in Scotland with trepidation, shocked at an anointed queen being imprisoned by her subjects. She did not want other European heads of state believing that she supported her detention, fearing them taking revenge on her. Leicester, who also opposed Cecil, told Throckmorton of Elizabeth's attitude to Mary's treatment: 'She breaks out to all men her affection and says she will be utter enemy to the Scots if the Queen perish. He [Leicester] thinks her punishment most unnatural, though her acts be loathsome and foul for any Prince. Lethington ought not to let private security banish due pity. The Queen deserves better consideration at some of her servants' hands. Let Lethington know what he says.'[10] Elizabeth fulminated from afar, saying: 'They have no warrant nor authority, by the law of God or man, to be as superiors, judges or vindicators over their prince and sovereign, for an example to all posterity. Though she were guilty of all they charge her with, I cannot assist them while their Queen is imprisoned.'[11] Cecil had to dissuade her from war, but she sent Throckmorton to negotiate Mary's restoration and to offer to bring up James as her ward in England. Maitland made clear that Scotland would expect the English Parliament formally to recognise James's 'title to the [English] succession with suitable provision for his state and train'.[12]

Elizabeth and Leicester had criticised Maitland's disloyalty and ingratitude for moving to join the Confederates. He responded that 'if Elizabeth was genuine in her concern for Mary, she should forbear from aggressive posturings, demanding Mary's immediate release'.[13] He continued his theme of a crime of passion by explaining: 'The Scots had not forgot the manifold benefits they had received from their Queen and meant her no harm. But she was at present like a sick person with a burning fever whose appetites ought not to be followed. When they see moderation of her passion, she shall have nothing but good at their hands.'[14]

Although Throckmorton had instructions to visit her, Maitland refused him access, and Home escorted him back to Edinburgh with 400 horse. He remained extremely concerned for Mary's safety. Nevertheless, Elizabeth's show of support may have saved her life. She hoped that Mary would be left as a titular monarch with Moray in authority, but this would not solve Cecil's determination to provide England with a Protestant succession. Throckmorton now recognised that Mary's rehabilitation depended on Mar's support. When he asked Mar to protect her, he replied: 'To save her life by endangering her son or his estate, or by betraying my marrows, I will never do it, my Lord Ambassador, for all the gowd in the world.' He had been taken in by the propaganda against her, and, with his absolute control of the prince, his 'incorruptible integrity' sealed her fate. He backed the Confederates and signed the agreement committing her to Lochleven. He now supported her deposition to allow his nephew, Moray, to become regent.

On his return to Edinburgh on 13 July, Throckmorton found 'the most part of Scotland incensed against the Queen'. Even Huntly and Herries supported Moray. Yet Elizabeth continued to argue that Mary's offences were nothing compared to the outrage committed 'by those that are by nature and law subject to her'.[15] Throckmorton again explained Elizabeth's concerns to Maitland, but, despite seeming 'wise and reasonable', Maitland would still not allow him to visit Mary. He claimed that she needed to be 'guarded very straitly because she had refused to lend herself to any plans to seek out the murderers of her husband'. This was untrue, but he cited her passion for Bothwell to justify her continued imprisonment. Given a choice between her kingdom and her husband, he claimed that she 'avoweth constantly that she would rather live and die with him a simple damsel; she could never consent that he should fare worse or have more harm than herself'.[16] Throckmorton explained that Elizabeth wanted the Confederates to 'commend their cause to God, instead of using force against their anointed sovereign'. Maitland retorted: 'The advice may be good for the soul, but not safe for the body, and hard to be followed.'[17] With Throckmorton being 'nothing contented', Maitland then spoke out, 'as of himself', that he:

> would talk to him more frankly than he would have done to any other Englishman, except Leicester and Cecil. You see our humour here, and how we be bent. Let the Queen your sovereign be well advised, for surely you run a course which will breed us great peril and trouble, and yourselves most of all. Do you not see that it doth not lie in my power to do that I fainest would do, which is to have the Queen my mistress in estate and honour? ... This is not the time to do her good ... Therefore take heed that the Queen your sovereign do not lose the goodwill of this company irrecoverably. For though there be some among us which would retain our Prince, people and amity to England's devotion, yet I can assure you, if the Queen's Majesty deal not otherwise than she doth, you will lose all.[18]

He was warning that however much Elizabeth might desire Mary's reinstatement, this would only lead to the restoration of the Auld Alliance with France. To retain Scotland's amity with England, Mary had to be deposed. Any attempt to garner English support for her would endanger her life.

'Personally Throckmorton did not approve of the instructions on which he had to act. He would have liked to pursue a more conciliatory course. He knew that the Confederate Lords were the only true friends of England, and that on them Elizabeth would, in the long run, have to depend. He was apparently satisfied that the sequestration of the Queen had been a necessity.'[19] Nevertheless, he was obliged to follow Elizabeth's instruction. He sent messages to Mary carried in Robert Melville's scabbard to advise of Elizabeth's desire to help her, but also warning her to give up Bothwell. Melville returned with Mary's response that she was 'seven weeks gone with child', and despite her despair, divorce would make it a bastard and forfeit her honour. This was no protestation of undying love for Bothwell, as Maitland claimed.

Throckmorton advised her that although the Confederates sought her abdication, forcing her to sign documentation under duress would not be enforceable. When Maitland learned of his continued meddling, he sent Throckmorton with a letter to Elizabeth from the Confederates explaining that they had to imprison Mary as she was reasserting 'the vehemence of her passion, and there was a need for breathing time and leisure to go forward in the prosecution of the murder'. Throckmorton made no mention of the Casket Letters, said by Morton to have been found on 19 June, as he surely would have done if they then existed. On receiving the Confederates' letter, Elizabeth defied Cecil and her Council by replying on 27 July that she was unimpressed with their 'colourful defences' of their actions and would not negotiate while Mary remained imprisoned.[20] She told Cecil to threaten war if Mary were deposed or executed. Despite knowing of Mary's imminent deposition and having advised Moray in Paris to return to Scotland, Cecil told Elizabeth that the Confederates remained undecided how to act.

After Moray's initial communication from Cecil, Sir James Melville reached Paris in early July to bring him the Council's formal offer of the regency. He set out for London immediately, seeing Cecil on 23 July. He then met Elizabeth to confirm his innocence and made a show of sympathy for Mary by sending his secretary, Nicholas Elphinstone, on to Scotland to complain at her harsh treatment. He told Elizabeth that he:

> could not fail to strive for her liberty because, besides being her brother, he was much beholden to her; but still, [Bothwell's] business and the King's murder had much grieved him and had caused him to leave the country. He returned now to see what could be done in these troubles, although he feared they would be difficult to mend. Many of those concerned in the Queen's detention were his closest adherents ... He would therefore find some means by which she should remain Queen, but without sufficient liberty to do them any harm, whilst punishing at the same time the authors of the King's murder.[21]

Cecil will have carefully briefed him on what to say. Moray had no intention of protecting Mary on her throne but was unaware that she had already signed abdication papers. Moray also explained that the discovery of the Casket Letters made Mary's abdication unavoidable. He had told Cecil of the content of one letter, which 'proved beyond doubt that she had been cognisant of the murder of her husband' but had felt unable to discuss it with Elizabeth. He added that in his opinion, Mary's worst crime was to 'pet and fondle' Darnley only hours before his murder. De Silva was not taken in by Moray's show of loyalty to his sister. He was 'more inclined to believe that he will do it for himself, if he has the chance'.[22]

Some time between 20 and 24 July, Mary miscarried twins. Although this became well known in diplomatic circles, it was hushed up to limit upwellings of sympathy. They seem to have been conceived at Dunbar in April, shortly before her marriage. Being separated from Bothwell, there were soon rumblings of disquiet at her continued captivity. Despite their outward show of unity, the Confederates continued to differ on how to treat her. Seton and her traditional allies, who had never wavered in their loyalty, met at Dumbarton during June to seek her freedom. They were joined by Atholl, Herries, Huntly, Lord John and Archbishop Hamilton. Perhaps more surprisingly, Argyll, who had signed the Craigmillar bond, also appeared. The Marians, as they would come to be known, signed a bond to seek her liberty, but could not agree how to achieve it. On 29 June, the Bishop of Ross withdrew to his see after finding them 'all being full of tumult'. Lord John Hamilton, who rather hoped to marry Mary himself, went to the General Assembly on 27 July to plead for her release, but was refused attendance. He then wrote to Throckmorton to seek Elizabeth's help, but with most Marians being Catholic, she refused. Despite placating her European counterparts with expressions of horror at Mary's imprisonment, she never actively opposed the Confederates prior to Mary's deposition and saw merit in Moray becoming regent.

Moray's allies found the prospect of his regency far more appealing than leaving Mary on the throne. She would be twenty-five in December, the age at which she could recall grants of land made earlier in her reign. Many nobles stood to lose. This provided a further incentive for her deposition. The Confederates sent Lindsay, in 'boasting humour', to obtain her signature on her abdication papers and he threatened to cut her throat if she refused. There were three documents: the first confirmed her deposition; the second confirmed Moray as regent; and the third appointed Châtelherault, Argyll, Morton, Glencairn and Mar as a Council of Regency until his return. Melville, who was with her, was shocked at how she was treated. She was extremely unwell from her miscarriage, but still demanded the promised parliamentary enquiry. She now had to rely on Throckmorton's assurance that her signature given under duress would be invalid.

James's coronation took place on 29 July. Mary learned of it when Sir William Douglas lit bonfires and discharged artillery in the garden at Lochleven. She assured him that James would avenge her. Throckmorton, who was under instruction from Elizabeth not to attend, unsuccessfully sought to defer it. He now sought consent to return to England but was told to continue working for Mary's freedom. He was to make clear how much Elizabeth disliked *their* doing, but Cecil transformed her meaning by changing *their* to *her.* Nevertheless, her expressions of support greatly comforted Mary and she was still relying on it when she fled Scotland. On 29 July, Robert Melville reported to Elizabeth that Mary 'would rather herself and the prince were in your realm than elsewhere in Christendom'.

On 5 August, Throckmorton reported that Mary's miscarriage made him more optimistic that she would agree to divorce Bothwell, making any possibility of a rescue attempt more remote. With Mary's hopes of restoration dwindling, Throckmorton focused on saving her life. By 7 August, after learning that she had signed abdication papers, Elizabeth contemplated sending English troops or funding the Hamiltons on her behalf. Maitland was dismissive of this threat, claiming that if England invaded, Scotland would turn to France for support. On 9 August, he sent an assurance that Mary 'shall not die any violent death unless some new accident chance', causing Throckmorton to believe that he had saved her life.[23]

On 31 July, Moray had left London for Scotland to be installed as regent for James. Only he had the charisma and diplomatic skills to justify holding Mary imprisoned, and he received a rapturous welcome on arrival in Edinburgh on 11 August. After assuming control, he rode to Lochleven on one of Mary's horses and, to her amusement, fell off into the loch. She noticed that he was addressed as 'your grace', despite his apparent reluctance to accept high office. She greeted him with 'great passion and weeping', but he distressed her with a pious sermon on her wrongdoings, 'in such injurious language as was likely to break her heart'.[24]

Mary was mortified to be threatened with execution. Moray told her that, even though she was innocent before God, she should have had regard to her reputation in the eyes of the world, 'which judges by the outward appearance and not upon the inward sentiment'.[25] Nau recorded: 'The injuries were such as they cut the thread of love betwixt him and the Queen for ever.' She objected to his appointment as regent, insisting that she was 'innocent of all that could be laid to her charge', as God would 'manifest' in the end.[26] Moray swept out, leaving her 'with nothing but the hope of God's mercy', but his sincerity and lofty sermonizing impressed Throckmorton, 'as if he were leading his people like the ancient prophets of Israel'.[27]

With his calculated but cynical approach, Moray showed Mary that he was now in control. On the following day, he found her more conciliatory. He told her that he could not free her, but 'would assure her of her life and, as much as lay in him, the preservation of her honour' by preventing the publication of her letters. If she persisted in her affection for Bothwell, her life would be in danger, and he would be unable to protect her. Conversely, if she were penitent and confirmed her abhorrence at Darnley's murder and did not seek revenge on the lords 'so it might appear she detested her former life', she might 'one day be restored to the throne'.[28] She kissed him and, in a show of trust, begged him to accept the regency. He told her he would do so only as a special act of kindness. Even on 30 August, he told Cecil that he had no real wish for it and privately shunned such grandeur and ambition, but he might be able to serve her while others would ruin her. This show of modesty met with Elizabeth's approval. As soon as Moray was installed as regent, she withdrew Thockmorton, but never formally recognised his regency. In the arena of European politics, she could not be seen to condone Mary's deposition. Moray told Cecil: 'Although the Queen's Majesty your mistress outwardly seems not altogether to allow the present state here, yet doubt I not that Her Highness in her heart likes it well enough.' He was correct. Elizabeth made no serious effort to restore Mary or to overthrow him, despite what she might say publicly.

Moray remained closely allied to Cecil and they had probably agreed to keep Mary imprisoned without trial. Although the Marians sought her release, Maitland told Throckmorton that even Archbishop Hamilton wanted her executed so that the nobility could meet without fear of the future. For once, Maitland was probably telling the truth. For a temporary period after Mary's abdication, the Hamiltons undertook to support Moray, so long as their legitimacy was not questioned. They insisted on Charles Stuart, Lennox's second son, being debarred from the succession. If Mary were executed, only the life of an infant child now stood between them and the Crown.

Moray's and Maitland's treatment of Mary was, of course, outrageous. She knew they were far more implicated in Darnley's murder than her, but she did not realise that they had induced her to marry Bothwell as the means of bringing her down. Providing evidence for her complicity in Darnley's murder would be difficult. Nevertheless, the propaganda was well organised and proved sufficiently credible at the time, losing her the support of Catholics abroad, even if today it fails to stand up to close examination. By keeping her at Lochleven without trial, her Scottish supporters could not rescue her.

According to Nau, Mary provided Moray with a sting in the tail, warning: 'He, who does not keep faith where it is due, will hardly keep it where it is not due.'[29] If she, a born queen, faced rebellion from her people, he, a bastard by birth and origin, would endure much more.

It was not until 28 November 1567 that Drury reported a meeting of the lords to discuss the content of the silver casket, which was to be produced at the forthcoming December parliament. The Act of Council beforehand claimed: '[On the evidence of] divers her privy letters written and subscribed with her own hand and sent to James, Earl of Bothwell, chief executioner of the horrible murder, it is most certain that she was privy, art and part, and of the actual devise and deed of the murder of the King.'[30] This was signed by Morton, Maitland and Balfour – all signatories of the Craigmillar bond – and twenty-seven others. The Council debated whether to refer to the letters publicly, 'as the manifestation thereof may tend to the dishonour of the Queen', but it concluded that they must 'open and reveal the truth of the whole matter from the beginning, plainly and uprightly'.[31]

When the Marians met at Dumbarton on 12 September 1568, they commented on what the Council had seen more than nine months earlier, saying: 'And if it be alleged that Her Majesty's writing should prove Her Grace culpable, it may be answered that there is no place mention[ed] in it by the which Her Highness may be convicted, albeit it were her own hand-writ, which it is not ... And also, the same is devised by themselves [the Regency] in some principal and substantial clauses, which will be clearer nearer the light of day.'[32] They were saying that that the 'writing' contained incriminating additions, even if it were not a complete forgery. They implied it was an original rather than a transcript, but probably only a single letter, referred to as 'it', which may well have been the one described to Cecil by Moray.

With progressive additions and changes being made in an effort to provide more plausible evidence, Buchanan faced an issue in keeping his *Detectio*, first published in Latin in June 1568, up to date. Initially he referred to '*litterae*' being found (and this can be translated to mean one letter or several), in which 'the whole wicked plot was exposed to view'. Yet in the English version of his *Detectio*, known as the *Book of Articles*, published shortly before Morton's declaration of the letters' authenticity, he described them as: 'Such letters of the Queen's own handwriting direct to [Bothwell] and other writings as clearly testified that, as he was the chief executor of the murder, so was she of the foreknowledge thereof, and that her ravishing [seizure] was nothing else but a coloured mask'.[33]

Despite their shortcomings, the letters provide the only remotely plausible evidence for accusing Mary of involvement in her husband's murder. As Cecil undoubtedly realised, they would never withstand detailed scrutiny in court and Mary was never permitted to see them. Moray was always reluctant to provide the originals, but quite improperly showed transcripts to the English commissioners before the conference at York to assess their sufficiency as incriminating evidence. After seeing them, the commissioners sought to have them 'huddled up', and never permitted their cross-examination. Elizabeth's limited objective was to justify Mary's retention under house arrest in England, but to avoid having them submitted in evidence. Du Croc later told Elizabeth that he understood the lords had letters proving Mary's foreknowledge of the murder plan, but she replied: 'It was not true, although Lethington had acted badly in the matter.' She added that if she saw him: 'She would say something that would not be at all to his taste.'[34] This implies that she knew of his part in manipulating them.

It is hardly surprising that in 1584 the original Casket Letters mysteriously disappeared. Without them, their authenticity cannot be categorically disproved. After being handed back to Moray by Cecil in January 1569, he returned with them to Scotland and, eventually, on 22 January 1571, returned them to Morton (twenty-one of the twenty-two were received by him and the whereabouts of the remaining one is unknown). Although further copies were made, these seem to have vanished immediately. After Morton's execution, one of his illegitimate sons passed them to the Earl of Gowrie (Ruthven). In 1584, Gowrie was also executed with his estates being forfeited, so the letters probably passed to James VI. They were never seen again. Although Gowrie could have destroyed them, it is much more likely to have been James. He was by then determined to restore his mother's reputation and had already arranged for Parliament to ban Buchanan's *Detectio* and *Book of Articles*. If they were found to be fraudulent, it was Mary and not him who was the rightful Scottish monarch. Destroying them removed this complication.

Following Bothwell's departure from Carberry Hill he was unable to assist Mary and had a hair-raising escape with several of his henchmen on two ships to Norway, then part of Denmark. Despite being followed by Kirkcaldy and Tullibardine, he outsailed them, only to be arrested as a suspected pirate north of Stavanger. He was taken to the castle at

Bergen, where his luck ran out. A former mistress, Anna Throndssen, who was living there, sued him for breach of promise to marry her. He was forced to hand over one of his ships and to promise her an annuity. Seeing him as a potentially lucrative hostage, Frederick II had him moved to Malmö, then part of Denmark. Unfortunately, the Scots had no interest in his repatriation. After writing his somewhat fanciful memoirs, he was moved to Dragsholm in Jutland, living there until his death on 14 April 1578.

Chapter 20

Mary escapes and Maitland's signs of sympathy

Moray had popular support, and, once in power, he showed firmness and courage as an administrator with 'unscrupulous adroitness'. By the middle of October, he told Cecil that Scotland was quiet. Even the Borders were settled, and, by January 1568, Drury reported that they had not been more peaceful for forty years. To provide money for the regency, Moray took control of Mary's jewellery, selling some and giving other pieces to his wife. He also tried to silence rumours of his involvement in Darnley's murder. Despite wanting to avoid bringing Bothwell to trial, he secured convictions for his henchmen. Morton was restored as Lord Chancellor with other supporters taking key positions. Kirkcaldy replaced Balfour as governor of Edinburgh Castle 'being the better man for the job', but Balfour became President of the Court of Session.[1] Moray also fostered better relations with Huntly, Argyll and Herries, although these proved short-lived and they soon demanded Mary's release.

Mary settled down to captivity with a better grace and improving health. In September, Mary Seton was permitted to join her with a small retinue of staff. Bedford reported that she was 'merrily disposed', dancing and playing at cards, and gave no indication of pining for Bothwell. She had begun to work her charms on the younger brother of Sir William Douglas, the eighteen-year-old 'pretty Geordie'. When she heard that Parliament was to meet in December, she asked to be allowed to 'vindicate her innocence, and to answer the false calumnies which had been written about her since her imprisonment'. She went on to say: 'There is no law which permitted anyone to be condemned outright without his cause having been heard, if it touched but the welfare of the least of subjects. It was much more reasonable, then, that justice should be done to her, their Queen, in a matter which touched her honour, which was dearer to her than her life.'[2]

Moray paid no attention. On 4 December, at a secret meeting of his adherents attended by Maitland and Kirkcaldy, Mary was formally accused of complicity in Darnley's death and of intent to murder her son, but no evidence was submitted. When Parliament met on 15 December, Maitland acted as Speaker. A Casket Letter was referred to, but was probably not tabled, and Moray made a show of being reluctant to produce it to save her honour. Her abdication in favour of James was deemed 'lawful and perfect [complete]', but an undertaking was given to protect her 'person'.[3] With her twenty-fifth birthday approaching, all earlier grants of land made by her were reconfirmed to prevent them being revoked.

Despite Moray's success, euphoria at his return was soon evaporating. The charge that Mary was involved in Darnley's murder was already seen as a hollow gesture and those in power, including Moray, were thought to be implicated. Seton joined the Hamiltons in openly supporting Mary. On 10 April, to limit further defections, Moray called a convention in Edinburgh to broker peace. He temporarily imprisoned the Hamiltons and Herries when they refused to sign an act pronouncing Mary guilty of the murder. He sent his secretary, Nicholas Elphinstone, to London with the Act, which confirmed Mary's abdication, but Elizabeth would still not involve herself in Scottish domestic affairs. He needed Mary kept securely in captivity to prevent her becoming a catalyst for opposition.

There is no doubt that, at this time, Maitland accepted the need for Mary's deposition and for the infant James to be crowned in her place, but he still seemed to believe that he could persuade her that it was politically desirable for her to become Protestant. If she did, he would help her to regain freedom and some semblance of authority. He remained in the Confederate camp and served Moray loyally but began calling for conciliation. Moray did not accept the need for this, and Morton, whose involvement in Riccio's and Darnley's murders left him most at risk from a compromise with Mary, was closely supportive of taking a hard line. Despite Maitland writing the Casket Letters and being similarly implicated in Mary's undoing, Moray became increasingly suspicious of him and banned him from the Council. Maitland was undoubtedly offended to find that his advice as Scotland's pre-eminent politician and diplomat, as he saw himself, was being ignored.[4]

In March 1568, Maitland sent a ring to Mary at Lochleven, ostensibly from Mary Fleming, enamelled with a lion and a mouse from Aesop's fable. Maitland, the mouse, was now gnawing away at the net surrounding Mary, the lion. There can be little doubt that Mary Fleming was placing him under pressure to gain Mary's release. There is no evidence that this was to support her restoration, and he remained sided with Moray at Langside. The prospect of union with England would be far more likely under Moray's regency for James. Nevertheless, he shared Kirkcaldy's concern that her abdication made under duress could be called into question and some agreement on her future status was desirable. She could not be left imprisoned indefinitely and the charge that she had conspired in Darnley's murder was unsustainable, as Moray, Morton and Balfour all knew.

It was Mary's personal charisma that melted the hearts of those around her to organise her escape. On 28 November, Drury reported 'a suspicion of over great familiarity' with pretty Geordie, saying 'this is worse spoken of than I write'.[5] She had enticed him into 'a fantasy of love for her'. In December, he irritated Moray, his half-brother, by seeking to marry her, but Moray saw his suit as 'overmean' for her (beneath her rank). In February 1568, Drury reported what seems to have been a recurrence of Mary's gastric ulcer, but the rumour-mongers put it down to pregnancy. Geordie was banished, but promptly approached Seton to assist in her escape. Maitland, who was hoping to negotiate Mary's release on acceptable terms, claimed that Argyll was trying to arrange her marriage to his brother, Colin Campbell, who was his heir.

It was Willy Douglas, an orphaned cousin of Sir William, who ultimately organised Mary's escape, acting as a go-between with Geordie and Seton. He craftily removed the keys to the main gate from Sir William while he was dining and was able to let Mary out when the guard went off duty. She lay under the seat of the boat while it was rowed ashore and was freed at last after ten-and-a-half months on the island. Willy and Mary, riding two of Sir William's horses, accompanied Seton and Geordie to Seton's palace at Niddry, where they were met by the Hamiltons. On reaching the Hamilton stronghold at Cadzow, they were joined by Argyll, Herries and other Marians. By 8 May, Mary had 6,000 supporters seeking her restoration. The Hamiltons did not wait for Huntly, whose route from the north was being blocked by Ruthven. Time was of the essence, and they hoped to take early advantage of their numerical superiority.

Moray learned of Mary's escape while in Glasgow, but quickly gained support from the Protestant lords, who were more cohesive than the Marians. Kirkcaldy, with his formidable military reputation, and Maitland arrived from Edinburgh. Although Mary told Maitland that she would be willing to negotiate a settlement, the Hamiltons were spoiling for a fight, and the opportunity was lost. Moray's objective was to prevent the Marians from reaching Fleming's garrison at Dumbarton, which offered access for French support. He made a stand at Langside, two miles south of Glasgow, where the approach up a long, narrow street could be defended from behind garden walls. As the Marians attacked, Argyll, who was in command, suffered an epileptic fit. His highlanders, who comprised a large proportion of their force, would not advance without him.

Mary's fate was sealed in a skirmish which lasted only forty-five minutes. With the route to Dumbarton blocked, Herries and a small party of supporters led her south-west on a nightmare journey. Having cut off her auburn hair to avoid recognition, she travelled ninety-two miles through inhospitable countryside without rest, spending 'three nights like the owls'.[6] Her most obvious plan was to seek help from France, where she had lands and income. Herries claimed that he could hold the south-west for forty days in her absence, rallying support in Dumfries and Galloway while awaiting her return. Moray did not chase after her but returned with Maitland to Edinburgh. He made himself unpopular by meting out severe treatment on her supporters as he went and seizing the property of those he captured. This caused his position as regent to be questioned in Parliament. De la Fôret, the French ambassador in London, estimated that Mary now had support from two-thirds of her countrymen.

Once more, however, Mary took the wrong decision, ignoring the advice of those with her. Being determined to throw herself on Elizabeth's mercy, she later wrote to Bethune: 'I commanded my best friends to permit me to have my own way.'[7] She realised that by setting out for France any hope of the English throne would be lost. Choosing England was a big romantic gamble, but she trusted in the filial bond between two 'sister' queens. With Elizabeth having little reason to help a committed Catholic, she saw Mary as a political embarrassment, particularly given Cecil's close alliance with Moray and Maitland. With fatal misjudgement, Mary moved to Dundrennan Abbey, south-east of Kirkcudbright, for her last night in Scotland. On the next day, 16 May, a fortnight after escaping from Lochleven, she embarked on a fishing boat at Abbeyburnfoot (near Maryport) to cross the Solway Firth to England. She would never see Scotland again.

On arrival, Mary wrote to Elizabeth for help, accusing Moray and his supporters of 'subscribing and aiding' Darnley's murder: 'for the purpose of charging it falsely upon me, as I hope fully to make you understand. I, feeling myself innocent, and, desirous to avoid the shedding of blood, placed myself in their hands. They have robbed me of everything I had in the world, not permitting me either to write or speak, in order that I might not contradict their false inventions.'[8]

This was only the truth. She was conducted to Carlisle, arriving on 18 May, and reported that she had been 'right well received and honourably accompanied and treated'.[9] She expected to be back in Scotland at the head of an English or French army 'about the fifteenth day of August'.

With the eyes of the world watching, Elizabeth confirmed that Mary should be honourably received with her restoration being discussed. The Venetian ambassador reported a palace being prepared for her in London. Cecil, though, had no desire to see the overthrow of the Scottish government he had worked so hard to install, and strongly opposed any show of sympathy. He wrote himself another of his private memoranda, in which he suggested various alternative ways to deal with her: 'If the criminality be excessive to live in some convenient place without possessing her kingdom. If restored she and her son may reign jointly, the Regent retaining office till the son's majority. If she should go to France, then England would be surrounded by very powerful enemies and France is superior in force to us. If she stays, she will embolden all the evil subjects here. If she returns to Scotland the friends of England will be abased and those of France increased.'[10]

Cecil took little comfort from Mary's arrival and reminded Elizabeth that she had been plotting against her for years. He recommended that she should be returned to Moray, but Elizabeth refused to send her to inevitable death, but would not provide military support for her restoration. As a compromise, she agreed to hold Mary in custody until the 'vehement presumption' of her complicity in Darnley's death was established.[11] If found innocent she should be restored to her throne, but if not, an arrangement might be found for her to remain as a titular queen while Moray continued to govern. Sir Francis Knollys was sent from

London to welcome Mary and to join Henry, 9th Lord Scrope of Bolton, the senior English official at the western end of the Scottish border. He was a close ally of Elizabeth, being married to her first cousin, Catherine Carey, and was soon under Mary's spell.

Handling Mary required extreme delicacy. When she sent Herries and Fleming to seek Elizabeth's support in London, Elizabeth prevaricated. She needed time for Mary's innocence to be established with impartiality. For once, Cecil approved of her being indecisive. Mary was to be retained under house arrest with the status and trappings of a queen. When Mary asked the French to send 2,000 foot and 500 horse to Dumbarton, to be paid for out of her French estates, Elizabeth feared a restoration of the Auld Alliance and made clear that this would be regarded as a renewal of old quarrels. She did not need Mary as a focus for Catholic opposition and refused her request to travel to either France or Spain. The famous auburn hair would no doubt grow back, and Mary was dangerously charismatic.

While at Carlisle, Mary did nothing to cause Elizabeth concern. She preferred to be seen as a guest, not a prisoner, but was told that there would have to be an investigation into the murders. Mary was well informed. She told Knollys that Morton and Maitland had planned Darnley's murder 'as it could well be proved'. She also complained that the Confederates had rebelled to prevent her from revoking grants made to them before her twenty-fifth birthday.

With Marian support in Scotland growing, Carlisle was too busy and too close to the Scottish border for comfort. Its castle could not be adequately defended against cannon and Mary might escape. Nevertheless, Elizabeth wanted her kept in the north, away from contact with the French who might land troops on Scottish soil. After six weeks at Carlisle, she was moved more remotely to Scrope's heavily fortified home at Bolton, fifty miles away in Yorkshire. On arrival, she was greeted by Scrope and his Catholic wife, Margaret Howard, who was Norfolk's sister. Despite its austere appearance, Bolton's early central heating system made it warm and comfortable. Knollys soon reported that Mary was 'void of displeasant countenance'.[12]

With Scrope supervising the Border region, Knollys remained as Mary's guardian, while Margaret Howard entertained her in style, arranging a meeting with English Catholics in sympathy with her predicament. Knollys became embarrassed at Mary's unresolved legal status and continued to request better evidence for detaining her without investigation. Neither Elizabeth nor Cecil had any intention of releasing her but needed a pretext for continuing to hold her. It was about now that Mary heard for the first time of the Casket Letters and their intended use as evidence at an enquiry. She wrote furiously to Elizabeth, excusing her bad writing, and claiming: 'These letters, so falsely invented, have made me ill.'[13] At the same time, Knollys reported Mary's hopes that Maitland was manoeuvring to her advantage, having blocked a blanket forfeiture being imposed on Marian supporters. This resulted in Moray bringing him to the Conference at York only as a 'necessary evil'.[14]

It is worth exploring Maitland's attitude at this stage. He had masterminded Mary's downfall, having failed to mould her as a suitable catalyst to unite England and Scotland. She remained determinedly Catholic and had married the unacceptable Darnley. In tandem with Moray and Cecil, Maitland had provided a scheme to implicate her in the murder of her husband as a crime of passion with Bothwell, the murderer. Although he knew she was innocent, he was still in the course of manipulating her correspondence to provide evidence to demonstrate her guilt. At some point, while Mary was being held at Lochleven, he had suggested that a compromise should be reached so that Mary could regain her freedom, but this did not extend to her restoration to the Scottish throne. While accepting that her Catholicism made her unacceptable as the means of uniting Scotland and England, he believed that her faith alone was insufficient cause for continuing to keep her in detention. It is reasonable to assume that Mary Fleming's influence played a part in his trying to mitigate Mary's predicament, but he was not deterred from his political obligation to provide the evidence to incriminate her. Moray mistrusted his softening attitude, and the divergence in their views did not stop there. Maitland's negotiation to promote Mary's marriage to Norfolk without, initially at least, envisaging her return to the Scottish throne, is another example of why Buchanan later dubbed him the 'chameleon'. On his return from the conferences, he became the Marian spokesman for her restoration, while also supporting Norfolk and his patrician allies against Cecil. History has had little sympathy for his change of heart. It has depicted Moray, Cecil and Morton as the upholders of sound Protestant government, but all three played their part in the underhand scheming that Maitland had begun, and which lost Mary her throne and ultimately led to her execution.

Chapter 21

The Conferences at York and Westminster

On 8 June 1568, Elizabeth wrote to Moray, no doubt for public consumption, accusing him of 'very strange doings' against a sovereign prince. She advised him that Mary was 'content to commit the ordering of her cause to us' (although Mary had only agreed to her conducting a private review), and that he should provide his defence 'against such weighty crimes as the Queen has already, or shall hereafter, object against you'.[1] She also told him to stop harassing Mary's supporters in Scotland. When Drury delivered this message, Cecil sent a warning that an English review of Mary's case was inevitable. He will have told Moray that he needed to provide convincing evidence to allow the English to protect his government. Cecil was only too aware that if Elizabeth ultimately restored Mary, the regency would become untenable.

The Scottish propaganda machine had already swung into action. Maitland was engrossed in going through Mary's and Bothwell's correspondence to produce the Casket Letters. On 21 May, five days after Langside, Moray sent his private secretary, John Wood, to London to 'damage the cause of Mary with Queen Elizabeth and the English nobility'. He was instructed to 'resolve' Elizabeth's mind of anything she 'might stand doubtful to'.[2] He brought transcripts of Maitland's letters in Scots (although these would not have been in their final form), principally to establish their acceptability as evidence. Nau records that 'after Elizabeth had heard what [Wood] had to say, her kindness towards Mary diminished somewhat'.[3] Nevertheless, Moray was nervous of using fraudulent evidence to accuse Mary of involvement in her husband's murder. If letters were tabled and Elizabeth still felt obliged to return Mary to the Scottish throne, there would be no room for compromise. He urgently needed to establish with Cecil how Elizabeth would react to Mary being found guilty. He wrote: 'It may be that such letters as we have of the Queen that sufficiently, in our opinion, proves her consenting to the murder of the King, shall be called in doubt by the judges.'[4] If genuine, he would not have been worried. Outrageously, he asked for English translations of the transcripts to be shown to them, to gain confirmation that, so long as they tallied with the originals, they would be sufficient to prove his case.

Cecil also approached Lennox, who was visiting his wife in Chiswick, to provide evidence. Lennox needed no further prompting, and asked Wood to draft a letter to Moray seeking information for inclusion in his *Supplication* to Elizabeth. This later formed the basis for his *Narrative,* setting out his version of events. He had two principal sources, Crawford, the gentleman of Darnley's bedchamber in Glasgow, and Thomas Nelson, Darnley's servant, who had survived the blast at Kirk o' Field. He blended their authentic evidence with fabrications designed to implicate Bothwell and Mary. It was clearly produced hurriedly without cross-referencing to Buchanan's *Detectio*. Although they often conflicted, the more glaring inconsistencies were later corrected. The *Supplication* referred only to one Casket Letter but claimed: 'There is sufficient evidence in her own handwriting to condemn her.'[5]

Cecil and Elizabeth played their own devious game. Cecil secretly assured Moray that Mary would not be returned to the Scottish throne, regardless of the outcome. It is not clear that this had Elizabeth's authority, but he had to avoid being implicated himself, as much as to protect Moray. Meanwhile, Elizabeth reconfirmed to Mary that she would be restored as queen, whether or not found guilty. Only if the investigation found against her were the regency's supporters to go unpunished. She also implied that Mary could attend to give evidence at a review to take place at York in October. However, on 30 June, she asked Mary to provide evidence to 'any noble personage sent to her by herself', confirming: 'I assure you I will do nothing to hurt you, but rather honour and aid you.'[6] Her change of heart seemed to relate to her concern that Mary might demonstrate the fraudulent nature of the evidence. Elizabeth met Herries in London to explain this but confirmed that no formal judgement would be given. She told Herries to reiterate to Mary that if she agreed to a public review, 'as her dear cousin and friend, I will send for her rebels and know why they deposed their Queen. If they can[not] allege some reason for doing so, which I think they cannot, I will restore Mary to her throne – by force if necessary'.[7] She then added conditions. These included: Mary renouncing her claim to the English throne during the lifetime of Elizabeth and any issue; abandonment of alliance with France, which was to be replaced with an alliance with England; abandonment of the Mass in Scotland to be replaced by Common Prayer in the English form; and ratification of the Treaty of Edinburgh. Even if the Scottish lords should prove their case, Mary would be restored to the throne with conditions, but, whatever the outcome, they were to go unpunished and 'continue in their state and dignity'.[8]

On 28 July, after four days of agonising indecision, Mary, who was in no position to bargain, accepted all these unpalatable requirements in return for the promise of restoration. Yet, in a private message to Moray, Elizabeth compounded her duplicity by confirming Cecil's earlier assurance that if found guilty, Mary would not be returned to her throne. Meanwhile, on 13 July, Moray had formally agreed to attend but was disappointed to find himself as the defendant. Elizabeth's private agenda was clear; she did not want Mary back on the Scottish throne but needed sufficient evidence to condemn her.

On receiving Elizabeth's advice, Mary instructed her supporters in Scotland not to provoke the situation and to lay down their arms if Moray had done the same. This was another fatal error. At the parliament on 16 August, Moray attainted the Hamiltons, Fleming and the Bishop of Ross. Mary retaliated by telling Herries to accuse Moray publicly of involvement in Darnley's murder. This forced Elizabeth to step in to enable him to continue as regent. Fearing that Bothwell might be called to provide evidence, Moray sent a message urgently to Denmark hoping to arrange his demise.

On 6 September, Moray at last received a safe conduct to attend the York Conference. Mary now realised that this would not be an investigation of the Protestant lords for having deposed her but an inquest into her involvement in Darnley's murder. She refused to attend as the investigation had no jurisdiction over her. She told Elizabeth: 'I will never plead my cause against theirs unless they stand before you in manacles.' Her non-attendance suited Cecil, who was extremely nervous of her undermining Moray's evidence. When Elizabeth barred her anyway, Mary was outraged. Given that she was in effect the accused, this breached natural justice.

Both Mary and Moray appointed 'commissioners' to represent them at the conference, which was to be conducted by English commissioners headed by Norfolk, the senior English peer, and supported by Thomas Radcliffe, 3rd Earl of Sussex, and Sadler, with his wide experience of Scottish affairs. There would be no judgement as Elizabeth lacked authority to try the Scottish queen and wanted to avoid her being found guilty. Her objective was to establish a pretext for continuing to hold her, both as a political bargaining counter and to enable the English to continue to manipulate Scottish domestic affairs to their advantage. Moray wanted Mary branded as a murderess and adulteress to justify her continued imprisonment so that he could continue to govern Scotland unhindered.

Moray headed the Scottish commissioners. Although Maitland was called upon to assist, their relationship was frosty, but he was needed, in part to prevent his involvement in any mischief in Scotland, and also because he was still its finest advocate and most experienced diplomat and might need to assert the Casket Letters' authenticity. Buchanan, who was considered more reliable, was appointed secretary. Mary chose a broadly based group of Catholics and Reformers headed by Herries and the Bishop of Ross, but none was noted for their advocacy. 'They had no confidence in their own case and dreaded the production of the Letters.'[9]

While Moray wanted Mary found guilty, Maitland later claimed that he tried to shield her. He wanted her reconciled to Moray as a precursor to her restoration in a subordinate role. He was anxious to avoid the evidence being examined too closely as it might implicate him. Neither Mary nor Moray trusted him, and she instructed her commissioners to treat Moray and her other 'disobedient subjects' only as defendants. On 9 September, she wrote:

> In case they allege to have any writings of mine which may infer presumptions against me, ye shall desire that the principals be produced, and that I myself may have inspection thereof, and make answer thereto; for ye shall affirm in my name I never wrote anything concerning that matter to any creature, and if any such writings be, they are false and feigned, forged and invent[ed] by themselves, only to my dishonour and slander; and there are divers in Scotland, both men and women, that can counterfeit

my handwriting, and write the like manner of writing which I use as well as myself, and principally such as are in company with themselves; and I doubt not, if I had remained in my own realm, I should before now have discovered the inventors and writers of such writings, to the declaration of my innocence and the confusion of their falsehood.[10]

It can be implied that she knew Maitland had perpetrated them.

Despite her instructions, Mary's commissioners sought a compromise to gain her restoration, but without necessarily dismissing Moray's case. They, too, wanted to prevent damaging evidence being tabled, whether true or false. Norfolk was unimpressed, believing that Mary had better friends on Moray's side than on her own. She was not above dissembling herself. On 29 September, she instructed her commissioners to say that she would consider embracing religious conformity with England after her restoration, despite recently having assured the gathering of Catholics at Bolton and the Spanish queen of her continued adherence to Catholicism.

In public, Elizabeth continued her even-handed approach. She asked the Scottish commissioners to 'bring a good end to the differences, debates and contentions grown between her dear sister and cousin, Mary Queen of Scots, and her subjects'.[11] They were told that if the case against her were 'plainly proved', Elizabeth would deem her 'unworthy of a kingdom', but if not, she would be restored. This conflicted with her private undertaking to Mary that she would be restored whatever the outcome, and with Cecil's assurance to Moray that she would not be restored under any circumstances. The English commissioners were instructed to press Moray to table his evidence so that Mary had a case to answer. On 20 September, Elizabeth reassured him that although it was reported that Mary would be restored to the throne even if found guilty, this was not the case. This was reaffirmed by Cecil five days later.

Norfolk headed the English commissioners in his capacity as Earl Marshal, a role which gave him judicial responsibilities. Although outwardly Protestant, he had strong Catholic sympathies and was one of a group of patrician Conservatives at the opposite end of the political spectrum to the 'low-born' Cecil. He disapproved of Cecil's interference in Scottish domestic affairs and for supporting the Confederates against Mary. He strongly backed Elizabeth in refusing to place religion ahead of dynastic right when contemplating the English succession. With his Conservative allies, he was suspicious of the Scottish regency, seeing an attack on Mary in Scotland as a threat to Elizabeth's divine authority in England. He also doubted England's jurisdiction to try Mary, which was only defended by Cecil on an old but doubtful argument that Scotland was an English suzerainty (see Endnote 11).

Mary welcomed Norfolk's appointment, taking comfort from Lady Scrope's assurance that her brother would be sympathetic. Nevertheless, he was a pragmatist with a role to support the English government. From the outset the English commissioners accepted that they were to avoid implying Mary's guilt. This suited Norfolk, as will be seen. There can be little doubt that they were aware that their quasi-legal investigation was a charade and that the Casket Letters had been fabricated as a pretext for keeping Mary, at least temporarily, off her throne. The only people who did not understand this were Mary, her commissioners and Lennox. She was not permitted to attend to defend herself, and Lennox, one of the principal sources of evidence against her, was also barred. He had already provided his *Supplication* to Elizabeth and, on 18 August, reminded Cecil that he had received no response. As he was 'the party whom the matter touchest nearest', he believed that his appearance at the enquiry might be thought necessary.[12] However, Cecil knew that his evidence conflicted with the Casket Letters.

The English wanted the door left open for Mary's restoration at some future point should circumstances change. Cecil told Norfolk privately to make clear that they were looking for evidence to justify keeping her imprisoned in England, but it should be found too obscure to make her culpable of her husband's murder. This was a fine line to tread. By 23 September, Cecil had already told Sussex that, if Mary were found guilty, she would not be returned to the Scottish throne, but Elizabeth did not want a guilty verdict. The English commissioners needed to see final transcripts of the Casket Letters to judge their quality as evidence before submission into the public domain.

Mary was personally convinced that Elizabeth would arrange her restoration after causing 'the reduction of our said disobedient subjects to their dutiful obedience of us'.[13] Her supporters assumed that her case hung on refuting the veracity of the evidence. It was not only Mary denying the letters' authenticity. It has already been seen that, on 12 September, her Marian supporters, meeting at Dumbarton, had branded them as forgeries. By now, the contents of the silver casket had progressively increased to twenty-two documents. On 16 September, Moray took custody of the originals from Morton, although transcripts in Scots had already reached London. Buchanan's *Book of Articles* (the English translation of his *Detectio*) was updated with a detailed postscript relating to them.

Mary's supporters were outraged that the conference had become an investigation of the queen without her being present. At the meeting at Dumbarton, they declared: 'There was nothing done in their [December] Parliament that could prejudice the Queen's honour in any sort, Her Grace never being called or accused. It is against all law and reason to condemn any living creature without first hearing them in their defence.'[14] Mary had never formally been accused of involvement in Darnley's murder, and had never been asked to defend herself. Now she was to be examined in her absence, using fraudulent evidence to condemn her without trial.

With the conference at York scheduled to start on 4 October, Moray left Edinburgh with his fellow regency commissioners on 25 September, bringing the Casket Letters and Buchanan's *Book of Articles*. On arrival, before the conference began, he provided Norfolk with transcripts to enable the English commissioners to assess the evidence. Before showing them publicly, he wanted confirmation that they had authority to pronounce on her guilt and, if established, that she would either be returned to Scotland for punishment or be kept imprisoned in England. He told Norfolk that up to now he had been reluctant to reveal what he knew (notwithstanding having sent Elizabeth the Act of Parliament accusing her of her husband's murder and having provided earlier versions to Cecil). He asked for written assurance, if Mary were found guilty, that Elizabeth would recognise the regency for James.

When Norfolk saw the transcripts, he was concerned at their highly incriminating nature. He wrote Elizabeth a carefully constructed report, although both she and Cecil will have been in no doubt what he was trying to say. He was particularly shocked by the love poem and Casket Letter II (the long letter purportedly written by Mary from Glasgow), and reported that they did 'discover such inordinate love between [Mary] and Bothwell, her loathing and abhorrence of her husband that was murdered, in such sort as every good and godly man cannot but detest and abhor the same'. He explained:

> The matter contained in them [was] such as could hardly be invented or devised by any other than by herself, for they discourse of some things which were unknown to any other than to herself and Bothwell, and it is hard to counterfeit so many, so the matter of them is such, as it seemeth that God, in Whose sight murder and bloodshed of the innocent is abominable, would not permit the same to be hid or concealed ... The chief and special points of the letters, written, as they say, with her own hand, to the intent it may please Your Majesty to consider them, and so to judge whether the same be sufficient to convict her of the detestable crime of the murder of her husband, which in our opinions and consciences, if the said letters be written with her own hand, is very hard to be avoided.[15]

While implying disingenuously that they seemed to be genuine, Norfolk's point is clear. Either the letters were genuine, and she would inevitably be convicted of complicity to murder, or they were fraudulent, and she would be found innocent. Neither of these were outcomes that Elizabeth and Cecil wanted.

As Norfolk now had the transcripts, Maitland, MacGill, Buchanan and Wood showed Sussex and Sadler privately 'such matter as they have to condemn the Queen of Scots of the murder of her husband'.[16] They produced a copy of the Ainslie's Tavern bond with a warrant, dated 19 April 1567, signed by Mary approving it, the two marriage contracts from the casket, and another letter that has not survived, but has been mentioned earlier and which apparently demonstrated that Mary had incited a quarrel between her half-brother, Lord Robert Stewart, and Darnley at Kirk o' Field in the hope of Lord Robert killing him to save Bothwell from having to do so. They also provided transcripts of Casket Letters I, II, VI and VII and the love poems already shown to Norfolk.

On seeing them, the English commissioners strongly discouraged the use of the letters as evidence. Norfolk wrote privately to Cecil during the conference with his views on the Scottish nobility, saying:

'This cause is the doubtfullest and most dangerous that ever I dealt in; if you saw and heard the constant affirming of both sides, not without great stoutness would you wonder! You shall find in the end [that] as there be some few in this company that mean plainly and truly, so there be others that seek wholly to serve their own private turns.'[17]

Norfolk now realised, even if he had not known earlier, that the Scots had no interest in justice. In their eagerness to vindicate themselves, 'they care not what becomes neither of Queen nor King [James]'.[18] Sussex held a similar view, which he confirmed to Cecil after the adjournment of the conference. He was disgusted at their inconstancy, claiming that the Hamiltons only wanted Mary's restoration because they hated Moray and did not want him promoted ahead of them in the Scottish succession. He concluded: 'Thus do you see how these two factions, for their private causes, toss between them the Crown and public affairs of Scotland, and care neither for the mother nor child, but to serve their own turns.'[19] The English commissioners were now aware that many of Mary's closest advisers had formed a conspiracy to murder Darnley, and Moray was trying to cover it up.

Mary's commissioners reached York on 2 October, a day ahead of the other parties involved. Quite improperly, they were not advised that Moray had shown transcripts of the evidence to Norfolk. As the plaintiffs, Mary's commissioners were heard first. On 8 October, they set out their complaints against Moray and his supporters, who, they said, had taken up arms against their sovereign, had deposed and incarcerated her, had usurped the regency and had compelled her to seek justice from Elizabeth. They had also ruined her reputation by 'feigned and false reports'. Moray responded that the Confederates had been intimidated into signing the Ainslie's Tavern bond by the presence of Bothwell's armed retainers, that Mary had relinquished sovereign power to the traitorous Bothwell and, after Carberry Hill, had threatened everyone who had taken up arms against her. This had obliged them to keep her imprisoned until Darnley's murderers had been brought to justice. He insisted that she had abdicated voluntarily and that his regency had been ratified by Parliament. He did not accuse her of involvement in Darnley's murder and, to Norfolk's relief, did not refer to the Casket Letters. Like Moray, Norfolk would be at risk if required to pronounce her guilty of adultery and murder on trumped-up evidence, and she was then returned to her throne. She was

Elizabeth's dynastic heir and, if she inherited, would not readily forgive those involved in the process of condemning her.

Both sides asked for time to reply. When Mary's commissioners needed her advice on how to answer, Norfolk asked them to obtain authority to act without needing discussion with her so they could 'treat, conclude and determine of all matters and causes whatsoever in controversy between her and her subjects'.[20] On 16 October, they delivered Mary's formal written reply. This argued that, even if Bothwell had murdered Darnley, she was unaware of it when she married him – by which time he had been acquitted – and the lords now accusing him had encouraged it. She had been miserably deceived at Carberry Hill by Kirkcaldy's fair words to put her trust in them. She stressed that she had abdicated only after being threatened with execution. All this was the truth.

Despite their political differences, Norfolk supported Elizabeth and Cecil in their desire to keep Mary imprisoned without finding her guilty. He wanted it thought that he believed the evidence, making the decision not to table it seem like an effort to avoid incriminating her. It was now that Maitland's chameleon-like stance came to the fore. Although his role was to support Moray, on 11 October he sent Mary Fleming to Mary with a transcript of at least one of the Casket Letters and a note offering his assistance to combat evidence that he had produced. He did not, of course, reveal his part in creating it, but his conscience must have been troubling him. Mary may not have trusted him, as she replied, neutrally enough, that he should try to pacify Moray, speak favourably of her to Norfolk and treat the Bishop of Ross as a friend, while doing what he could to 'stay these rigorous accusations'.[21] Maitland even told her commissioners that the letters had been shown to Norfolk and his colleagues privately. They warned Mary, who advised Knollys that '[if the Scottish commissioners] will fall to [this] extremity, they shall be answered roundly and to the full, and then we are past all reconciliation'.[22]

On 15 October, Knollys told Norfolk that Mary was aware that he had seen the evidence. This placed Norfolk in a delicate position. Concerned that it might become public knowledge, he sought advice from London on how to proceed, having reported seeing it unofficially 'for our better instruction'.[23] He adjourned the conference and went hawking about ten miles away at the Archbishop of York's residence at Cawood, where he was joined by Maitland. It might seem surprising that Norfolk should agree to meet a key witness privately in the middle of an investigation he was supervising, but it is a tribute to Maitland's persuasiveness. Maitland lost no time in confirming, if Norfolk did not already know it, that the Casket Letters were almost certainly forged, since many people could imitate Mary's handwriting. Norfolk showed no surprise, and Maitland came to his main objective. He suggested that Norfolk should consider marrying her, as she needed a husband on whom Moray and Elizabeth could rely, and even that his daughter, Margaret Howard, should marry Prince James. He did not propose restoring Mary to her throne, but hoped to neutralise her politically, vesting power and authority in her husband. This could lead to her or her heirs gaining the English Crown if Elizabeth died childless. Even now, Maitland had not lost hope of using Mary to establish the union, but with Norfolk at the head of a new royal house to govern both Scotland and England. Maitland's only request was to receive absolution for any earlier crimes.

Perhaps surprisingly, the recently widowed Norfolk was receptive, notwithstanding that a clause in his contract as a commissioner threatened treason to anyone contemplating marriage to Mary. He was aged thirty-three, while Mary was twenty-six, and arguably their marriage would satisfy English interests, ultimately paving the way for her restoration in Scotland. It also resolved the problem of what to do with her after the conference. Norfolk explained that Elizabeth had no intention of restoring Mary or finding her guilty, but would hold her in England, leaving the door open for her restoration if circumstances changed. Maitland advised him to explain this to Moray to deter him from tabling the Casket Letters. Norfolk was forgetting that the marriage would be completely unacceptable to Moray, who would lose authority in the process. Nevertheless, the discussion was left in abeyance until the conferences ended.

Marriage to Mary struck a chord with Norfolk and his Conservative allies. They wanted peace with France and Spain to end the threat of foreign invasion, and they opposed Cecil's alliance with the Huguenots. Hostility to Spain conflicted with England's commercial interests in the Low Countries and they hoped to restore friendship by returning treasure usurped by English privateers, and by removing Cecil and his supporters from power. As Elizabeth was showing public support for Mary's restoration, they were confident that she would approve.

Maitland quickly hinted to Mary's commissioners that Norfolk would consider marriage. It fitted well with their hope of restoring her to the Scottish throne in a titular capacity, leaving a regency acceptable to Elizabeth to run the government. He discussed it with the Bishop of Ross, who asked Norfolk to confirm privately if 'he bore a certain goodwill' towards her.[24] Despite Maitland's ambivalence, the bishop still hoped to gain Mary's restoration. Norfolk now had good reason for wanting Mary cleared, although Elizabeth would need persuasion to support their marriage. Norfolk took Maitland's advice, telling Moray that, although his role as a commissioner was to hear the accusations against Mary, Elizabeth did not want her found guilty, and urged him not to use the Casket Letters in evidence. He argued that, 'albeit the Queen had done, or suffered harm to be done, to the King her husband', it was better for her son's sake that she should not be accused or dishonoured as 'our future Queen'.[25] Moray confided this to Maitland and Melville but remained undecided on whether to table them.

Elizabeth and Cecil in London must have gained wind of the behind-the-scenes discussions at York. They gave instructions for the conference to be adjourned so that the evidence could be laid before the Privy Council at Westminster, where they could control what was going on. Elizabeth wanted to establish why Moray and his colleagues had failed 'to charge the queen with guiltiness of the murder'.

Mary had been advised by her commissioners that Norfolk might consider marrying her and told Knollys that she would 'not greatly mislike' a union with Elizabeth's second cousin (through Anne Boleyn). With Lady Scrope being her constant companion, there can be little doubt that she was also encouraging it. Nevertheless, Mary recognised the difficulty of obtaining Elizabeth's approval. 'She wished them first and foremost to get the Queen's assent, lest the matter might turn to her hurt and the Duke's whereof she had had experience before in her marriage with Lord Darnley contracted without her assent.'[26]

On 20 October, Knollys reported to Cecil that Mary favoured the marriage, adding that, in his opinion, she could not be detained with any honour 'unless she be utterly disgraced to the world'.[27] Isolated at Bolton, Mary remained optimistic that Elizabeth would approve, seeing it as her means of extricating herself from imprisonment. On 21 October, she instructed her commissioners to seek a divorce from Bothwell, secretly sending papers for his signature to Denmark. This was on the grounds that she had been taken by force and that his earlier nullity from Jean Gordon was invalid. She made no show of sadness, and, by June 1569, Bothwell had confirmed his agreement. Papers were sent to Rome for the Pope's signature, and, in November 1570, Sir Henry Norris, the English ambassador in Paris, reported that the Pope had granted it. But there is no record of this at the Vatican, and Norris seems to have been mistaken.

Notwithstanding the secret negotiations with Mary, Norfolk was furious at Cecil moving the proceedings from York and tried unsuccessfully to have him removed from office. Cecil retaliated by posting him on a futile mission to the northern frontiers until preparations to reopen the conference in London were complete. Norfolk took exception to being marginalised, but Elizabeth felt threatened by the marriage proposal and decided to tackle him herself. She told him 'to beware on which pillow he leaned his head'. Realising that marrying Mary might be treasonable, he quickly denied his suit, saying: 'What! Should I seek to marry her, being so wicked a woman, such a notorious adulteress and murderer? I love to sleep upon a safe pillow.' He went on: 'And if I should go about to marry her, knowing, as I do, that she pretendeth a title to the present possession of your Majesty's crown, your Majesty shall justly charge me with seeking your own crown from your head.' Elizabeth kept an eye on him, but his denial did him little credit. Elizabeth's ambassadors told Mary 'to bear herself quietly, lest she saw ere long those on whom she most leaned hop headless'.[28]

On 22 October, after the commissioners had left for London, Sussex outlined the likely outcome to Cecil. As he did not believe that Moray's evidence could be sustained, his attitude was entirely political. If Mary were to be kept imprisoned:

> This matter must at length take end, either by finding the Scotch Queen guilty of the crimes that are objected against her, or by some manner of composition with a show of saving her honour. The first, I think, will hardly be attempted for two causes: the one, for that, if her adverse party accuse her of the murder by producing her letters, she will deny them, and accuse most of them of manifest consent to the murder, hardly to be denied, so as, upon trial on both sides, her proofs will judicially fall best out, as it is thought. I think the best in all respects for the Queen's

Majesty [Elizabeth], if Moray will produce such matter [privately] as the Queen's Majesty may find the Scotch Queen guilty of the murder of her husband, and therewith detain her in England at the charges of Scotland.[29]

The only realistic choice was for 'the matter to be huddled up with a show of saving her honour'.[30] Sussex undoubtedly believed that Darnley's murder was a conspiracy arranged by the Scottish nobility, and the testimony was unlikely to stand up to examination. If Elizabeth wanted Mary to remain imprisoned, then her guilt needed to be implied without a public trial. Mary should not attend the conference in London as she would refute the evidence. It was preferable for Elizabeth to deal with matters quietly in a show of shielding Mary's honour. Cecil agreed with him and arranged the outcome pretty much as Sussex had proposed. Sussex believed that, if Mary confirmed Moray as regent, he could be persuaded to withdraw his accusations and repeal the parliamentary acts declaring her guilty of Darnley's murder.

On reaching London, the Scottish commissioners' principal concern was to be assured of their continued control of the regency. As Mary had accused Moray of complicity in the murder, Herries and his Marian colleagues argued that control should pass to Châtelherault, James's presumptive heir, who had reached London after returning from exile in France. Moray's allies retorted that he had been properly nominated by Parliament. He was anxious to avoid being absent from Scotland for a lengthy period and sought a speedy conclusion to assure his continued authority.

Mary was initially enthusiastic that the conference would be reconvened at Westminster. She believed that Elizabeth's review of the findings at York could only be helpful. On 17 October, she wrote to Cassillis of these 'good proceedings'.[31] Elizabeth, however, followed Sussex's advice by telling her that her presence was unnecessary, as she had no case to answer, but her commissioners would be invited.

By now, Elizabeth was closely sided with Cecil on how to deal with Mary, whatever she might say for public consumption. She wanted her under house arrest in England, despite knowing that the evidence was fraudulent. On 24 October, Cecil reported that she did not want Mary's credit to be advanced by marriage to Norfolk. He knew that Elizabeth disapproved and was aware that she regarded Bothwell's continued existence as a safeguard. This explains why Cecil wanted to remove Norfolk from controlling the process at York. There was little in his handling to have caused complaint.

Cecil carefully prepared the ground for the reconvened conference. On 30 October, to persuade Moray to produce his evidence, Elizabeth authorised the Council to confirm that Mary would not be returned to the Scottish throne if found guilty. It was agreed that she would be moved to Tutbury, an ancient motte and bailey castle near Burton-upon-Trent. The outcome was already prejudged. On 21 November, Cecil wrote himself another memorandum, confirming that 'the best way for England, but not the easiest, was for Mary to remain deprived of the crown and the state to continue as it is'.[32]

Although Elizabeth remained at Hampton Court at a tactical distance from Westminster, she met with each of the parties beforehand. She assured the Bishop of Ross and Gavin Hamilton of her desire to see 'some good end'. She then met with Maitland and MacGill, who came on behalf of the Scottish commissioners to confirm the Council's agreement that, 'if it may certainly appear to Her Majesty and her Council that the said Queen was guilty, then Her Majesty will never restore her to the crown of Scotland but will make it manifest to the world what she thinketh of the cause'.[33] The Bishop warned Mary that she would let Moray and his colleagues say 'all they could to your dishonour'. She would not pass judgement, but would 'transport you up in the country and retain you there till she thinks time to show you favour, which is not likely to be hastily, because of the fear that she has herself of your being her unfriend'.[34] Despite being assured that the adjournment had been arranged so that 'her restitution may be devised with surety to the Prince her son and the nobility that have adhered to him', Mary's optimism evaporated.[35]

On 13 November, Elizabeth received Moray privately at Hampton Court. She reconfirmed that if the evidence were found to be genuine, Mary would be handed over to the Confederates with assurances for her safety, or else she would be kept under house arrest in England. She would also recognise him as regent. He now felt able to charge Mary with complicity in Darnley's murder. When Mary heard of this private audience, she told her commissioners to complain at her lack of similar treatment. If Elizabeth would not permit her to appear before the English nobility and foreign ambassadors to answer all that 'may or can be alleged against us by the calumnies of our rebels', they must 'break the Conference and proceed no further therein'.[36] She was stunned that, despite Elizabeth's earlier assurances, she would bring her to trial.

Prior to restarting the conference, Cecil and a range of senior Privy Councillors were appointed as additional English commissioners. With most being Protestant and hostile to Mary, this moved the balance in Moray's favour. Although Thomas Percy, 7th Earl of Northumberland, and Charles Neville, 12th Earl of Westmoreland, both Catholic, were appointed, they had insufficient time to travel from the north. At the outset on 25 November, the Bishop of Ross declared that Mary, as a sovereign princess, would not be bound by any judgement, but he was given assurance that this was not a judicial review. The commissioners then met Moray privately, explaining that, after his evidence had been presented, they would report their views to Elizabeth, who would pronounce what she thought to be true. They reconfirmed that, if Mary were found guilty, Elizabeth would recognise James as king and Moray as regent.

On the following day Moray presented his 'Eik' as an 'amplification of his accusations'. He implied that he had previously delayed producing it in order to protect Mary's honour. He stated unequivocally 'that as Bothwell was the chief executor, so was the Queen of the foreknowledge, counsel, and devise, persuader and commander of the same murder to be done'.[37] After breaking for the weekend, the commissioners stayed at Hampton Court, although the Eik's content was not discussed with Elizabeth. On the Monday, Moray repeated it. A written copy was provided for Mary's commissioners, who withdrew to discuss it, but returned to say that they needed time to consider their answer. Nevertheless, they thought it strange that he and his colleagues should make such accusations in writing against their queen, who had always been so generous to them. At this point, Lennox appeared in defiance of Elizabeth's orders, and submitted 'in writing, briefly but rudely, some part of such matter [against Mary] as he conceived to be true, for the charging of the Queen of Scots with the murder of his son'.[38] With the English commissioners looking for a far cosier solution, this annoyed everyone.

On the next day, Mary's commissioners again asked for time to answer Moray's Eik. Mary had instructed them to seek permission for her to attend in person 'since they have free access to accuse us'. If this

216

were refused, they were to withdraw.[39] This became an ongoing bone of contention. Both Herries and Leslie again protested that Mary had a right to defend herself. Herries then claimed that the lords had rebelled to stop Mary from revoking grants made before her twenty-fifth birthday, not because of Darnley's murder, and that some of them had themselves signed bonds to arrange it, but he could say no more without authority.

On Thursday 2 December, some of the English commissioners visited Elizabeth at Hampton Court, returning with a summons for Mary's commissioners to attend Elizabeth on the next day. On arrival, they repeated their protest that Mary should be permitted to attend, but Elizabeth did not want her to be able to refute the evidence being presented. She promised an answer the following day, when she accepted that it was 'very reasonable that [Mary] should be heard in her own cause, but was insistent, for the better satisfaction of herself' that Moray's evidence should be presented first and she needed to confer with the Scottish commissioners. On the same day, she told the English commissioners and the Privy Council that she would not receive Mary so long as she remained accused.

Herries and the Bishop of Ross were now so pessimistic that they asked for a second audience with Elizabeth without having Mary's authority, proposing a compromise to limit further damage to Mary's reputation. As they saw it, there were only three acceptable outcomes: firstly, Mary could ratify her abdication, living in retirement in England; secondly, she could rule Scotland jointly with James, but with Moray retaining the regency; and thirdly, she could remain as queen of Scotland, but live in England, while Moray acted a regent in her name. Elizabeth knew that Moray would reject the latter two courses and did not want a compromise. She argued that, as Moray had levelled charges, Mary needed to defend herself. A compromise would be interpreted as proof of her guilt. She explained that Moray's evidence should be scrutinised so that, when seen to be unfounded, he and his colleagues could be punished for 'so audaciously defaming' her. However, as Mary was determined to defend herself only before Elizabeth, the danger remained that she would show up the shortcomings in the evidence. Elizabeth told Herries and the Bishop of Ross that she did not believe Mary's honour to be sufficiently at risk to require her attendance in person, and it would be degrading for her to have to deny the charges publicly. When Herries and the bishop made a final request for Mary's attendance, she flatly refused.

When the conference reconvened on 6 December, Mary's commissioners followed her instructions by withdrawing. Although this should have brought proceedings to an end, Cecil claimed that their departure was not in accordance with the terms agreed. Although Moray would continue providing evidence, they could no longer hear it or receive a record of the proceedings, despite being required to remain at Westminster. With Mary's commissioners sidelined, Sir Nicholas Bacon told Moray that Elizabeth saw it as strange that he should accuse their sovereign of 'so horrible a crime' and he demanded the evidence. With a show of great reluctance, Moray now started to present his documentation. He tabled Buchanan's *Book of Articles*, the December 1567 Act of Parliament confirming Mary's abdication, the depositions of key witnesses, and Lennox's *Narrative*. The *Book of Articles* was retained but was read out on the following morning. In an attempt to avoid having to produce the Casket Letters, Moray then asked whether the English commissioners were satisfied of Mary's guilt, but they would offer no opinion. Believing that they needed more evidence, Moray tabled the two marriage contracts, the evidence of Bothwell's trial and acquittal and, finally, the silver casket containing Casket Letters I and II. On the next day, he tabled the remaining Casket Letters and the love poem, all in French, with a journal setting out the events from James's birth to the Battle of Langside, and depositions from four of Bothwell's henchmen, all now deceased. Both Crawford and Nelson arrived to confirm revised versions of their earlier testimonies. The Scottish commissioners then swore on oath that the Casket Letters were 'undoubtedly' in Mary's hand. After arranging for copies to be made, the English commissioners returned the originals to Moray, but made no comment on them. On 9 December, Mary's commissioners again protested that the conference was a travesty of justice and demanded the arrest of those accusing her. When this was refused, they again withdrew.

Elizabeth was having cold feet. Her limited objective was to protect herself by keeping Mary under house arrest, leaving open the possibility of her future return to the Scottish throne. She had to be seen to be even handed, and Moray's revelations, if not rebuffed, would preclude this. She could not be seen to condone a fix and believed that the Casket Letters had been manipulated. She suspended the conference for a second time. Believing in safety in numbers, she added all her remaining Privy Councillors, together with George Talbot 6th Earl of Shrewsbury and Huntingdon, as commissioners. She then confirmed that she would personally supervise a two-day meeting at Hampton Court, starting on 14 December.

When the conference reconvened, Cecil again took the minutes, and recorded:

> There were produced sundry letters written in French supposed to be written in the Queen of Scots' own hand to the Earl of Bothwell. Of which letters, the originals ... were then also presently produced and perused, and being read, were duly conferred and compared for the manner of writing and fashion of orthography with sundry other letters long since heretofore written and sent by the said Queen of Scots to the Queen's Majesty. And next after these was produced and read a declaration of the Earl of Morton, of the manner of the finding of the said letters, as the same was exhibited on his oath of the 9 December.[40] In collation whereof no difference was found.[41]

Although Cecil was implying that the handwriting test was passed, he was only saying that the letters reviewed were the same as on the list collated by Morton. An exhaustive handwriting check could not of course have been done that quickly, and the Bishop of Ross quite rightly protested that a handwriting comparison constituted no legal proof of Mary having written the letters. It is unlikely that her 'scribbled' hand from Glasgow would have been remotely comparable to her carefully crafted formal letters to a fellow queen.

Elizabeth expressed shock, declaring that the letters 'contained many matters unmeet to be repeated before honest ears, and easily drawn to be apparent proof against the Queen'.[42] Yet she was not saying that she thought them genuine, and they did not meet her limited objective. Cecil's minutes confirmed that Mary's guilt was 'upon things now produced made more apparent, and they could not allow it as meet for Her Majesty's honour to admit the said Queen to Her Majesty's presence, as the case now did stand'.[43] De Silva hinted that the commissioners were not unanimous and sought to control 'the unseemly violence of Cecil's attitude towards the Queen of Scots'.[44]

None of the English commissioners, and certainly not Norfolk, appeared to take the Casket Letters seriously, and Maitland was not called to give evidence. It can be concluded that they were seen as a carefully constructed ploy to justify maintaining Mary, somewhat tarnished in reputation, in detention. When Mary learned what had happened, she again wrote to Elizabeth demanding permission to attend personally. Although this was again refused, Elizabeth warned Moray that the proceedings could only continue if Mary would depute someone to answer the charges against her or would speak to a deputation that she sent. Mary reiterated that she would only answer to her face.

Elizabeth now ended the conference without conclusions being reached. Mary was not found guilty and Elizabeth 'saw no cause to conceive an ill opinion of her good sister of Scotland'. Nor was she found innocent, and to the world at large she remained tainted with suspicion. The matter was 'huddled up' exactly as Sussex had proposed. While Moray could return to Scotland and privately received £5,000 from Elizabeth to help him to defeat Mary's supporters there, she remained incarcerated at Bolton. The commissioners were sworn to secrecy, and the evidence was not made public. Elizabeth retained a hold over Scotland and could restore Mary whenever she wished. This kept the Scottish government closely aligned to English foreign policy.

Moray was anxious to return to Scotland to settle disorder, which had arisen in his absence. With Mary unlikely to offer a defence, Cecil told him that he could go, but might need to return to deal with Mary's 'answers to such things as have been alleged against her'.[45] When Mary heard this, she told her commissioners to charge him and his allies with their part in the king's murder. They advised Cecil of this in Moray's presence, although they were still awaiting copies of 'the pretended writings given in against their mistress'.[46] Cecil would not let Mary see the evidence, but Moray was required to stay until 19 January, when, at a farewell audience, Elizabeth promised to maintain him as regent.

Elizabeth worried that Mary's refusal to offer a defence made the conference proceedings illegal. Either Mary had to be persuaded to do so, but preferably not in public, or she should confirm her abdication. Even Herries and the Bishop of Ross urged Mary to defend herself, arguing that failing to do so might be seen as an admission of guilt. Mary ignored them, refusing to 'answer otherwise than in person' before Elizabeth. She demanded copies of the evidence, with the originals to be shown to her commissioners. She would then meet Elizabeth so 'that our innocence shall be known to our good sister, and to all other princes'.[47] For Elizabeth and Cecil the important issue was not Mary's guilt, it was England's security, but her detention needed to stand up to legal scrutiny.

In the meantime, Mary belatedly drew up charges against Moray, declaring that he had, 'falsely, traitoriously and miscreantly lied, imputing to us the crime whereof they themselves are authors, inventors, doers and executors'. By now the English commissioners had closed ranks behind Elizabeth, convinced by the soundness of Moray's case against Mary. This belies disquiet behind the scenes, and it cannot have been what Norfolk wanted. On 4 January, Henry FitzAlan, 12th Earl of Arundel advised Elizabeth that one sovereign could not tell another to leave her crown simply because her subjects would not obey her. 'It may be a new doctrine in Scotland, but it is not good to be taught in England.'[48] Elizabeth, though, had made up her mind.

On 5 January 1569, Mary asked Huntly and Argyll to confirm a written record that she had prepared of events at Craigmillar two years before. It stated that: '[With regard to] the murder of the said Henry Stuart following, we judge in our consciences that the said Earl of Moray and Secretary Lethington were authors, inventors, devisers, counsellors, and causers of the said murder, in what manner or by whatsoever persons the same was executed.'[49] This was sent for their signature, but was intercepted by English spies before reaching them. Even so, as they had signed the Craigmillar bond, they might not have agreed. Mary also persuaded the French ambassador to ask Elizabeth to furnish her commissioners with copies of the evidence. Elizabeth promised to deliver everything the following day but failed to do so. When she again sought Mary's abdication, Mary confirmed: 'My last breath shall be that of a Queen.'[50] Mary realised that the English had colluded with Moray and wrote plaintively to Mar to guard James well and not to let him out of his control without her express permission. She wrote bitterly to Elizabeth at her treatment. She had come to England seeking support to be revenged on her rebels and to recover her honour. She had regarded Elizabeth as her 'nearest kinswoman and perfect friend', but now realised that she had been mistaken and Cecil was an implacable protagonist. Despite her demand for permission to return to Scotland, Cecil would not agree.

With negotiations having failed, Mary's commissioners retired to Scotland. On 8 January, Mary wrote to Philip II, protesting her innocence and seeking his help: 'I am deprived of my liberty and closely guarded.'[51] She instructed her secretaries: 'Tell the ambassador, if his master will help me, I shall be Queen of England in three months, and the Mass shall be said all over the country.'[52] She needed the support of 10,000 men from France and Spain and hoped for English Catholic support. Yet Philip feared that, if Mary gained the English throne, she would inevitably ally with France.

Mary now donned a mantle as 'an obedient, submissive and devoted daughter of the holy Catholic and Roman church, in the faith of which I will live and die'.[53] In May 1569, the Bishop of Ross published a pamphlet in France, entitled *The defence of the honour of Queen Mary*, to refute Buchanan's *Book of Articles*. No longer was she the advocate of religious tolerance, but a Catholic icon spearheading an English Counter-Reformation. She wanted the English throne; restoration in Scotland would follow. Norfolk began a secret and affectionate correspondence with her. He sent a diamond and they were secretly betrothed. She was now moved from the relative comfort of Bolton to Shrewsbury's supervision at draughty Tutbury. She was never to regain her freedom. She was losing her lustre, was unwell, depressed, stooped and prematurely aged, needing wigs to cover her greying and thinning hair.

Chapter 22

A last hurrah for the Marian cause

Although Mary continued to be cherished by an intimate circle of Scottish courtiers, including the Flemings, Livingstons, Setons and Bethunes, they could offer little political or military support. Many of them had faced attainder, and Seton had been forced to escape to Holland, where he reputedly scratched a living as a wagoner. Despite this, the Marians had grown in numbers and 'run riot in [Moray's] absence'.[1] They now included Argyll, Mary's brother-in-law, Atholl, Huntly, Cassillis, Herries, Boyd, Kirkcaldy, the Bishop of Ross and several Border lairds. With Mary Fleming being Atholl's sister-in-law, Maitland joined their fold on his return to Scotland and became their spokesman in the Scottish Parliament. He also attracted support from the Hamiltons and Gordons, whose primary objective was to destroy Moray, but were also attracted by the opportunity to offer Mary much needed political guidance. Together with Argyll and Atholl, the Hamiltons and Gordons transformed the Marians into a force to be reckoned with. Despite their lack of cohesion, they controlled north and west Scotland with troops which collectively outnumbered those of the regency. Nevertheless, on Moray's return, he took immediate steps to reassert control. On 12 February 1569, he called a convention at Stirling to approve the actions he had taken at the conferences. With his financial support from Elizabeth, he mustered an army at Glasgow to 'overaw' the Marian rebels, who immediately sued for peace. They agreed to recognise his regency in return for the cancellation of their forfeitures.

As a sop to the foreign ambassadors, Elizabeth paid lip service to Mary's restoration. She needed to be seen to treat her in a manner acceptable to both Spanish and French interests. Despite giving assurances to both Cecil and Moray that she would retain her in England, she wanted to diffuse English and Continental Catholic dissent and to end the cost, political embarrassment and anxiety of retaining her under house arrest. She now referred to Mary as 'the daughter of debate that eke discord doth sow'.[2]

In April, she approached Moray with a choice of three 'degrees' to establish Mary's future: firstly, for her to reaffirm her abdication; secondly, to grant her joint sovereignty with James; and thirdly, to grant her full sovereignty, but safeguarding the interests of her regency allies.[3] Moray did not reply immediately – he was probably awaiting Cecil's advice – but then he came out firmly in favour of Mary reaffirming her abdication. To reinforce this, on 13 May he again accused her of complicity in Darnley's murder. This caused irretrievable enmity with the Marians. When Châtelherault and Herries refused to acknowledge James as king, they were imprisoned in Edinburgh Castle. Although Elizabeth made a show of fury at Moray's refusal to repatriate Mary, she had no real desire or expectation that he would agree and saw his regency as the means of providing Scotland with assured Protestant government.

The more difficult issue was the prospect of Mary's marriage to Norfolk, which was made more complicated because Elizabeth, officially at least, was not aware of the proposal, and it was uncertain how she would react to it. Initially Moray had concluded that she favoured the plan as a convenient means of resolving Mary's continued detention. When he showed signs of supporting it, Maitland gave him his wholehearted backing. It was only when Elizabeth's opposition became clear that he changed his tune. He did not want Mary linked to such a powerful magnate as Norfolk, who would inevitably seek to dominate Scottish government. His changing view may have been coloured by an attempt on his life by a Norfolk supporter as he travelled from London. This left him sufficiently alarmed not to voice his disapproval, and he failed to warn either Elizabeth or Cecil of the negotiations for the marriage taking place behind their backs.

To open the way for her marriage to Norfolk, Mary asked Moray 'to submit to the courts her demand for a legal divorce from Bothwell'.[4] On 28 July, Moray called a convention of the nobles at Perth, during which Maitland attempted 'to traffic for the Queen's return to Scotland' by supporting the divorce submission. With Moray's allies closing ranks behind him, her divorce was refused by a majority of forty votes to nine. It was the first time that Maitland had openly opposed Moray. At the beginning of September, when he attended a commission at Stirling, Crawford went down on one knee and, in a carefully orchestrated plan, accused Maitland of being of the 'counsel, device, and execution of the late King's murder'.[5]

Maitland was arrested and found himself with Châtelherault and Herries in Edinburgh Castle under the supervision of Kirkcaldy, whose loyalty Moray still trusted. Although Maitland was beginning to suffer from paralysis in his legs, this did not prevent him from continuing to work for Mary's restoration, but 'with his life in imminent danger, he began with increased activity to organise a party for his own security'. When he came to trial, Mary appealed from Tutbury for him to be protected, and Marians appeared in great numbers. In the face of a threatened riot, Moray thought better of pursuing the charges against him. Maitland knew too much, and, on 9 September, Kirkcaldy helped him escape. A month later, they met at Kelso, after which Maitland confirmed secretly to Mary that Kirkcaldy was holding Edinburgh Castle on her behalf. This defection greatly disappointed the regency.

Kirkcaldy and Herries shared Maitland's view that, with Mary separated from Bothwell, she should be restored to her throne. Maitland argued that her marriage to Norfolk would find favour with Elizabeth, who was still giving every impression of wanting her restored to the Scottish throne, albeit with her authority limited. He knew only too well that the evidence of her approval of Darnley's murder was false. Whether Mary Fleming knew the devious part he had played is difficult to judge, but certainly he felt contrition. It might prove a futile gesture, but his final roll of the dice on Mary's behalf was to promote her marriage to Norfolk as a demonstration of loyalty as much from himself as from his wife.

Although the English Parliament saw Mary as a 'monstrous dragon', Elizabeth was shaken to find her gaining support among the patrician and more Catholic-orientated wing of the English nobility. Maitland's confirmation to Norfolk of her innocence was now widely circulated. This 'Conservative' group backed Mary's marriage to Norfolk and her restoration to her Scottish throne. Despite Mary's perceived shortcomings. the Catholic powers saw her as their chief weapon to restore papacy, but realised that her rehabilitation would need the approval of Elizabeth, who was now being seen as the 'great bulwark of the reformed cause, and the patron of heresy and rebellion in their own dominions'.[6]

Elizabeth now faced a schism within her Council. With his stranglehold on government, Cecil had been striking out boldly to injure and humiliate Catholic powers on the Continent, fearing that England would be their next target. He licenced piracy, authorised the seizure of Spanish treasure, and provided supplies to Huguenot and Dutch rebels. With support for him dwindling, Norfolk's allies sought peace with Spain and wanted the captured Spanish booty to be restored as a precondition to a new alliance. Norfolk gained Spanish and French support to lead a plot aimed at Cecil's downfall and at ending the dispute over the succession by nominating Mary as Elizabeth's heir. As an anointed queen, Mary had never accepted Elizabeth's right to detain her and had not been found guilty of any wrongdoing. The scandals that had surrounded her in Scotland, whether true or false, would soon be forgotten. She would condone any realistic plot for her liberation, perhaps by gaining support from Philip II or Charles IX.

Although Elizabeth remained officially unaware of Mary's proposed marriage to Norfolk, she knew that it would reinforce Mary's claim to the English throne and could only view it as a Catholic threat. She steadfastly backed Cecil to enable him to weather the political storm. Cecil was also horrified at the marriage proposal, which would threaten his position as Secretary of State, but he decided to play along with the plan, knowing that Elizabeth opposed it. He thus cast himself in the role of conciliator in the hope of establishing more detail but had to warn Elizabeth that the marriage of itself would not amount to treason.

In September, Moray at last warned Elizabeth and Cecil of Norfolk's plan to marry Mary. Despite the progress made by Maitland and the Marians, they would need assistance from Norfolk and his allies to achieve Mary's repatriation, but Elizabeth's and Cecil's opposition made this increasingly unlikely. Maitland's diplomacy in promoting the marriage plan had simply placed both Mary and Norfolk in great danger. Although Elizabeth dined with Norfolk to establish his intentions, he admitted nothing. Nevertheless, his allies were already contemplating a full-scale rebellion to be led by Northumberland and Westmoreland. Leicester, who had initially supported Norfolk as the means of reducing Cecil's authority, broke ranks and confided in Cecil, who advised him to confess to Elizabeth everything he knew. Leicester begged her for forgiveness. When she summoned Norfolk to court, he feigned illness, escaping to East Anglia to raise troops. On finding the ports closed, he was unable to contact the Duke of Alva, commanding the Spanish forces in the Low Countries. When told to appear at Windsor, he again pleaded illness, but was instructed to come by litter. Taking a cue from Moray's treatment of Maitland, on 11 October, Elizabeth sent Norfolk to the Tower. Mary's apartments at Wingfield were searched by men armed with pistols, and she was returned to Tutbury. When the Bishop of Ross was interrogated, he assured Elizabeth that Mary had not signed a marriage contract with Norfolk and only wanted to do what she desired. Elizabeth blamed Moray for not keeping her better informed. He now divulged all he knew, claiming, justifiably, that he realised she would turn the marriage proposal down on hearing of it and did not want to face further risk by openly opposing it.

Norfolk sent a belated message to Westmoreland from the Tower, warning him not to stir, but the 'Northern Rising' was on the move. Northumberland and Westmoreland marched south, intent on rescuing Mary from Tutbury and on having Cecil dismissed. With Yorkshire failing to provide its expected support, everywhere further south held solidly for Elizabeth. Most English Catholics would back their Protestant anointed queen rather than a crusading Catholic army with overseas backing to support Mary. When she was moved south to the relative distance of Coventry, the rebels were forced to retreat. They were chased by an army under Sussex, which scattered their followers, driving their leaders into Scotland. Moray, who was waiting with 5,000 men, arrested Northumberland, holding him at Lochleven, but Westmoreland and Lady Northumberland escaped to the Continent, hoping to raise money from Alva and the papacy. Those captured were severely treated, with 600 being hanged.

Elizabeth had been thoroughly rattled and was excommunicated by Pope Pius V. She had to decide how to deal with Norfolk, who hotly denied any involvement, and it is most uncertain that either he or Mary approved of the rising. Despite exhaustive investigation, Cecil had no evidence against them, and the Bishop of Ross testified that Mary tried to prevent it. In August, Norfolk was released into a loose form of house arrest, after undertaking never to deal in the marriage again. This did not prevent him from continuing his correspondence and exchanges of gifts with Mary, causing her to be 'deeply compromised'.[7]

The Hamiltons blamed Moray for Mary's undoing. On 23 January 1570, they arranged his assassination in the streets of Linlithgow. Mary wrote to Archbishop Bethune in Paris 'expressing her indebtedness to the assassin, all the greater, she said, that he had done the deed without instructions from her and promising him a pension from her dowry to support him in his compulsory exile'.[8] Although Maitland strongly disapproved of the murder, he did not support those seeking to avenge it, arguing that Moray had 'sought his own life, fame and inheritance'.[9] He also opposed resultant efforts to secure Mary's permanent deposition. 'He was impelled by ... a very cordial dislike to the policy of the Protestant party, which he regarded as narrow and divisive, and subversive of the ancient social and political order.'[10]

With Moray dead, Maitland wrote to Cecil hoping to be recognised as the leader of Scottish affairs. He was still officially Secretary of State but was only nominally part of the regency government. After playing on their longstanding friendship, he sought Elizabeth's help to effect a reconciliation between Mary and the Scottish nobility. Cecil, who had no time for his 'pretentions', did not respond. He was well-aware of his underhand scheming for the Norfolk marriage and his suspected sympathy for Moray's assassins. Both Cecil and Elizabeth recognised that English security depended on the maintenance of a Protestant regency. After hearing rumours of a Spanish invasion from the Low Countries to support the Marians, they wanted them brought to heel.

Maitland was carried away with his belief in his ability to coerce and conciliate the Scottish nobility into supporting their queen, regardless of their religious affiliation, and was 'misled by his own aristocratic bias'.[11] He wanted Mary restored, albeit in a titular capacity. This was a futile ambition. Although he remained committed to his 'lifelong zeal for the union of the two realms, and for the English succession as the way to it', he had long ago concluded that Mary, as a determined Catholic, would not enable this, but that was not grounds for her deposition.[12] He had only to wait for the young king, being brought up as a Protestant, to take power for the achievement of his objectives of union. Mary Fleming's influence is obvious, but it was more than this. He could not say so, but he did not want Mary left incarcerated when the evidence against her had been falsified, largely by himself. He was lucky that his underhand plan to implicate her in her husband's murder had not leaked beyond Moray, Morton, Balfour and Cecil.

Moray's death caused great distress in both England and Scotland. Although Morton was his natural successor, 'his character and career had not won for him anything like the same respect and confidence, even within his own party ... He was everywhere more regarded than loved.'[13] By resolutely opposing Mary's restoration, he now became Maitland's formidable enemy. Although each knew the other's part in Darnley's murder, Morton was determined to secure the regency for James and believed that Mary's restoration would risk everything. He had support from Knox and the Kirk, and the backing of the barons, lairds and burgesses of the towns. He made every effort to conciliate with the Marians, releasing Châtelherault and Herries from Edinburgh Castle. Even Maitland was 'purged of the privitie to the murder of the king or regent'. This left him sufficiently secure to rejoin Atholl in Perthshire as the acknowledged Marian spokesman.

If Elizabeth had been prepared to recognise James as her heir, Maitland would have supported her, but as we have seen, she would not do this. It would signal to France and Spain that she had condoned Moray's rebellion. Nevertheless, her indecisive approach encouraged the Marians to lobby for Mary's release. Maitland continued to argue that Mary had support from the English nobility, and Elizabeth needed an excuse to free her. By using delaying tactics to thwart the appointment of a new regent, Scotland was left without legal government. This bought time for him to gain French support. With Moray dead, he had brokered Argyll's return to the Marian fold by ending his long-running feud with Atholl, and linking up with the Hamiltons, Boyd and later Huntly in Glasgow. Kirkcaldy continued to control Edinburgh Castle. If the Marians solicited help from France, or from Alva in the Low Countries, and retained control of Dumbarton, an invasion force could be landed in the Clyde.

Elizabeth's principal objectives were to hold the Scottish nobility together, to retain their Reformation, and to avoid James being sent to France. She confined the Bishop of Ross in London and called for the repatriation of the rebel leaders of the Northern Rising. Morton and five other Protestant lords formed a provisional council to govern Scotland until a regent was appointed. They confirmed their continued adherence to Moray's policies and undertook to seek Elizabeth's approval before a new regent was chosen. When Randolph came north, they pressed him to seek Elizabeth's support. With Mar seeking English protection for James, she recognised her need to back them, but did not want this publicly known. Despite their erstwhile friendship, Randolph waited a month before visiting Maitland at Lethington, but found him bedridden and sadly broken: 'His legs clean gone, his body so weak that it sustained not itself, his inward parts so feeble that to endure to sneeze he could not, for annoying the whole body, only his heart whole and stomach good. To this the blessed joy of a young wife hath brought him.'[14] Maitland needed a litter but remained mentally alert. Randolph had to explain that his former friends in London strongly disapproved of him breaking faith with Moray.

Under Maitland's influence, the Marians fought on determinedly. This made him the butt of regency propaganda, of which Buchanan's *Chameleon* is the best known. He called a convention of supporters to meet at Linlithgow on 9 and 10 April, which was attended by Huntly and Atholl, along with Westmoreland and other English rebels. Maitland even invited Morton and the regency supporters to attend, but they refused. The French envoy, Verac, came with promises of men and money. The attendees signed a letter seeking Elizabeth's assurance of support for Mary's restoration. To try to prevent an English incursion into Scotland, they were carrying out nightly raids across the English border with as many as 4,000 men, who included English rebels being sheltered after the Northern Rising. Elizabeth now had a clear motive for supporting the regency party. With Morton and his allies being outnumbered, they needed her help, but she was still weighing up her desire to invade Scotland against the threat of French or Spanish intervention. It became a race against time. The Marians moved to Edinburgh to challenge Morton's authority. On 8 May, they proclaimed Mary as queen, though Maitland insisted on James being protected, as he was now the key to the union. On hearing of this support for Mary, Morton arranged for James to be 'vehemently' proclaimed.

Following a convention of the regency party in Edinburgh on 1 May, Robert Pitcairn, Commendator of Dunfermline, who was now acting as their Secretary of State, came to Elizabeth in London to gain her undertaking to provide support for the king. He reaffirmed that they would seek her confirmation before appointing a new regent. On 29 April, despite Elizabeth's continued concern that it would trigger French and Spanish intervention, the Privy Council in London secretly confirmed financial and military aid for the regency party and instructed Sussex to lead a punitive expedition into Scotland.

On reaching Berwick, Sussex announced that he was 'entirely friendly to all but the English rebels and their predatory allies, who disturbed the peace in both countries'.[15] Maitland warned that, if he crossed the border, he would face Marian opposition supported from overseas, and Elizabeth would be better occupied 'in peaceful mediation'.[16] Sussex paid no attention. On 17 April, having divided his forces into three groups spread across the border, he sent the English wardens into Scotland. They took 'dire revenge' for Marian incursions, levelling 'ninety strong castles, towers, and dwelling houses' including Ferniehirst and Buccleuch, and garrisoned Home and Fast Castles, which were found deserted. They then destroyed 'three hundred towns and villages' in rebel areas.[17]

On 11 May, Sussex sent Drury to Edinburgh with 1,000 men to join Morton's allies, who had raised a larger force, to end border incursions and bring the Hamiltons and their allies to book. Although the Marians challenged Morton, hoping to overwhelm him before Drury's arrival, Sussex sent them a warning not to attack the friends of England. Although he demanded Maitland as a hostage, this was refused, and Maitland took refuge in the castle.

Lennox came with a second English force, which gained control of Glasgow. When Châtelherault left Linlithgow to challenge him, his well-armed force was again dispersed by Drury, who appeared at Stirling. With Drury having destroyed the town of Hamilton and Châtelherault's properties at Cadzow, Kinneil and Linlithgow, Lennox asked him to bring artillery from Berwick to take Dumbarton, but, fearing Continental reprisals, Elizabeth vetoed the plan.

With Maitland being seen by Sussex as a 'traitor to all he dealt with', he left for Blair Atholl, foiled and discredited.[18] On 2 June, when Elizabeth believed that the 'rebel' Marians were 'reasonably chastised', Drury was instructed to withdraw to Berwick having decisively re-established regency authority. With the Marians permanently damaged, Morton called for English guns to take Edinburgh Castle.

From imprisonment, Mary complained to France. The French ambassador in London, Bertrand Salignac de la Mothe Fénélon, demanded her restoration, threatening to send a French force to the Marians' aid. (It is an amusing aside that Maitland called for the French to be led by Henry de Valois 'Le bâtard d'Angouleme', who was Mary Fleming's half-brother, arising from her mother's misalliance with Henry II. Maitland believed that his 'Scottish provenance would offset the popular revulsion against French intervention'.)[19]

Having come to a truce with the Huguenots, Catherine de Medici had now dispensed with Guisian advice. This relaxed pressure on the French government to support Mary's restoration. They made no plans to send troops to Scotland, despite continuing to deliver supplies to Dumbarton, but any hint of a threat from France was enough to deter Elizabeth. She released the Bishop of Ross after three months' confinement and agreed to send an envoy to Scotland to discuss Mary's restoration. Sussex and Randolph tried to resign in fury. Maitland concluded that Elizabeth 'was inconstant, unresolved and fearfull', but her vacillation allowed his standing with the Marians to be restored.[20] Nevertheless, she had no real intention of restoring Mary and sent Cecil, who would never agree to it, as her negotiator.

Despite Maitland's incapacity, he remained the Marians' chief spokesman. His kinship through his wife with many of the Marian supporters was a strong and binding influence in what was not a naturally cohesive group. In a lengthy correspondence with Sussex, he complained at Mary's continued imprisonment. Sussex responded that she was maintained in state and enjoyed much personal liberty, and that Maitland was being hypocritical as he had played a significant part in arranging her imprisonment and deposition in Scotland. Maitland replied that a statesman had a right to change his mind and he had never sought her 'destruction' nor 'ill to her person'.[21] While imprisonment for a few days, or 'a season', might be reasonable, 'seven years' or a lifetime was not. He had encouraged Moray to conciliate with her, but his death had caused him to change his attitude.

With the Protestant lords needing to appoint a regent, they ultimately proposed Lennox. Having arrived in Scotland in support of his grandson, he had helped his own cause. Morton continued to lack universal support, despite being head of the Douglas clan and the regency's most powerful figure. Elizabeth accepted Lennox (although according to Russell, she would have preferred Morton), and he was elected on 13 July 1570. This did not prove popular with the Marians. 'The selection of this angry, old man was always more likely to antagonise than to conciliate.'[22] Kirkcaldy refused to attend his instalation or to fire a salute from the castle guns. Despite lacking political acumen, Lennox acted forcibly, with constant support from the burghs, and sought Elizabeth's help to take Edinburgh and Dumbarton castles. When the Marians attempted to call their own Parliament at Linlithgow to discuss an alliance with the Spanish, they were refused entry to the town, and the meeting had to be moved closer to Maitland at Dunkeld.

With the regency now firmly in control, it would not accept Mary's restoration on any terms, but Elizabeth failed to provide Lennox with support, forcing him to battle on unassisted. Pitcairn's appointment to replace Maitland as Secretary of State was formally confirmed, and Buchanan agreed to supervise the four-year-old James's education. He also wrote his *Chameleon* to depict Maitland as a traitor to the Protestant lords. Although this was not published until 1710, it was circulated in manuscript.

Lennox's first decisive blow was to send Darnley's former ally, Crawford of Jordonhill, to capture Dumbarton Castle. This involved a plan of 'unparallelled daring' using 100 picked men. On 2 April 1571, they used ropes to scale the rock in a heavy mist carrying their harquebuses with ladders strung between. They clambered over the wall at a point considered inaccessible and captured the guns before the garrison could react. Although Fleming escaped by boat, Verac, the French envoy, and Archbishop Hamilton were captured. Verac was permitted to depart for France, but the Archbishop was taken to Stirling for execution after admitting complicity in Moray's murder. The Marians' port of access for French support had now been removed.

After eluding capture, Fleming found his way into Edinburgh Castle to join Kirkcaldy, but its position as the last remaining Marian stronghold was now precarious, despite Kirkcaldy strengthening its defences. He was also joined by his son-in-law, Kerr of Ferniehirst, smarting at the loss of his ancestral stronghold to the English. With his seventy spearmen, he was deployed on diversions away from Edinburgh. This allowed Kirkcaldy to hold the castle for more than three years despite reproach from his former regency colleagues. Ferniehirst successfully gained control of the town of Edinburgh, and when Kirkcaldy brought in Châtelherault with Hamilton troops, hostile Edinburgh citizens were given six hours to leave. Many went to Leith, and even Knox departed in fear of his life, leaving Ferniehirst to be elected provost.

With Maitland realising that his days were numbered, he was determined to provide moral support for Kirkcaldy. On 11 April 1571, he was carried on a litter from Blair Atholl, his legs paralysed, his body weak and his head in need of support. After reaching Leith by ship, he was assisted into Edinburgh Castle by his brother, John (later Lord Maitland of Thirlestane). Herries and his nephew John 8th Lord Maxwell soon joined them.

Having been excluded from the capital, the regency lords held a parliament in the Canongate, outside the walls. On 14 May, this approved Maitland's attainder for his part in King Henry's murder. Not to be outdone, the Marians held a rival parliament in the Tolbooth to declare James's coronation 'null and void', although this was never likely to meet general acceptance and their forfeitures of regency supporters could not be enforced. Recognising their precarious position, Argyll, Eglinton, Cassillis, and Boyd tried in vain to persuade Maitland and Kirkcaldy to come to terms, before signing their own agreement with Morton, Mar and Glencairn. Realising which way the wind was blowing, Balfour joined them. With French support dwindling, the Marians were greatly weakened. Nevertheless, Eglinton soon returned to their camp.

Maitland and Kirkcaldy maintained their bravado. A deputation of Reformist leaders, headed by Spottiswood and Knox's deputy, Craig, arrived to tell them that holding the castle for Mary was 'an offence against god'. Maitland, who referred to Knox as a 'drytting [shitting] prophet' and describing him as an atheist, told them that they owed allegiance 'to the principals of the nobility of Scotland' at the castle, and that 'they that are in the Canongate are far inferior in rank'.[23] When Spottiswood complained at Maitland's change of allegiance, he in turn lectured them on 'resisting lawfully established authority'.[24] Spottiswood replied that the regency had 'proceeded upon an honest and constant ground' in the need to punish the murder crime and had not shifted its stance as Maitland had done.[25] As Parliament had authorised the king's coronation, the regency should be obeyed until Parliament reversed it. When Maitland disputed the 1567 Parliament's authority, Spottiswood pointed out that it was this Parliament that had confirmed the Scottish Reformation. Craig asked how Maitland, Balfour and Kirkcaldy 'could deny the King's authority, since they had been the chief instruments in erecting it and had sworn allegiance to it'.[26] If the queen were guilty of the murder, which Maitland did not deny, how could they want her to have authority to punish others for it? Maitland, for once, seems to have lost the argument, but he still complained at the queen's abdication from the throne being obtained by compulsion. This left the Reformist leaders to return to Leith having failed to make progress.

At the end of May, Elizabeth at last sent Drury back to Edinburgh to negotiate an end to hostilities. He was to seek Lennox's consent to meet Kirkcaldy and Maitland and to argue that fortifying the castle incited civil war. He was to instruct them to vacate it, but also to assess the level of English aid required to take it. Kirkcaldy for his part was continuing to make lightning forays to disrupt regency forces from concentrating on the siege. Drury's arrival heralded 'a large body of horse and foot issuing towards Leith, where Morton lay with a force ready to meet them'.[27] Morton got the better of Kirkcaldy's force, killing about thirty men and taking prisoner some 160 others, including Home and Captain James Cullen, an explosives expert, who had assisted Bothwell in Darnley's murder. Home was imprisoned at Tantallon, but Cullen was executed for his part played at Kirk o' Field, although 'to the end that [Morton] might the more freely enjoy the favour of his fair wife', with whom he now lived openly.[28]

Kirkcaldy was still hoping for French reinforcements, and Verac returned in a pinnace with 200 men ready to support the castle. When this was seized in the Firth of Forth, Verac was arrested together with its cargo and some incriminating papers. A second pinnace laden with French provisions was landed at Blackness by Kirkcaldy's brother, James, but the castle was surrounded by regency troops and his valuable cargo was again captured. At the end of August, Norfolk was caught attempting to send gold to Herries to support the castle, resulting in him being rearrested.

With the Castle's credit from Edinburgh merchants exhausted, the mercenaries supporting them were threatening mutiny for want of pay. When Seton went to France seeking aid, he was not welcomed as Catherine de Medici was negotiating a settlement with Elizabeth. He moved on to Brussels in hope of a better reception. Catherine's negativity was coloured by reports that the Spanish were planning to support the Marians with an invasion through Aberdeen, apparently arranged during Seton's visit to Alva in the Low Countries. Although probably untrue, it caused her to instruct her ambassador, du Croc, to side with the regency. The report came from Roberto Ridolfi, who, as is now known, had become Walsingham's double agent. Walsingham's objective was to make the Spanish threat seem greater than it was, but there is no plausible evidence that they had any plans to invade either Scotland or England at this time.

The two sides in Scotland remained at daggers drawn. When the regency assembled for a parliament at Stirling, from 28 August to

7 September, Kirkcaldy brought a force, under cover of darkness, to gain control of Lennox and his regency allies. When they were forced from their lodgings, Morton resisted arrest, causing enough delay for the townspeople to counterattack and drive the Marians out. During the mêlée, Lennox was treacherously shot from behind, apparently on orders from Huntly and Lord Claude Hamilton, in revenge for the execution of Archbishop Hamilton. Morton was lucky to survive unscathed. Lennox survived long enough to commend the Protestant nobles' unflinching support to the young king and to send a touching message to his wife, 'Meg'. His bleeding body made a lasting impression on the boy. His death, by Maitland's own admission, did the regency more good than harm, by ridding it of its greatest political liability. Mar, who remained James's guardian, replaced him as regent, and Elizabeth confirmed that 'no one more meet could have been chosen'.[29] 'She assured him of her intention to help them to a universal quietness by a general obedience to the King.'[30] Morton remained Lieutenant-General and, with Mar being unwell, 'held him in his pocket'.

Elizabeth's desire to settle the war in Scotland was shared by Catherine de Medici. This fitted with Catherine's decision to sign a defensive agreement with England at Blois on 19 April 1572 for protection against Spain. By holding back money and provisions, the English and French may have hoped to stifle the conflict in Scotland. It was in retaliation for Catherine's more conciliatory stance that the Guise inspired Massacre of St Bartholomew's Day was launched against the French Huguenots in the following August. This had the effect of making Elizabeth act more decisively and it allowed her to see the merit of Mary's demise.

The Marians in Edinburgh Castle were now offered honourable capitulation with protection of their lives and property, which Huntly and Herries accepted. This would have ended Maitland's political career, and, despite his declining health, he would not consider it. He demanded the acknowledgement of joint rule by Mary and James, and that Kirkcaldy 'should be provided with revenues and a garrison sufficient for the safekeeping of the Castle till the Queen's return, or till the King should reach the age of fifteen'.[31] The English could not believe that he was serious, but he knew that Elizabeth would want to avoid military action. Randolph concluded: 'In so weak a body as Lethington's, he had never found a man less mindful of God, or more unnatural to his country.'[32] The English, however, did not trust the regency party, which was supposedly its ally. When it asked for money, the English eventually granted £1,000, which was one quarter of what was needed to pay its men. Mar took steps to stamp out Marian opposition elsewhere by sending John Lyon 8th Lord Glamis to challenge the Gordons in the north and by reaching a compromise with Livingston. Elizabeth assisted by refusing to restore Home Castle, which was still in English hands, to Home's wife.

Although Norfolk was executed on 2 June 1572 for his complicity in the Northern Rising, Elizabeth wanted to avoid having Mary's blood on her hands. She approached Mar and Morton, offering to repatriate her with assurance of her life, but in the secret expectation that they would arrange her execution. Morton saw through Elizabeth's objective, and said that the regency would agree only if Mary were publicly executed in the presence of 2,000 English troops. These were then to be employed to remove the last vestiges of Marian support in Edinburgh. Initially, Mar saw Mary's execution 'as the only salve for the cures of the whole Commonwealth', but the reality so horrified him that he became speechless. 'He departit to Stirling, where for grief of mynd he deit' on 29 October.'[33]

On 24 November, Knox also died, and Morton presented the eulogy at his funeral. On his deathbed, Knox strongly rebuked Kirkcaldy for deserting the regency lords, but would have strongly approved of Morton's appointment as regent. Although the Marians tried to arrange for Argyll to succeed Mar, Morton was elected by a considerable majority. He made his acceptance conditional on receiving Elizabeth's clear support and did not announce his appointment until this was confirmed. She at last agreed to send a force to regain Edinburgh Castle.

Morton's first objective was to reconcile rivalries. He offered Kirkcaldy an amnesty, but, as this did not include the Hamiltons and other Marians, Kirkcaldy turned it down as a point of honour. Nevertheless, Herries, Maxwell and Robert Melville submitted. Although Balfour sought a reprieve, he was still seen as chiefly culpable for Darnley's murder and was forced into exile in France. On 5 July, Fleming had accidently been shot in the knee by a French soldier, whose bullet ricocheted after his firing piece was discharged. Although he remained for a time at the castle, he died on 6 September after being moved to Biggar on a litter. Still mentally alert, Maitland knew the game was up, but remained at the castle. Morton was in no mood to compromise. He was ruthless to those upsetting the peace process and was determined to destroy Hamilton and

Gordon power. On 10 February 1573, he took Blackness Castle, which had been held by Lord Claude for more than a year. This persuaded Châtelherault to be reconciled with the regency. Morton now approved an amnesty for the Hamiltons and Gordons, signed at the 'Pacification of Perth', on terms negotiated by Argyll. This confirmed that further enquiry into Darnley's, Moray's and Lennox's murders would be ended.

The final task was to dislodge Kirkcaldy and Maitland from Edinburgh Castle. Morton sent Rothes to offer terms, which were refused, and he now concluded that Maitland would never submit. He called up Drury from Berwick with 1,500 men. They disembarked their heavy guns at Leith, and, on 17 May, started a devastating cannonade lasting four days, which destroyed the castle's eastern front. Maitland was carried to the vaults below St David's Chapel as he 'could not abide the shot'. On 28 May, Crawford stormed the spur of the castle and contaminated the water supply. Kirkcaldy was left without water and short of provisions. On the following day, he surrendered his garrison of 164 men, thirty-four women and ten boys. Hoping for leniency, he handed the keys to Drury, who treated him with great courtesy. Although Marian bribes were offered to save Kirkcaldy's life, Morton was determined to stamp out lingering opposition and saw his 'sacrifice' as essential to his security.

Maitland was probably at his side but needed to be carried down the High Street to the jeers of the long-suffering Edinburgh townsfolk. He was housed with Drury and subsequently moved to his quarters at Leith, while Drury supervised the reshipment of his guns back to Berwick. Kirkcaldy had been handed over to the regency and, on 3 August, was executed on the gibbet at the Market Cross 'as a stern necessity as he had exasperated public feeling'. He was unrepentant. Maitland had made a last appeal to Burghley on 29 May, recognising 'we dout not your lordship Cecil, now Lord is sore offended with us and perhaps not without caus'.[34] Maitland had hoped to be taken to England, but Elizabeth insisted on him being handed over to Morton. On 9 June, he was found dead in his bed and it is assumed that he took poison to kill himself 'after the old Roman fashion'. He was aged forty-five. He was left unburied, as befitted a traitor, but, within a few days, his body had become a feasting ground for maggots.[35] Mary Fleming approached Burghley to secure him a decent burial and Elizabeth wrote to Morton to assure this. On hearing of his death, Mary Queen of Scots kept her feelings to herself. Shrewsbury reported that she made 'little show of grief, and yet it nips her near'.[36]

It is difficult to fathom the determination of Kirkcaldy and Maitland to hold out to the bitter end. Kirkcaldy's political judgement had always been questionable, and he rejected ample face-saving opportunities for an honourable surrender. He seemed to relish the military challenge of defending the castle against all odds. His achievement cannot be doubted, and he stands at the forefront of the military commanders of his age. Sir James Melville described him as 'humble, gentle, meek, like a lamb in the house, and like a lion in the field, a lusty, stark and well-proportioned personage, hardy and of magnanimous courage'. Maitland, for his part, may never have trusted the regency's offers of amnesty. He was dying and may have seen their stand as a last gesture to support his wife's sympathy with a queen, for whose downfall he had been largely responsible.

Conclusion

It was an extraordinary achievement for Maitland, the son of a laird, albeit with a respected Anglo-Norman pedigree, to remain at the heart of Scottish politics and court life as Secretary of State for almost his entire adult existence. During this period, he retained 'at times magisterial influence over the course of events', with an instinct for self-preservation (despite his changes in allegiance).[1] Although he was not coloured by strong religious belief, his academic brilliance enabled him to debate with theologians on an equal footing and placed him at the forefront of those seeking a Scottish Reformation. While he maintained his steadfast belief in the benefits for Scotland of union with England, his Anglophile affiliation waned in his later years as he battled Elizabeth's indecisive policy towards Scotland and her government's determination to thwart Mary's restoration. Despite coming to realise that Mary could never be the catalyst to achieve union with England, he ultimately concluded that her Catholic faith alone did not provide adequate grounds for her deposition. Nevertheless, his ambitions paved the way for her son, James, to inherit the English throne. His determination brought about a huge change in policy for the Scots, and without him the British Isles would have faced a far more confrontational future.

Maitland freely admitted to changing his political allegiances during his career. For this inconsistency he has been justifiably branded a 'chameleon', but he saw a flexibility to change one's views as a political virtue.[2] His approach to government was little different to that of Burghley, his role model. But while Burghley could control his own propaganda and has been assessed as the ultimate Elizabethan political figure, Maitland was dubbed 'Scotland's Machievelli' after betraying Mary of Guise and masterminding the murders of Riccio and Darnley.

After her imprisonment, Mary Queen of Scots came to respect Maitland's efforts to ameliorate her lot, even though she may have recognised his role in causing her downfall. She appreciated his extraordinary skills as a politician and diplomat. Although she granted him the valuable estates of Haddington Abbey, he was never knighted or ennobled. Her later memoirs, dictated to Nau, were far more critical of Moray, Morton and Balfour. Maitland seemed to believe that she would win out in the end and would restore him to his rightful position as her most influential adviser.

It is difficult to assess the involvement of Mary Fleming in Maitland's changing political stance. His paralysis must have been a heartache for a young wife, but there is no suggestion that she attempted to deter him from his dangerous stance on behalf of the Marian cause. All we know for certain is that she remained steadfastly loyal to his memory, though we do not know when they last saw each other. It is most unlikely that she was with him in Edinburgh Castle, despite his need for nursing care, as she had an infant daughter, Margaret, by that time, in addition to her son, James. There is no mention of her visiting him while being held by Drury before his death, though it seems likely that they would have wanted a last meeting. Most frustratingly, almost nothing is written about her or their relationship and no correspondence seems to remain. There is simply a natural consensus that she must have influenced his changing political stance. She was, after all, the granddaughter of James IV and a member of the highly influential Fleming family. History has portrayed the four Maries as a fairly homogenous group and individual character traits are not easily discerned. Yet she was probably Mary Queen of Scots' closest friend, being her cousin, and nearer in age than the other three. At various stages, when the queen was nervous for her own security, they even shared a bed together. Neither during their time in France, nor back in Scotland, is there any mention of the Maries balancing any political involvement with what seems to have been a gilded lifestyle at court.

What we do know is that Mary Fleming became the conduit for her husband's communication with Mary Queen of Scots while imprisoned, and she seems to have swayed him into supporting her. She eventually remarried George Meldrum of Fyvie while Mary Queen of Scots was still imprisoned in England and, in view of this, turned down a request to join her, but there is no record of when the marriage occurred or that she had more children by him. In 1583, with help from Maitland's brother, John, now Lord Thirlestane, she arranged to reverse the forfeiture on Lethington. She raised her children as Catholic, but with great respect for their father's memory. Their son, James, reconfirmed his mother's loyalty by publishing a defence of his father's honour, but does not mention his parents' relationship. He married Agnes Maxwell, Herries's daughter, and they had a son, Richard. After recovering control of Lethington, he sold it to Thirlestane and moved to Brussels. Perhaps the thought of a life in Scottish politics was too much for him. His sister, Margaret, married Sir Robert Ker of Cessford, who was created Lord Roxburghe in 1600 and Earl of Roxburghe in 1626.

It was Thirlestane who survived all the vicissitudes of the regency for James to become Lord Chancellor and to fulfil the role in Scottish government that Maitland had envisaged for himself.

Endnotes

Endnote 1

Both Châtelherault and Lennox were descended from Princess Mary, the daughter of James II of Scotland, who had married James Hamilton, 1st Lord Hamilton. Princess Mary had two children, James, 2nd Lord Hamilton, who was created Earl of Arran in 1503, and Elizabeth, who had married Matthew Stewart, 2nd Earl of Lennox, becoming the 4th Earl's grandparents. Arran married twice. His first wife, Elizabeth Home, had received a divorce from her first husband, Sir Thomas Hay, Master of Yester, to enable her to remarry Arran on 28 April 1490. Fourteen years later, on 15 November 1504, Arran received the Pope's authority to divorce Elizabeth Home, who had not provided him with children, on the grounds that her original divorce from Sir Thomas Hay had not been valid and she was not free to remarry. This was reconfirmed by the Papacy on 11 March 1510.

Some time before November 1516, Arran remarried Janet Bethune, the cardinal's first cousin, who became Châtelherault's mother. On 8 September 1543, the cardinal, who wielded complete authority as papal legate, met with Châtelherault to wean him away from the English alliance, which was to be confirmed by Mary marrying Prince Edward and Châtelherault's son marrying Princess Elizabeth. He threatened him with excommunication if he did not revert to Catholicism and questioned his legitimacy. He argued that Elizabeth Home had in fact received a valid divorce from Sir Thomas Hay and had thus been repudiated by the 1st Earl without cause. He also argued (entirely against the interest of the Catholic Church) that if papal authority were rejected in Scotland, then the Pope had no right to grant the divorce. Thus the 1st Earl's later

243

marriage to Jane Bethune was invalid, making Châtelherault illegitimate. Châtelherault seems to have accepted this argument, but there can be no doubt that the cardinal was using it as a ruse to prevent the English marriages and to preserve the Catholic Church in Scotland. Given that the original repudiation of the divorce had received papal authority, it is difficult to give any credence to the cardinal's argument made nearly forty years after the event.

Endnote 2

It has generally been argued that the two letters written by Maitland and Lord James were carefully coordinated. While this is just possible, they cannot have been written at similar times. It is clear that Maitland wrote before knowing the outcome of Lord James's discussion with Mary in France, being unaware that she had agreed to accept the religious status quo. His letter shows that he was fearful of her gaining French support to launch a Counter-Reformation. Lord James's letter can only have been written after meeting her.

Endnote 3

Lord Robert Dudley had been Elizabeth's childhood friend. His father, Northumberland, had failed in his attempt to install Lady Jane Grey on the English throne in order to avoid Mary Tudor's Catholic succession. This resulted in his attainder and execution, leaving the family in a parlous state. Yet by selling land the Dudleys had given Elizabeth comfort when imprisoned on suspicion of supporting Wyatt's rebellion. She fell passionately in love with the handsome Lord Robert, resulting in rumours of them conducting an affair. He was closely associated with the Conservative faction in English politics, which disapproved of the 'low-born' Cecil and wanted to weaken his political hold over Elizabeth. Cecil feared that his careful planning to protect England from Continental aggression would be undone if Elizabeth married this fourth son of the attainted duke and would open up all the petty jealousies among Elizabeth's senior advisers. Although Dudley had been married to Amy Robsart for ten years, by September 1560 she was extremely ill, probably suffering from breast cancer. Cecil spread rumours that Dudley was poisoning her, but she died from breaking her neck in a fall down some stairs at her lodging. With Dudley at the height of his romance with Elizabeth, the natural question, fuelled by Cecil, was to ask if her fall was suicide, or was she pushed? Although Dudley was exonerated, the rumours persisted, and Elizabeth realised that she should not marry him. She needed to be loved by her people, and this would only bring dissent. When faced with a similar choice, Mary would fail to show similar sensitivity.

Endnote 4

Catherine Grey had stupidly gained Elizabeth's enmity. Her Protestantism was pragmatic, and the Spanish ambassador considered her sufficiently compliant to be the means of restoring England to the Catholic faith, even contemplating her kidnap to marry Don Carlos. Elizabeth retained her as a Lady of the Bedchamber to keep a careful watch on her. Her marriage as a child bride to the Earl of Pembroke's son and heir, Henry Herbert, had been annulled, but she clandestinely escaped from court to marry and hurriedly bed Edward Seymour, Earl of Hertford (later 2nd Duke of Somerset) without Elizabeth's consent, as required by the Royal Marriage Act of 1536. The only known witness was Hertford's sister, Jane, who died of consumption shortly after. By early 1561, Catherine was obviously pregnant, and after confessing, was thrown with her husband into the Tower. When cross-examined, neither Hertford nor Catherine would name the priest who had married them, claiming that he had been hauled in off the street. If there were other witnesses, they wisely did not show themselves, and Catherine had lost the marriage certificate. The couple were brought before the Court of Star Chamber, where Hertford was fined £15,000 (which was never paid), and the marriage was annulled, making them guilty of 'fornication'. On 24 April 1561, Catherine gave birth to a son, and while still in the Tower, had three more children, although all were declared illegitimate to debar them from the throne. Their jailer, Sir Edward Warner, was removed from his post and imprisoned for his leniency. At the age of twenty-seven, Catherine stopped eating in a vain attempt to gain sympathy and died in 1568.

Endnote 5

Arran was only released on a caution of £12,000 on 2 May 1566, by which time he was completely insane and could no longer speak. He remained in confinement in the care of his mother at Craignethan Castle, living on unmarried until 1609. Eventually James VI allowed his next brother, John (later Marquess of Hamilton), to take the Arran title before his elder brother's death.

Endnote 6

Elizabeth's decision not to marry Dudley requires explanation. Cecil had been determined to prevent it, as it interfered with diplomatic negotiations on the Continent to provide her with an appropriate dynastic alliance. He seems to have persuaded her to assess Dudley's moral and religious integrity by testing whether his ambition to marry her was of more importance to him than his puritan rectitude. In February 1561, Dudley asked his brother-in-law, Sir Henry Sidney, to approach de Quadra to seek Spanish backing for the marriage. According to de Quadra, he told Sidney that, if Spain would support it with armed force if necessary, Elizabeth would restore Catholicism, would extirpate heresy and would also regard Philip as the arbiter of English policy at home and abroad.[1] Sidney confirmed to de Quadra that when granted the Crown Matrimonial, Dudley 'would thereafter obey your Majesty [Philip II] as one of your own vassals'. According to Hume: '[Dudley] was without shame, scruple, or conscience ... his sole objective was to force or cajole the Queen into marrying him, and he grasped at any aids towards it.'[2] De Quadra, who was well known for failing to keep his mouth shut, was incredulous, and Sidney is unlikely to have made such a proposition unless genuine. Despite his scepticism, de Quadra wrote to Philip that the marriage would be in the Spanish interest. When he next met Elizabeth, he told her that Philip had always regarded Dudley with great affection. She immediately backed off, replying that she could not deny 'having some affection for [him], for the many good qualities he possessed, but she certainly had not decided to marry him or anyone else'.[3] De Quadra confirmed that Philip would support the marriage, and this seemed to please her. Afterwards, Dudley thanked de Quadra profusely, asking him to continue to promote his suit, which would leave Philip in control of English government policy.

Without de Quadra being the unimpeachable source of this story, it would not seem realistic. It is inconceivable that Elizabeth would genuinely have been prepared to forgo the Religious Settlement of 1559 that she had worked so hard with Cecil to achieve, or to allow Spanish troops to massacre her subjects. It seems equally unthinkable that Dudley would be prepared to desert his long-held puritan beliefs to satisfy his matrimonial ambitions. Elizabeth must have been testing him, and he came up short, so she could never marry him herself. There is a more detailed account in *Elizabeth's Secret Lover: Robert Dudley, Earl of Leicester* (Pen & Sword, 2020).

Endnote 7

The right to the Angus title had been disputed since Lady Margaret's father, the 6th Earl, had changed its entail limiting it to heirs male, thus promoting his nephew rather than his daughter to succeed him. Although she had remained on good terms with her father, he strongly disapproved of Lennox's support for the English during the Rough Wooings. His nephew, David, thus succeeded as the 7th Earl, but died in 1557, so that the title devolved to David's infant son, Archibald, as 8th Earl. With David's younger brother, James, inheriting as 4th Earl of Morton in right of his wife, he now acted as ward for his nephew, thereby retaining the revenues of the Angus estates until his nephew's majority.

Endnote 8

In 1599, Jean eventually married Ogilvy, by which time her second husband, Alexander, 12th Earl of Sutherland, and Mary Bethune were both dead.

Endnote 9

It is known that Yaxley's diplomacy while in Brussels had promoted Darnley as the man most likely to achieve a Counter-Reformation in Scotland and caused the Pope to overestimate the level of Catholic support for the couple. His letter led Mary to believe that the Papacy would support her claim to be the rightful English queen.

Endnote 10

Ruthven was already crippled from inflammation of the liver and kidneys, which resulted in his death in Newcastle three months later. His involvement in the murder was conditional on Darnley solemnly swearing not to reveal the plan to the queen, which was unhesitatingly agreed. George Douglas had been involved in Cardinal Bethune's murder. He was Lady Margaret Lennox's illegitimate half-brother, the son of Archibald, 6th Earl of Angus. As a young man, he had become a priest, having 'seized the lucrative office of Postulate of Arbroath, despite being a lacklustre preacher, a fornicator, and a devious and violent ruffian'.[1] Melville reported that he incited Darnley, by putting into his head 'such suspicion against Riccio'.[2]

Endnote 11

The argument that Scotland was an English suzerainty does not stand the test of history. After the death, on 26 September 1290, of the seven-year-old Margaret, Maid of Norway, while en route to Scotland to take the throne, there were two pretenders to the Scottish Crown, John Baliol and Robert Bruce. Edward I was asked to arbitrate on their rival claims. Edward preferred Baliol, who was prepared to submit to him as Lord Paramount, but Bruce challenged him and freed Scotland from English domination at Bannockburn on 24 June 1314. Baliol was forced to flee, leaving Bruce to become King Robert I.

Bibliography

Bannatyne, R., *Bannatyne Manuscript*, ed. and intr. By W. Tod Ritchie, Vols. I to IV, Scottish Text Society, 1934 ("Bannatyne MS")

Black, J. B., *The Reign of Elizabeth*, 1959 ("Black")

Bowen, Marjorie, *Mary, Queen of Scots, The Daughter of Debate*, London, 1934, reprinted 1971 ("Bowen")

Buchanan, George, *Detectio Mariae Reginae, etc.* Edinburgh, 1571, 1572 ("Detectio")

Buchanan, George, *TheTyrannous Reign of Mary Stewart*, ed. and trans. W. A. Gatherer, Edinburgh, 1958 ("Buchanan")

Calderwood, David, *The True History of the Church of Scotland from the Beginning of the Reformation unto the End of the Reign of James VI*, 1646, ed. T. Thomson and D. Laing, The Wodrow Society, Edinburgh 1842–9 ("Calderwood")

Camden, William, *Annales Rerum Anglicarum et Hibernicarum Regnate, Elizabetha*, Trans. R. Norton 1635 and T. Hearne, p1717 ("Camden")

Cecil papers; A Collection of State Papers, ed. Rev. William Murdin, Hatfield House ("Cecil papers")

Cockburn, H., and Maitland, T., eds. *Les Affaires du Conte de Boduel*, Bannatyne Club, Edinburgh, 1829 ("Cockburn and Maitland")

Crawford of Jordonhill, Thomas, *Deposition*, ed. CSP Scottish Cambridge University Library ("Crawford")

Donaldson, Gordon, *The First Trial of Mary Queen of Scots*, Greenwood Press, 1983 ("Donaldson")

Diurnal of Occurrents, Bannatyne Club, Edinburgh, 1833 ("Diurnal of Occurrents")

Fleming, David Hay, *Mary Queen of Scots from her birth until her flight into England*, London, 1897 ("Fleming")

Fraser, Lady Antonia, *Mary Queen of Scots*, Weidenfeld & Nicolson, 1969 ("Fraser")

Gee, H. *The Elizabethan Prayer Book,* London, 1902 ("Gee")

Goodall, W., *Examination of the [Casket] Letters Said to be written by Mary Queen of Scots to James, Earl of Bothwell,* Edinburgh and London, 1754 ("Goodall")

Gore-Browne, R. *Lord Bothwell,* London, 1937 ("Gore-Browne")

Graham, Roderick, *An Accidental Tragedy, The Life of Mary Queen of Scots,* Berlinn Limited, 2008 ("Graham")

Guy, John, *My Heart is My Own,* Harper Perennial, 2004 ("Guy")

Herries, Sir John Maxwell, Lord, *Historical Memoirs of the Reign of Mary, Queen of Scots,* Abbotsford Club, ed. R. Pitcairn, Edinburgh, 1836 ("Herries")

Hosack, J., *Mary Queen of Scots and her Accusers,* Edinburgh, 1969 ("Hosack")

Hume, Martin Andrew Sharp, *The Great Lord Burghley; A Study in Elizabethan Statecraft,* Longmans, Green and Co., New York, 1898 ("Hume")

Jenkins, Elizabeth, *Elizabeth & Leicester,* Victor Gollancz, 1961 ("Jenkins")

Keith, Robert, *History of the Affairs of Church and State in Scotland from the beginning of the Reformation until 1585,* ed. J. P. Lawson and J. C. Lyon, Spottiswoode Society, Edinburgh, 1844, 1845, 1850 ("Keith")

Knox, John, The History of the Reformation, ed and trans. W. Croft Dickinson ("Knox, Dickinson")

Knox, John, *The Works of John Knox,* ed, D. Laing, Edinburgh, 1895 ("Knox, Laing")

Labanoff, Prince (A. I. Labanoff-Rostovsky), *Lettres de Marie Stuart,* London, 1844 ("Labanoff")

Leslie, John, Bishop of Ross, *The Historie of Scotland,* Ed. Fr. E. G. Gody and William Murison, Scottish Text Society ("Leslie")

Levine, Mortimer, *Early Elizabethan Succession Question from Tudor Dynastic Problems,* California, 1966 ("Levine")

Loughlin, Mark, *The career of Maitland of Lethington c.1526–1573,* University of Edinburgh, 1991 ("Loughlin")

MacNalty, Sir Arthur Salusbury, *Mary Queen of Scots: The Daughter of Debate,* London, 1960 ("MacNalty")

Maitland, James, *A Narrative Of The Principal Acts Of The Regency, During The Minority Of Mary Queen Of Scotland, From The Original*

Ms. Of James Maitland, R. Root, Ipswich, 1842 -Paperback, Scholar Select, 2018 ("Maitland, *Regency*")

Marshall, Rosalind K. *Queen Mary's Women,* John Donald, 2006 ("Marshall")

Melville, Sir James, of Hallhill, *Memoirs of his own life 1549–1593,* ed Francis Steuart, 1928, ed. Gordon Donaldson, The Folio Society, 1969 ("Melville")

Mumby, Frank Arthur, *The Fall of Mary Stuart: A Narrative in Contemporary Letters,* London, 1921 ("Mumby")

Nau, Claude, *Memorials of Mary Stewart,* ed. J Stevenson, 1883 ("Nau")

Neale, Sir J. E., *Elizabeth I,* Jonathan Cape, 1934 ("Neale")

Ovid, 5th book of the *Fasti* ("Ovid")

Oxford Book of English Verse, 1250–1900 ed. Arthur Quiller-Couch, ed.1919

Pedrina, Allessandra, *Machiavelli in the British Isles,* Routledge 2016 ("Pedrina")

Pitcairn, R., *Ancient Criminal Trials in Scotland,* Vol. I, Bannatyne Club, Edinburgh, 1833 ("Pitcairn")

Plowden, Alison, *Two Queens in One Isle; the Deadly Relationship of Elizabeth I and Mary, Queen of Scots,* Brighton, 1984 ("Plowden")

Pollen, J. H., *Papal Negotiations with Mary Queen of Scots,* Scottish History Society, 1st Series, Edinburgh, 1901 ("Pollen")

Prebble, *The Lion of the North; One Thousand Years of Scotland's History,* Londo1971 ("Prebble")

Protestation of Huntly and Argyll, The ("Protestation")

Robertson, Joseph, *Inventaires de la Royne d'Ecosse, Douairière de France, 1556–1569,* Bannatyne Club, Vol. III, Edinburgh, 1863 ("Robertson, J")

Robertson, William, *The History of Scotland during the Reigns of Queen Mary and of King James VI til his Accession to the Crown of England,* London, 1759 ("Robertson, W")

Russell, E., *Maitland of Lethington: The Minister of Mary Stuart, A Study of His Life and Times,* James Nisbett & Co, London, 1912 ("Russell")

Ruthven, William, Lord, *The Murder of Riccio, being Lord Ruthven's Own Account of the Transaction,* Holyrood Series, 1891 ("Ruthven")

Schutte, Kim, *A Biography of Margaret Douglas, Countess of Lennox, 1515–1578; Niece of Henry VIII and Mother-in-law of Mary Queen of Scots,* New York, 2002 ("Schutte")

Sitwell, Edith, *The Queen and the Hives,* London, 1962 ("Sitwell")

Skelton, John, *Maitland of Lethington: And the Scotland of Mary Stuart,* 3 Volumes, William Blackwood and Sons, Edinburgh, 1887 ("Skelton")

Spottiswoode, *The History of the Church of Scotland to the End of the Reign of James VI,* Bannatyne Club, London, 1851 ("Spottiswoode")

Stuart, John, *A Lost Chapter in the history of Mary Queen of Scots recovered,* Edinburgh, 1874 ("Stuart")

Teulet, A. *Papiers d'État relatives à L'Histoire de L'Écosse au 16e siècle,* Paris, 1862 ("Teulet")

Tytler, P. F., *History of Scotland,* 1841, and New Enlarged Edition, 1870 ("Tytler")

Weir, Alison, *Mary Queen of Scots and the Murder of Lord Darnley,* Jonathan Cape, 2003 ("Weir")

Wilson, Derek, *Sweet Robin: A Bigraphy of Robert Dudley Earl of Leicester 1533–1588,* Allison & Busby, 1981 ("Wilson")

Wormald, Jenny, *Mary Queen of Scots, Politics, Passion and a Kingdom Lost,* Tauris Parke Paperbacks, 2001 ("Wormald")

Manuscript sources

Ailsa Muniments

British Library, Additional Papers ("BL")

Calendar of Manuscripts at Hatfield House ("Hatfield MS")

Calendar of State Papers Foreign ("CSP Foreign")

Calendar of State Papers Scottish ("CSP Scottish")

Calendar of State Papers Spanish ("CSP Spanish")

Calendar of State Papers Venetian ("CSP Venetian")

Cotton Manuscripts, British Museum ("Cotton MMS")

Egerton Manuscripts ("Egerton MMS")

Hardwick State Papers ("Hardwick SP")

HMC, Talbot Papers ("Talbot Papers")

Public Records Office Chancery Lane, State Papers of Scotland, Elizabeth ("PRO. SP 52")

References

Preface

1. Calderwood, III, p285
2. Pedrina, p35

PART I: A BRILLIANT BUT DEVIOUS SECRETARY

Chapter 1: Maitland establishes his standing under Mary of Guise

1. Russell, p15
2. Loughlin, p91
3. Cited in Fraser, p29
4. Loughlin, p15
5. Russell, p4
6. Loughlin, pp20–22
7. Russell, p4
8. ibid.
9. ibid. p13
10. ibid. p9
11. ibid. p10
12. Cited in Wormald, p88
13. Loughlin, p37
14. Russell, p11
15. Knox, Laing, I, p273; cited in Russell, p42
16. Maitland, *Regency*, p17
17. Russell, p13
18. ibid. p14
19. Loughlin, p.25
20. Russell, pp8–9

21. ibid. p7
22. Spottiswoode, p263: cited in Loughlin, p36
23. Loughlin, p37

Charter 2: The Lords of the Congregation challenge French authority

1. Knox, Laing, IV, p373; cited in Fraser, p177
2. Loughlin, p15
3. PRO SP 52.10.11; cited in Loughlin, p4
4. Russell, p102
5. ibid. p103
6. Loughlin, p37
7. CSP Foreign, I, pp168–9; cited in ibid. p41
8. Robertson, W, ii, pp273–80; cited in ibid. p51
9. Russell, p.27
10. Knox, I, Laing, p320
11. Russell, p22
12. ibid. p25
13. Wormald, p94
14. CSP Scottish, I, 223; cited in Loughlin, p38
15. Loughlin, p38
16. Cecil, *The Distresses of the Commonwealth* in Gee; cited in Loughlin, p38
17. Russell, p43
18. ibid.
19. Loughlin, pp46–7
20. ibid. p38
21. Russell, p44
22. ibid. p38
23. Fraser, p112
24. Loughlin, p91
25. Russell, p49
26. CSP Scottish, I, p326; cited in Russell, p52
27. Skelton, I, pp254–5 and Loughlin, p54
28. Russell, p58
29. CSP Scottish, I, p427; cited in Russell, p19
30. Russell, p20
31. ibid. p72
32. ibid.
33. ibid.

34. ibid. p.21
35. Loughlin, p64
36. Russell, p86
37. ibid.
38. Keith, App. 193–255; cited in Russell, p88
39. Loughlin, p65
40. Russell, p82
41. CSP Scottish, I, p477; cited in Russell, p82
42. Russell, p100
43. Keith, p154; cited in ibid. p84
44. Loughlin, p91
45. ibid. p84
46. CSP Scottish, I, 58i; cited in Loughlin, p90
47. Loughlin, p88
48. BL, 23,109, f.7; cited in ibid. p90
49. Loughlin, p89
50. ibid. p91
51. Keith, p156; cited in Russell, p93
52. Loughlin, p90
53. ibid. p85
54. PRO SP, 52.5.21; cited in Loughlin, pp83–4
55. Loughlin, p85
56. Russell, p94
57. Knox, Laing, II, p132; cited in ibid.
58. Russell, p96
59. ibid. p97

Chapter 3: The return of the widowed Mary Queen of Scots

1. Russell, p97
2. ibid. p101
3. ibid. p95
4. ibid. p102
5. ibid. p115
6. ibid. p104
7. ibid. p105
8. ibid.
9. ibid. p117
10. ibid. p118
11. ibid.

12. Loughlin, p99
13. Spottiswoode, 372; cited in ibid.
14. Loughlin, p100
15. Russell, p106
16. Loughlin, p65
17. Russell, p119; cited in Guy, p129
18. ibid.
19. Russell, p101
20. ibid. p132
21. Knox, Dickinson, II, p7; cited in Loughlin, p113
22. Knox, Dickinson, I, p.8
23. Fleming, p246
24. Guy, p140
25. Russell, p136
26. Weir, p34
27. Russell, p136
28. ibid.
29. Knox, Laing, IV, p373; cited in Fraser, p177
30. CSP Scottish, I, p551; Knox, Laing, VI, p132; cited in Fraser, p178
31. Knox, Dickinson, II, p13 et seq.; cited in Fraser, p178
32. Cited in Guy, p148; and in Wormald, p127
33. CSP Scottish, I, pp552,555,574; cited in Russell, p144
34. Buchanan; cited in Fraser, p219
35. Weir, p31
36. Loughlin, p115
37. Guy, p149

Chapter 4: Diplomatic efforts to establish Mary as Elizabeth's heir

1. Guy, p146
2. CSP Spanish, I, p27; cited in Wilson, p98
3. Loughlin, p155
4. Russell, p147
5. Levine, pp117–8; cited in Fraser, p186
6. Loughlin, p124
7. Hardwick SP, I, p173; cited in ibid. p123
8. Guy, p148
9. Fraser, p225

10. CSP Foreign, III, p573; cited in ibid. p189
11. Labanoff, I, p123; cited in ibid. p190
12. CSP Scottish, I, p559; cited in Marshall, p200
13. CSP Scottish, I, p588; cited in Loughlin, p129
14. Guy, p160
15. Russell, p157
16. Henry Sidney to William Cecil, 25 July 1562, CSP Scottish, 1547–1563, p641
17. Loughlin, p157
18. Guy, p166
19. ibid.

Chapter 5: Lord James (soon to be Earl of Moray) and Maitland establish authority

1. CSP Scottish, I, p582; cited in Fraser, p196
2. CSP Scottish; cited in Weir, p41
3. Fraser, p199
4. Buchanan, p79; cited in ibid. p221
5. Wormald, p125
6. Fraser, p225
7. Randolph to Cecil, 18 September 1562; cited in ibid. p226
8. Diurnal of Occurrents, p74; cited in Fraser, p230
9. Guy, p165
10. Keith, II, p182; cited in Fraser, p233
11. Guy, p168
12. ibid.
13. Russell, p205
14. Guy, p168

Chapter 6: The negotiations for Mary's remarriage

1. Guy, p170
2. Loughlin, p160
3. Russell, p170
4. ibid. p173
5. ibid.; Guy, p174
6. Russell, p176
7. Guy, p174

8. Loughlin, p164
9. ibid.
10. Russell, p180
11. CSP Foreign, VI, p221; cited in Fraser, p237
12. Guy, p183
13. ibid. p181
14. ibid. p182
15. ibid. p175
16. Loughlin, p173
17. Schutte, p182; cited in Marshall, p114
18. Guy, p194
19. ibid. p183
20. ibid. p185
21. ibid. p186
22. ibid. pp189–90
23. Fraser, p245
24. Guy, p192
25. Russell, p201
26. Fraser, p245
27. Guy, p193
28. Russell, pp202–3
29. ibid. p204
30. ibid. p209

PART II: MARY TAKES PERSONAL CONTROL

Chapter 7: Mary's effort to take up the reins of power

1. Russell, p196
2. Keith, II, p251; cited in Loughlin, p193
3. Guy, p224
4. Gore-Browne; cited in Guy, p225
5. Guy, p228
6. Cockburn and Maitland; CSP Scottish

Chapter 8: Marriage to Darnley

1. Melville, p45, cited in Fraser, p256
2. Randolph to Cecil, 8 May 1563; CSP Scottish, II, p156

REFERENCES

3. Russell, p213
4. Buchanan; cited in Sitwell, and Guy, p211
5. Russell, p246
6. ibid. p200
7. Guy, p205
8. Melville; cited in Weir, p59
9. Weir, p60
10. Guy, p207
11. ibid. p206
12. Russell, p211
13. Guy, p209
14. ibid. pp208–9
15. Russell, p246
16. Bannatyne MS; Oxford Book of English Verse, p176; cited in Fraser, p261
17. CSP Scottish; cited in Weir, p63
18. ibid. pp63,65
19. CSP Spanish; cited in Weir, p77
20. CSP Scottish; cited in Weir, p66
21. CSP Scottish, II, p159; cited in Russell, p216
22. Loughlin, p203
23. Cockburn and Maitland; cited in Weir, p67
24. CSP Scottish, II, p75; cited in Fraser, p257
25. Russell, p225
26. ibid. p219
27. Cited in Guy, p213
28. CSP Scottish; cited in Weir, p68
29. ibid.
30. Guy, p211
31. CSP Scottish; cited in Weir, p69
32. ibid.
33. Weir, p72
34. ibid.
35. Cited in Fraser, p263
36. Russell, p227
37. CSP Scottish; cited in Guy, p214
38. Russell, p222
39. ibid. p224
40. Randolph to Leicester in CSP Scottish; cited in Guy, p217
41. CSP Scottish; cited in Weir, p76
42. Melville; cited in Weir, p. 76–7
43. Russell, p232

44. CSP Scottish, II, p185; cited in Russell, p233
45. Teulet; cited in Guy, p217
46. Russell, p231
47. ibid.
48. Cited in Wormald, p157

Chapter 9: Moray's rebellion

1. Keith; cited in Weir, p78
2. Loughlin, p37
3. Knox, Laing, II, p162; cited in Weir, p79
4. Russell, p236
5. Guy, p231
6. Russell, p235
7. ibid. p238
8. Guy, p254
9. Russell, p243

PART III: MAITLAND RE-ESTABLISHES HIS STANDING

Chapter 10: Riccio's Murder

1. Guy, p240
2. ibid. p243
3. Fraser, p280
4. Russell, p244
5. Guy, p244
6. Russell, p247
7. ibid.
8. Weir, pp90, 94
9. CSP Scottish, II, p255; cited in Guy, pp245–6
10. Tytler, V, p334; cited in Guy, pp244, 247
11. CSP Scottish, II, pp261–4; cited in Russell, p256
12. Weir, p96
13. ibid. p102
14. CSP Scottish, Ruthven; cited in Weir, p102
15. Melville, p113; cited in Fraser, p161
16. Meville; cited in Weir, p109

17. Russell, p257
18. Nau; cited in Weir, p110
19. ibid.
20. ibid.
21. CSP Venetian; cited in Weir, p119
22. Labanoff, I, p351; cited in Fraser, p296
23. Melville; cited in Weir, p120
24. Russell, p259
25. Guy, pp260–1
26. Prebble; cited in Weir, p123
27. Russell, p259
28. Mary to Archbishop Bethune; cited in Guy, p260
29. CSP Scottish; cited in Weir, p127
30. Melville; cited in Weir, p122
31. Gore-Browne; cited in ibid.
32. Nau, p41; cited in Fraser, p303
33. Herries, p80; cited in Fraser, p302
34. CSP Spanish; cited in Weir, p128

Chapter 11: Restored as Secretary of State

1. CSP Spanish, 18 May 1566; cited in Weir, p130
2. Egerton MMS: cited in Weir, p131
3. Nau, p28; cited in Fraser, p300
4. Herries, p79; cited in Wormald, p163
5. CSP Foreign VIII, p114; Keith, III, p349; cited in Guy, p270
6. Weir, p145
7. ibid. p149
8. CSP Foreign; cited in ibid.146
9. Weir, p148
10. Nau, p30; cited in Weir, p312
11. Keith, II, p447, p450; cited in Fraser, p314
12. Privy Council to Catherine de Medici; du Croc to Archbishop Bethune; cited in Keith; cited in Guy, p272
13. Du Croc to Catherine de Medici, 15 October 1566; Keith, II, p451; cited in Guy, p272
14. Fraser, p315
15. Weir, pp158–9
16. Weir, p159

Chapter 12: Ending Mary's marriage to Darnley

1. Nau; CSP Spanish; cited in Weir, p163
2. Guy, p276
3. Cotton MMS, Protestation; Keith; cited in Weir, p170
4. Weir, p172
5. Guy, p283
6. ibid.
7. Keith, II, p475; cited in Weir, p174
8. Keith, III, p290; cited in Fraser, p321
9. Goodall; cited in Weir, p175
10. Guy, p285
11. ibid. p286
12. Melville; cited in Weir, p181
13. Robertson, J, pp61–9; cited in Fraser, p324
14. Du Croc to Archbishop Bethune; Fraser, p325
15. Loughlin, p240
16. ibid. p214
17. Du Croc to Archbishop Bethune; cited in Guy, p285
18. Knox; cited in Weir, p190
19. Loughlin, p239
20. Weir, p199

PART IV: DEVELOPING THE TALE OF A CRIME OF PASSION

Chapter 13: The Chameleon

1. Paraphrased from Loughlin, p250

Chapter 14: The plot to murder Darnley unfolds

1. Crawford; cited in Weir, p208
2. ibid. p209
3. Guy, p293
4. Nau; cited in Weir, p235
5. Weir, p201
6. Buchanan, *Detectio*; cited in Weir, p247
7. Pitcairn, *I, pt. 1, p. 502;* Herries, p84; cited in Fraser, p350

8. Sloane MMS; cited in Weir, p250
9. William Powrie's deposition in Pitcairn; cited in Fraser, p354
10. Cockburn and Maitland, p13; cited in Weir, p252

Chapter 15: Providing the evidence of a crime of passion

1. Loughlin, p244
2. ibid. p.249
3. Buchanan, *Detectio*; cited in Weir, p361
4. Guy, p401

Chapter 16: Enticement for Mary to marry Bothwell

1. Keith; cited in Antonia Fraser, pp353–4
2. Weir, p331
3. Guy, pp304, 313
4. Pollen; cited in Weir, pp280, 320
5. PRO. SP 52; CSP Scottish; cited in Weir, p308
6. Guy, p310
7. Weir, p318
8. Loughlin, p254
9. Teulet; cited in Guy, p313
10. CSP Spanish; cited in Weir, p327
11. Keith II, p532; CSP Foreign, VIII, p198; cited in Fraser, p360
12. CSP Spanish, de Silva to Philip II, 21 April 1567; cited in Weir, p331

Chapter 17: Bothwell is exonerated and marries Mary

1. Guy, p400
2. Weir, p300
3. Drury to Cecil, 15 April 1567, in Tytler; cited in Guy, pp323–4
4. Meville; cited in Weir, p339
5. Diurnal of Occurrents, p108; cited in Fraser, p361
6. Buchanan, *Detectio;* cited in Weir, p340
7. Keith, II, p558; cited in Weir, p341
8. Keith, II, p562, Cotton MMS; CSP Scottish; Anderson, Collections; cited in Guy, p326
9. Kirkcaldy to Bedford, 20 April 1567, State Papers of the PRO; cited in Guy, p327

10. Nau, p37; cited in Fraser, p363
11. Nau; cited in ibid.
12. Guy, p327
13. Pollen, p386; Labanoff; cited in Antonia Fraser, p364
14. MacNalty; cited in Weir, p352
15. De Silva to Philip II, May 1567; CSP Spanish; cited in Weir, p354
16. PRO. SP52; CSP Scottish; cited in Weir, p363
17. Keith; cited in Weir, p365
18. Guy, p331
19. Weir, p364
20. Melville; cited in Weir, p367
21. ibid. p362
22. ibid. p368
23. CSP Spanish; cited in Weir, p376
24. CSP Foreign; cited in Weir, p376
25. Stuart, p48; cited in Marshall, p134
26. Diurnal of Occurrents, p111; cited in Weir, pp374–5
27. Ovid; cited in Fraser, p372
28. Plowden; cited in Guy, p335

PART V: MARY'S ARREST AND MAITLAND'S CONTRITION

Chapter 18: The Confederates challenge Mary and Bothwell

1. CSP Scottish; cited in Weir, p379
2. Guy, p339
3. Labanoff; CSP Scottish; cited in Weir, p383
4. Weir, p375
5. Du Croc to Catherine de Medici, 18 May 1567, Teulet; cited in Guy, p337
6. Melville, p154; cited in Weir, p376
7. Drury in CSP Foreign; cited in Guy, p336
8. Weir, p377
9. Teulet; cited in Weir, p378
10. Pollen; cited in Wormald, p146
11. Black; cited in Weir, p382
12. Cockburn and Maitland; cited in ibid. p378
13. Weir, p378
14. Loughlin, p261
15. Russell, p340; cited in ibid.

16. CSP Scottish, II, 336; cited in Russell, pp316–7
17. Melville; cited in Weir, p380
18. ibid. p385
19. CSP Scottish; cited in Weir, p389
20. Cockburn and Maitland; cited in ibid p391
21. Nau; cited in ibid. p391
22. Cockburn and Maitland; cited in ibid. p392
23. ibid.
24. Melville; cited Weir, p392
25. ibid. p393
26. Nau, p48; cited in Fraser, pp383–4
27. Nau; cited in Fraser, p384
28. Nau, p52; cited in Weir, pp281, 294–5
29. Nau; cited in Weir, p395
30. Russell, p445
31. ibid. p446

Chapter 19: Negotiations while Mary is held at Lochleven

1. Calderwood, ii, p366
2. Du Croc to Catherine de Medici, 17 June 1567; Teulet; cited in Weir, p396
3. CSP Foreign; cited in ibid.
4. Nau; cited in Guy, p351
5. Guy, p352
6. Weir, p406
7. CSP Scottish; cited in ibid.
8. CSP Foreign, VIII, p269; cited in Fraser; p394
9. CSP Foreign; cited in Weir; p389
10. CSP Foreign, VIII, p311; Hosack, I, p363; cited in Russell, pp27–8
11. CSP Scottish; cited in Weir, p407
12. CSP Scottish II, p361; cited in Russell, p337
13. Loughlin, p263
14. Keith, *History*, II, p742; cited in ibid. p259
15. CSP Scottish; Keith; cited in Weir, p409
16. CSP Scottish; cited in ibid. p409
17. Keith, p417; cited in Russell, p339
18. Stevenson, p237; cited in Russell, p340
19. Russell, pp333–4
20. CSP Scottish; Selections from unpublished manuscripts; Keith; cited in Weir, pp412, 415
21. Weir, p416

22. De Silva to Philip II, 2 August 1567, CSP Spanish; cited in ibid. pp417–18
23. CSP Scottish; cited in ibid. p419
24. CSP Scottish; Keith; Nau; cited in Fraser, p401
25. ibid. p420
26. Nau; cited in Weir, p420
27. ibid.
28. CSP Scottish; cited in ibid. p420
29. Nau, p69; cited in Fraser, p402
30. Acts of Parliament Scotland, III, 27; cited in Guy, p397
31. Goodall; Calendar of Manuscripts at Hatfield House; CSP Scottish; cited in Weir, p425
32. Goodall; cited in Guy, p397
33. Buchanan, *Detectio*; cited in Weir, p402
34. De Silva to Philip II, 21 July 1567, CSP Spanish; cited in Weir, pp411–2

Chapter 20: Mary escapes and Maitland's signs of sympathy

1. CSP Scottish
2. Mary to Moray, 8 December 1567, Nau; cited in Weir, p425
3. Act of Parliament, 15 December 1567; cited in Fraser, p407
4. Russell, pp358–9
5. CSP Foreign, VIII, p363; cited in Weir, p424
6. Mary to the Cardinal of Lorraine, Labanoff, II, p117; cited in Fraser, p422
7. Nau, *Memorials,* p95; cited in Antonia Fraser, p424
8. Mumby; cited in Weir, p434
9. Talbot Papers, Vol. V, Appendix to Fifth Report, p615; Ailsa Muniments folio 17; cited in Fraser, p426
10. CSP Scottish II; cited in Graham, p301
11. CSP Scottish; cited in Weir pp435, 444
12. CSP Scottish, II, p457; cited in Fraser, p437
13. ibid. p443; cited in ibid. p437
14. Loughlin, p269

Chapter 21: The Conferences at York and Westminster

1. CSP Scottish; cited in Weir, p439
2. Nau; cited in ibid. p436
3. Nau

REFERENCES

4. CSP Scottish; Goodall; cited in Guy, p395
5. Cited in Weir, p440
6. CSP Scottish; cited in ibid. p443
7. ibid.; cited in ibid. p444
8. ibid.; cited in ibid.
9. Goodall, ii, pp111, 121–5; cited in Russell, p373
10. Cited in Guy, p435
11. ibid. p429
12. CSP Scottish; cited in Weir, p445
13. Cited in Fraser, p440
14. Goodall, cited in Weir; p447
15. CSP Scottish; Goodall; cited in ibid. p452
16. ibid. p451
17. CSP Scottish; Goodall; cited in Guy, p431
18. Cited in ibid.
19. Hatfield MS, I, p369; cited in Weir, p457
20. CSP Scottish; Goodall; cited in ibid. p453
21. Cecil papers, from evidence taken from the Bishop of Ross in 1571; cited in Weir, p453
22. CSP Scottish; Goodall; cited in Weir, p454
23. CSP Scottish, II, p526; cited in Fraser, p445
24. CSP Scottish; Goodall; cited in Weir, p455
25. ibid.
26. Camden, p129; cited in Fraser, p483
27. CSP Scottish; Goodall; cited in Weir, p456
28. Cecil papers, p180; cited in Weir, p458–9
29. Hatfield House, I, p369; cited in Guy, p431
30. Cited in Fraser, p446
31. Cited in Weir, p457
32. CSP Scottish; Goodall; cited in ibid. p459
33. ibid. p458
34. ibid.
35. ibid. p459
36. Cecil answer, 10 January 1569; Donaldson; cited in Weir, p459
37. Goodall, ii, p207; cited in Russell, p382
38. Cited in Weir, p461
39. Cited in ibid. p459
40. Cited in Guy, p433
41. Goodall, II, p. 256
42. CSP Scottish; Goodall; cited in Weir, p472
43. ibid.

44. CSP Spanish; cited in Weir, p476
45. Leslie; cited in Weir, p481
46. CSP Scottish; Goodall; cited in Weir, p482
47. ibid. p477
48. Cited in Neale, p173
49. Keith; cited in Weir, p480
50. Cited in Bowen; cited in Weir, p481
51. Cited in Guy, p436
52. Cited in Neale, p174
53. Cited in Guy, p436

Chapter 22: A last hurrah for the Marian cause

1. Russell, p384
2. Cited in Guy, p508
3. Russell, pp386–7
4. ibid. p391
5. ibid. p392
6. ibid. p387
7. ibid. p395
8. CSP Foreign, ix, pp173–93; cited in ibid. p399
9. Bannatyne MS, 15; cited in Russell, p396
10. Russell, p403
11. ibid.
12. ibid. p404
13. ibid. p402
14. CSP Scottish, ii; cited in ibid. p414
15. Russell, p420
16. Loughlin, p291
17. ibid. p293
18. Russell, p427
19. Loughlin, p290
20. CSP Scottish, III, p172–30; cited in ibid. p295
21. Russell, p431
22. Loughlin, p298
23. Russell, p444
24. ibid. p445
25. ibid. p446
26. ibid. p448
27. ibid. p449

28. CSP Scottish; cited in Weir, p493
29. Russell, p458
30. ibid. p459
31. ibid. p460
32. ibid. p470
33. Melville; cited in Weir, p149
34. Cotton Manuscripts, Caligula, C IV, f.58; cited in Loughlin, p332
35. Melville; cited in Fraser, p499
36. CSP Scottish; cited in ibid.

Conclusion

1. Loughlin, p343
2. ibid. p317

Endnote 6

1. Jenkins, p79
2. Hume, p104
3. Jenkins, p80

Endnote 10

1. Cecil Papers; cited in Weir, p96
2. Melville

Index

INDEX

with Morton, 43, 229
with Randolph, 229
with Lord James Stewart (Moray),
   15, 32, 42-3, 69-70, 72, 74, 89,
   128, 195, 197, 204, 210, 224,
   227-8, 230, 232
with Sussex, 232
with Throckmorton, 81, 184-6, 190
Malmö, 193
Mar, Earl of, see Erskine, John
Mar, Earldom of, ix, 56, 59, 82
March, Earldom of, 157
Marches, Middle, 15, 43
Marches, Western, 43
Margaret, Maid of Norway, 248
Margaret Tudor, Queen of Scotland, 45,
   47, 49
Marians (supporters of Mary), 88,
   100, 104, 172, 187-8, 190-1, 196-7,
   199-201, 203, 207, 214, 220, 223-6,
   228-38, 241
Maries, Four, 64, 74, 83, 147, 154, 162,
   165, 241
Marischal, Earl, see Keith, William
Marriage contracts among the Casket
   Letters, 142, 146, 208, 218
Mary Queen of Scots, ix-xiii, 2-3, 5-6,
   11-6, 19-20, 22-70, 72-92, 94-126,
   128-66, 168-92, 194-234, 236-41,
   243-5, 247
Mary, Infanta of Portugal, 33
Mary, Princess of Scotland (d. of
   James II), 243
Mary Tudor, Duchess of Suffolk, 49
Mary I (Tudor), 4, 6-10, 13-5, 33, 41,
   45, 48, 63, 244
Masques at court, 10, 51, 56, 76, 112,
   121, 147
Mass, 7, 27, 37, 39-40, 59-60, 63, 76,
   84-5, 87-8, 91, 94-6, 135, 170-1,
   203, 222

Massacre of St Bartholomew, 236
Maxwell, Agnes, 242
Maxwell, Sir John, later 4th Lord
   Herries, 22, 43, 89, 104, 107, 152,
   164, 165, 185, 187, 194-7, 199,
   202-4, 214, 217, 220, 223-5, 229,
   234-7, 242
Maxwell, John, 8th Lord Maxwell,
   234, 237
Medici, Catherine de, 33, 52, 62-5, 79,
   86, 98, 110, 115, 138, 150, 153,
   169-70, 232, 235, 238
Meggetland, 113
Meldrum of Fyvie, George, 241
Melrose, 116, 145, 172-3
Melville, Sir James, 40, 74, 76-7, 86,
   97, 102, 104, 109, 115, 121, 140,
   156, 159-61, 163-4, 172, 186, 212,
   239, 248
Melville, Sir Robert, 16, 29, 91, 108,
   168, 186, 188, 237
Memorials of Mary Stewart, 139
Menteith of Kerse, Janet, 6
Mercat (Market) Cross, Edinburgh,
   105, 238
'Middle way', 46, 59
Mondovi, Bishop of, see Laureo,
   Vincenzo
Montgomerie, Hugh, 3rd Earl of
   Eglinton, 157, 234
Montrose, Earl of, see Graham,
   William
Moray, Earl of, see Stewart, Lord
   James
Moray, Earldom of, 36, 56-7, 65
Moray estates, 56
Moray's rebellion, see Chaseabout Raid
Morton, Earl of, see Douglas, James
Mowbray of Barnbougle, Sir John, 106
Murray, Annabella, Countess of Mar,
   82, 111, 138